BLOOMSBURY, MODERNISM, AND THE REINVENTION OF INTIMACY

Bloomsbury, Modernism, and the Reinvention of Intimacy integrates studies of six members and associates of the Bloomsbury group into a rich narrative of early-twentieth-century culture, encompassing changes in the demographics of private and public life, and Freudian and sexological assaults on middle-class proprieties. Jesse Wolfe shows how numerous modernist writers felt torn between the inherited institutions of monogamy and marriage and emerging theories of sexuality which challenged Victorian notions of maleness and femaleness. For Wolfe, this ambivalence was a primary source of the Bloomsbury writers' aesthetic strength: Virginia Woolf, D. H. Lawrence, and others brought the paradoxes of modern intimacy to thrilling life on the page. By combining literary criticism with forays into philosophy, psychoanalysis, sociology, and the avant-garde art of Vienna, this book offers a fresh account of the reciprocal relations between culture and society in that key site for literary modernism known as Bloomsbury.

JESSE WOLFE is Assistant Professor of English at California State University, Stanislaus.

BLOOMSBURY, MODERNISM, AND THE REINVENTION OF INTIMACY

JESSE WOLFE

CAMBRIDGE
UNIVERSITY PRESS

CAMBRIDGE UNIVERSITY PRESS
Cambridge, New York, Melbourne, Madrid, Cape Town,
Singapore, São Paulo, Delhi, Tokyo, Mexico City

Cambridge University Press
The Edinburgh Building, Cambridge CB2 8RU, UK

Published in the United States of America by Cambridge University Press, New York

www.cambridge.org
Information on this title: www.cambridge.org/9781107006041

First published 2011

Printed in the United Kingdom at the University Press, Cambridge

A catalogue record for this publication is available from the British Library

Library of Congress Cataloguing in Publication data
Wolfe, Jesse, 1970 – Bloomsbury, Modernism, and the Reinvention
of Intimacy / Jesse Wolfe.
p. cm
Includes bibliographical references and index.
ISBN 978-1-107-00604-1
1. English fiction – 20th century – History and criticism. 2. Intimacy (Psychology) in literature. 3. Bloomsbury group. 4. Intimacy (Psychology) 5. Modernism (Literature) – Great Britain. 6. Literature and society – Great Britain – History – 20th century I. Title.
PR888.I64W65 2011
823′.91209353222
2010046600

ISBN 978-1-107-00604-1 Hardback

Contents

Figures

Tables

Acknowledgments

I owe thanks to many colleagues at Wisconsin and Stanislaus, as well as other institutions, friends, and family members for making this book possible. My dissertation director, Richard Begam, has been a friend and intellectual mentor for over a decade, helping to guide the project to completion. Also at Wisconsin, Susan Friedman provided extensive written notes, Rebecca Walkowitz met with me to discuss chapters in progress, Cyrena Pondrom shared her insights, and Claudia Card contributed her expertise as a philosopher. My colleagues Matthew Brown, James Mardock, Deirdre Egan, and Mike LeMahieu discussed the project with me globally and worked through notes with me at the Writing Center. Kate Merz provided extensive research assistance. I am indebted to UW–Madison not only for the help of these talented people, but also for the University Dissertator Fellowship that funded a semester's worth of work.

At Stanislaus, colleagues including Arnold Schmidt and the wonderful library staff including Arthur Buell and Tim Held have been generous with support. I owe thanks to the Museum of Modern Art, the Courtauld Institute, DACS, and Alessandra Comini for use of images in their possession, as well as for Professor Comini's warm encouragements. I'm grateful to Ray Ryan, my editor at Cambridge University Press, as well as to my two anonymous readers, who gave excellent feedback, and to *Modern Fiction Studies*, in which sections of Chapter 5 originally appeared.

Finally, my wife Alexandra Block has been my untiring editor and proofreader. My mother, Bonnie Wolfe, and my father, Thomas Wolfe, in addition to being my lifelong mentors, aided the book's progress with their responses to individual chapters and their consistent support. Naomi and Meyer Rothberg likewise encouraged me, opened their home to me as a work space, and even provided astute editorial suggestions. I am most indebted to my family and friends for helping to take my mind off the project when I most needed to. This historical investigation of intimacy would not have been possible without the sustaining intimate relationships to which I can return outside of work.

Introduction: narrating Bloomsbury

Popular and scholarly interests in Bloomsbury have been robust in recent years, with film adaptations of Virginia Woolf's and E. M. Forster's novels, homages by Michael Cunningham and Zadie Smith, biographies of several group members, critical examinations of its literary and philosophical importance, and studies of its role in the history of liberalism, feminism, pacifism, gay liberation, and other aspects of culture and politics.[1] This interest suggests that Bloomsbury illuminates many dimensions of modern life. The current turn in modernist studies – toward examining modern*ity* (a social phenomenon) as the context for modern*ism* (aesthetic responses to this phenomenon) – also suggests that Bloomsbury deserves a central role in the story of literary modernism.

The following six chapters accord Bloomsbury such a role, and explore how early-twentieth-century modernity, with its demographic and intellectual shifts, both inspired and resulted from a reinvention of intimacy that was a primary source of the group's finest work. From the increased frequency of divorce (which seemed ominous at the time, but seems more modest in retrospect), to the emergence of women in higher educational and professional institutions, to the rise of sexology, psychoanalysis, and subcultures – such as Bloomsbury – organized around loves that had dared not speak their name in the nineteenth century, the period that I examine (roughly 1900 to 1930) saw many signs that an old order was crumbling.

The challenges precipitated by these changes were multidimensional. Early-twentieth-century men and women felt themselves to be more courageous than their parents and grandparents in the kinds of intimacies they sought – sexually frank ones with spouses and lovers of the same or opposite sex, emotionally honest ones with friends – and believed nineteenth-century forms of association to be staid and unfeeling. Lytton Strachey accused Victorians in a 1903 letter of living in "the Glass Case Age. Their refusal to face any fundamental question fairly – either about people or God . . . was simply the result of an innate incapacity for penetration . . . It's damned difficult to copulate through a glass case."[2] In his disdain for his predecessors, Strachey expresses a value that Bloomsburians share with early-twenty-first-century men and women: their sense that the burden of a meaningfully lived life falls largely on its romantic and sexual partnerships. Because moderns felt their milieu in transformation, they were compelled to redefine, rather than inherit, their roles as friends, lovers, and spouses. This predicament at once threatened the stability of such relationships and held the promise that they could be deeply fulfilling.

This challenge both to forge intimacies and to figure out *on what grounds* to do so provoked theoretical questions – *What are men and women like?* – and practical ones – *What models of intimacy shall we advocate*, both in life and in literature? Regarding men's and women's natures, are the two sexes fundamentally alike or different? What place does sexual desire – including that for their own sex – occupy in their hierarchy of needs? Are male and female desires products of nature or culture, and if the latter, what kinds of desires are produced, satisfied, and frustrated by various epochs, including the Victorian and modern ones? Regarding models of intimacy, shall our attachments be sexual, platonic, or both? If sexual, erotic or agapic? Exclusive or polyamorous? Shall they assume marital, non-marital, or extra-marital forms? Shall they be exclusively heterosexual? Each text in this study gives answers to these two genres of questions that stand in productive tension with each other. The dual shapes of this tension – anti-essentialist accommodations to, and essentialist rejections of, such pillars of the Victorian middle-class social order as marriage and monogamy – will be my primary thematic foci. In close readings of works by three writers who were central to Bloomsbury – G. E. Moore's philosophical treatise, *Principia Ethica* (1903), Forster's *Howards End* (1910), and Woolf's *Mrs Dalloway* (1925) – and works by three writers within the group's orbit – Sigmund Freud's *Dora* (1905), D. H. Lawrence's *Women in Love* (1920), and Vita Sackville-West's *All Passion Spent* (1931) – I will discuss how the new century's transformed landscape of intimacy inspired, and was in turn enriched by, their ambivalent reactions to Victorian precedents, and how their ambivalence was one of their defining aesthetic strengths.

The form and style of these six works mold their treatments of intimacy, making them valuable illustrations of how moderns respond to Victorian precedent at once in philosophical and formal ways. Freud's and Woolf's texts are the most aesthetically radical, with his genre blending and her use of post-realist techniques such as free indirect style. Sackville-West's novel is the most aesthetically conservative: though an homage to *Mrs Dalloway*, it eschews Woolf's experimental methods. The other two novels occupy formal and stylistic middle grounds between Victorian realism and modernist experimentation. I will explore how the stylistic choices of all six works open up and close off opportunities for posing questions about modern intimacy.

While Bloomsburians did not employ the terms "essentialist" and "anti-essentialist," they did think through the ideas captured by these terms. Their Cambridge colleague Ludwig Wittgenstein codified what anti-essentialist thinking entails with regard to such concepts as "games,"[3] while Woolf put anti-essentialist principles to work in examining more existentially pressing concepts such as "femaleness." *Bloomsbury, Modernism, and the Reinvention of Intimacy* performs an "archaeological" study – to adapt a term from Foucault – of what "intimacy" meant to a diverse group of influential thinkers in the early twentieth century. Uncovering a layer of textual artifacts roughly a century old, we find that modernists' notions about healthy intimacy were not monolithic, but nonetheless the questions they asked share enough family resemblances to distinguish their quandaries from those of the Victorians, and also to distinguish them from our own.

As much as any twentieth-century movement, literary Bloomsbury made intimacy central to its work, interrogating its meaning and imagining models – both positive and negative – of intimate relations. Modernism is frequently associated with newness of various kinds, including a turn toward subjectivity, away from Victorian realism.[4] For Bloomsbury and its satellites, an examination of inwardness means an examination of intimacy: they bring to life the ways in which inwardness is not manifested *in vacuo*. In focusing on Bloomsburians' social approaches to subjectivity, in the context of couples, families, and friendships, this study sketches possible terrain for "New Modernisms," a scholarly movement which explores connections between modernist inwardness – so crucial to modernist newness – and the larger culture.[5]

Newness, then – new ideas and new ways of expressing them – will be a recurring motif through these six chapters. But although the years 1900 to 1930 witnessed the social transformations mentioned above, they also confirmed the durability of marriage as a social norm. They lie at the heart of what marriage historian John Gillis terms the "era of mandatory marriage,"[6] between 1850 and 1960. The 2001 British census attests to the distinctness of this era in its commentary on the "declining" percentage "of married couples in the population" beginning in the 1970s (see Tables 1–2 in Appendix).

Standing as we do on the far shore of the sexual revolution of the 1960s and 1970s, after which being single (for example) is less stigmatized than it used to be, we have a critical distance on Bloomsburians' predicaments. What can appear to our hindsight as an ongoing challenge – a debate about love and marriage spanning the Victorian and modern eras – often appeared to moderns as a crisis of intimacy, a sharp feeling of alienation from Victorian mores. Hence Lawrence says in the Foreword to *Women in Love* that "we are now in a period of crisis" – a period in which old ways of feeling (such as those excoriated by Strachey) were dying, and new ones were struggling for expression. He even begs excuse for the repetitive qualities of his novel, claiming that they capture this process of coming-into-expression. Woolf made a similarly sweeping claim about history, psychology, and the power of art – albeit in the guise of an aperçu – when, alluding to Roger Fry's Postimpressionist exhibition, she said that "on or about December 1910, human character changed."[7] And subsequent commentators concur with Lawrence's sense that modern thinkers were "smashing the frame,"[8] that their aesthetic experiments constituted a "cataclysmic upheaval," a "fundamental convulsion."[9]

But moderns had complex feelings about their relation to their parents' culture. Notwithstanding their revolutionary claims, they also saw themselves in more modest ways. "I belong to the fag-end of Victorian liberalism," Forster said.[10] Demonstrating his flair for the illuminating paradox, Strachey says that moderns "know too much" about the Victorian age to write a history of it, and lack the "requisite . . . ignorance, which simplifies and clarifies."[11] And Woolf wrestled with her connections to her mother's generation as much as she marked her distance from it. Little wonder, then, that recent scholars on modernism and Bloomsbury have focused more on continuities than on ruptures between the Victorian and modern eras.[12]

This study weighs claims of "crisis" such as Lawrence's against those of belatedness such as Forster's, but it also opens beyond the nineteenth and twentieth centuries. In addition to seeing the reinvention of intimacy in its late- and post-Victorian aspects, I follow the sociologist Anthony Giddens in viewing it through a wider lens, as part of a post-Enlightenment project of making equality and freedom (for men and women with opposite- and same-sex desires) into realities of daily, domestic life, not just of a male-dominated public sphere.

With this broader narrative in mind, notwithstanding the continuities in Western life since the French and American revolutions, my choice of 1900 to 1930 as a period of focus supports modernists' claims of their differences from Victorians: it suggests that the early twentieth century witnessed a renaissance of intimacies, a renewal of the radical promises of freedom and equality, after the pendulum had swung, through much of the nineteenth century, toward a model of stability and separate spheres. World War One falls in the middle, not at the beginning nor end, of these three decades; thus they open onto a cultural stage where domestic dramas, rather than geopolitical ones, can assume starring roles. Scholarship has long recognized connections between the war's cataclysms and the formal bravado of works such as *Guernica* and *The Waste Land*.[13] But the reinvention of intimacy helps to explain how avant-gardism was equally inspired by disorientation and ambivalence on the battlefields of familial love and friendship.

THE MODERN MIDDLE CLASS AND BLOOMSBURY'S AMBIVALENCE

The "crisis" so named by Lawrence did not exist merely in his passionate, nor Woolf's exquisite, imagination. It was acted out through massive demographic and conceptual changes, some gradual and others more sudden, centered in the middle classes but affecting all of society, as Britain, Europe, and the United States entered the twentieth century. Moderns continued several Victorian trends, including those of urbanizing and suburbanizing England. Eight years before the Queen's death, for example, in 1893 the 14-year-old Forster moved with his mother to Tunbridge Wells. This town's population has kept pace with the expanding national population for the last two centuries. Thirteen years after Victoria's passing, in 1914 the 32-year-old Woolf moved with her husband to Richmond. Like other suburbs in Greater London and elsewhere in Britain, Richmond grew more rapidly than the nation in the late-nineteenth and early-twentieth centuries, as the capital overflowed its boundaries, its population soaring from 950,000 in 1800 to 6 million in 1900. As they transported the matrimonial "mandate" into such crowded environs, modern couples altered the nature of wedded life. They blurred Victorian "spheres," negotiated the limits of female emancipation, and increasingly saw marriage in terms of equality and companionship, in contrast to their parents and grandparents. They differed from their ancestors also in more frequently owning their own residences. They formed small nuclear families, as opposed to Victorian families with multiple domestics and children. While not eager to forgo the convenience and prestige of domestic service, after World War One many households employed only one servant, and no "resident," or live-in, domestics. The latter were replaced by workers including charwomen, hired to perform discrete tasks, such as carpet cleaning, to whom home owners related on a contractual, rather than master–servant, basis (see Tables 3–9 in Appendix). With the "turning inward"[14] of these smaller, more atomized domestic societies, moderns could not only seek companionship, alone together as a family, but they could also indulge more frequently in independent thought and activity. Because new opportunities engender new expectations, and because high expectations can lead to disappointment, the specter of divorce haunted some modern households.

By today's standards, though, moderns' divorce rates were modest. It was within the context of mandatory (and usually lifelong) marriages that they fashioned new selves. The newfound spaciousness of rooms of their own, an increasingly feminized professional sphere, and the influence of sexology and Freudianism led some to develop anti-essentialist attitudes toward sexuality and selfhood. They doubted, for example, that all women share an essential nature that distinguishes them from men. Such doubts hastened the erosion of strict "masculine" and "feminine" roles in households and in society: demographic realities and anti-essentialist interpretations of them reinforced one another in a feedback loop.[15]

Their skepticism also made some moderns anti-foundationalists regarding institutions such as marriage, which they did not see as rooted in natural necessity or divine will, but instead viewed as a social creation, subject (perhaps) to reform. These anti-foundational sensibilities contained the seeds of revolutionary social attitudes.

In some of Bloomsbury's profoundest writings, however, these seeds did not flower into thorough rejections of the middle-class social order, but rather into critiques that balance a sense of belonging and not belonging to society, of loyalty and disloyalty to its dominant values. These writings, influential from their time through today, illustrate how reformist ideas can be as efficacious as revolutionary ones: the kinds of men and women who inhabited the roles of "husband," "wife," and "friend" in 1930 differed greatly from those in 1880. Moore, Freud, Lawrence, and Woolf both record and contribute to these evolutionary changes in the history of gender as they articulate four varieties of *anti-essentialist accommodations.* Though they doubt Victorian theories of "masculine" and "feminine" essences, they largely share Victorians' faith in the practical value of marriage.

Conversely, novels by Forster and Sackville-West articulate *essentialist rejections.* They largely reproduce Victorian treatments of gender, choosing not fully to explore the psychological and moral potential of an "intermediate sex," though characters in each novel provide them opportunities to do so. Such philosophical conservatism might seem to fit logically with a conservative defense of marriage on a "separate-spheres" model. Strangely, though, these two novels reject such marriages as prisons for women.

Each of these two groups of Bloomsburian texts is conceptually self-divided, and in each text the divisions play out in unique ways. But conceptual self-divisions are not necessarily drawbacks: more often than not, these works' internal tensions are sources of aesthetic strength, means to capture the complexity of intimacy as it is simultaneously dreamed of, logically analyzed, and actually experienced. I explore the aesthetic value of Bloomsbury's ambivalence by interweaving analyses of these six works and of other Victorian and modern discourses about sexuality and love. These non-Bloomsburian works often achieve rhetorical potency by articulating a tight fit between their ideas about sexual selfhood on the one hand, and about a good society or a healthy intimacy on the other hand. The contrast between their tight fits and Bloomsburians' ambivalences underscores both the productively disoriented – i.e., modern – nature of Bloomsburians' thought, and the avant-garde aesthetic strategies of Bloomsburian texts – from free indirect style to open endings – so useful for registering paradox and uncertainty.

THE VICTORIAN RIGHT, THE MODERN LEFT, AND THE VALUE OF AMBIVALENCE AS AN AESTHETIC TOOL

Conservative nineteenth-century authors, by contrast to Bloomsbury, conveyed no sense of confusion or crisis in their parallel answers to questions about sexual selfhood and good societies. Such thinkers held, first of all, that the sexes are innately distinct. Nature, and perhaps God – not mere social constructs – account for differences between masculinity and femininity, they believed. These attitudes were as often implicit in Victorian texts as they were carefully spelled out. Second, conservative attitudes toward marriage held that separate male and female "spheres" reflect a natural plan and afford the sexes their best route to shared happiness. Coventry Patmore's *Angel in the House*, a celebration of marriage for love's sake published in four volumes between 1854 and 1862, is a paradigmatic expression of these attitudes, and thus a useful foil for Woolf in her essay "Professions for women,"[16] to which the poem owes its place in the cultural canon. The poem expresses in a literary form a sexual ideology that many of Patmore's contemporaries propounded in magazine articles, newspaper editorials, and essays. Mary Poovey ably delineates this discourse that combines such elements as a conservative view of marriage, essentialist ideas of maleness and femaleness, religious symbolism, and national pride.

Even at the time of the poem's publication, but especially in the new century, this network of ideas about marriage, gender, and Britishness was challenged by an array of feminists and other social critics from what can broadly be called the left. Like many fictional and non-fictional socialist works, Cicely Hamilton's 1909 *Marriage as a Trade* depicted marriage in economic terms – the kind of rhetoric that raised Lawrence's ire – with the aim of exposing its injustice to women. Shaw's *Mrs Warren's Profession* likens nineteenth-century marriage not just to any trade, but to prostitution; other texts reiterate the idea that middle-class women prostitute themselves in legal and "respectable" ways when they trade their bodies to their husbands in exchange for comfort and security. Ibsen's *A Doll's House* employs an arguably bleaker trope, likening marriage to a prison.

Other feminist texts, rather than condemning present-day (or Victorian) marriages, articulate their hopes for the happiness the institution can bring to both sexes. Marie Stopes's 1918 sex manual *Married Love* champions female sexual desire – in contrast to Patmore's association of Vaughan's Wife with spiritual purity – seeing such desire, in the spirit of current science and psychology, as coincident with ovulation, and insisting that marriage should be a partnership of equals. (*Married Love* was banned as obscene by the US Customs Service until 1931, when Judge John Woolsey – who would do the same two years later for James Joyce's *Ulysses* – lifted the ban.) Stopes also edited the journal *Birth Control News* (founded by the American Margaret Sanger), which provided anatomically exact advice; and in 1921 Stopes founded the United Kingdom's first family-planning clinic. In the 1910s and 1920s the birth-control movement succeeded in disseminating contraceptive knowledge especially among the educated classes, and in the 1930s it did so increasingly with the working class as well (see Table 10 of Appendix). Birth rates fell, until war-related fertility concerns led them to rise again after 1941.[17]

Stopes's career was mirrored in the United States by Sanger, whose 1926 *Happiness in Marriage* also celebrated physical passion (Stopes suspected Sanger of stealing her premise). Sanger established the United States' first legal birth-control clinic with the help of her sister, and founded the American Birth Control League, which became Planned Parenthood. Her commitment to sexual emancipation led her to edit a 1928 volume entitled *Motherhood in Bondage*, made up of correspondence from women across America begging for birth-control options, and later to help smuggle contraceptives (then illegal) into the country.

Such non-literary activists as Stopes and Sanger provide limit cases of how thinkers of the twentieth-century left, enlivened by an Enlightenment tradition of scientifically informed social radicalism, could approach questions of sexual selfhood and love – much as Patmore is illustrative of the

Victorian right. For Stopes and Sanger, the two sexes are (at least at their best) rational, freedom-loving, pleasure-seeking, and equal. They believed that, given everything that men and women have in common, heterosexual intimacies thrive on mutual respect and physical attraction. Each believed that men and women, unfettered by religious taboos, should be free to control their sex lives, with the help of scientific knowledge and contraceptive technology. While it was not the business of *Howards End*, *Women in Love*, or *Mrs Dalloway* to expound on such topical issues as birth control, nor to prescribe how "married love" should work, such socially engaged polemics were by no means absent from the many works of Bloomsbury and its satellites. Bertrand Russell, for example, echoes many aspects of these two feminists' attacks on nineteenth-century sexual taboos and chauvinism.

In a series of articles, books, and debates over several decades, Russell variously broached the questions *What are men and women like?* and *How can happy marriages be sustained?* In the spirit of Voltaire and the Enlightenment, he argued against superstition and religion as reliable routes to happiness; largely sympathetic with psychoanalytic thought (though without its interest in polymorphous perversity), he echoed Freud's opposition to Victorian prudery, treating sexual desire as natural, even while aiming to assign it a proper (not excessive) value in a hierarchy of human needs.

His polemics were consistently informed by his sense of historical transformations whose unsettling and potentially liberating influences were conditions of modern family life, including the rearing of children. A 1916 article entitled "Marriage and the population question"[18] sees an "extraordinary change" taking place, with patriarchal authority breaking down, though reason and equality are not yet enshrined in its place. He wonders how marriage affects spouses' characters, confident that the Victorians' separate spheres had arrested (and continue to hinder) both sexes' development. He is sympathetic to modern women's decreased desire for children, but suggests that collateral damage could result from the push toward equality and the "individuality which springs inevitably from mental progress."[19] One danger with equal marriage is that couples may rely too heavily on their love for one another (what Birkin in *Women in Love* calls "egoïsme à deux"),[20] compromising their liberty and happiness, their ability to find pleasure in extra-marital friendships and activities.

Despite his concern for the possible collateral effects of modern morals, though, Russell advocated tirelessly for people's freedom to pursue happiness in what he saw as reasonable ways. His 1927 *New Republic* article entitled "Education without sex taboos"[21] examines free love, seeing infidelity as a fact of life, and wonders – in an anti-essentialist vein reminiscent of Woolf's comment on changes to "human character" – whether new social values could lead spouses to be less jealous. Asking such questions did not endear him to cultural conservatives, though he was by no means anti-marriage; in fact being a father of two (a happy one, he wrote) prompted his interest in education and the formation of children's characters. Later in 1927, at the American Public Forum, he debated on behalf of "trial marriage," a model that affords young couples practice at cohabiting, without the burdens of child rearing or a commitment to a lifelong partnership. Russell saw such marriages – with the help of birth control and divorce by mutual consent – as humane alternatives to the status quo, in which he thought many couples hurried into what Sanger termed "motherhood in bondage."

In expanded form, Russell's ideas about men and women (anti-Victorian, though less geared toward rethinking "human character" than Woolf's or Freud's work) and about marriage (critical of both its Victorian and current shapes, and determined to see it reformed in ways befitting modern experience) became the basis of his 1929 book *Marriage and Morals*, a wide-ranging anthropological, sociological, psychological, and philosophical study of love and marriage under matrilineal, patriarchal, Christian, non-Christian, primitive, and modern conditions. In awarding him the 1950 Nobel Prize for literature, the Nobel Committee noted this work among his varied writings championing "humanitarian ideals and freedom of thought." But such views as his support of premarital sex led to what Russell called a "witch hunt"[22] against him in America. In 1940 the New York Supreme Court deemed him unfit to teach philosophy and dismissed him from his appointment at the City College of New York.[23]

Russell, Shaw, Sanger, and Stopes were, of course, only several of many public figures whose ideas, deemed in one way or another sexually radical, aroused public and legal opposition. Radclyffe Hall's *The Well of Loneliness* was one of several lesbian-themed novels to appear in 1928 (others included Woolf's *Orlando* and Elizabeth Bowen's *The Hotel*), but only Hall's was banned for obscenity, likely because its treatment of this theme was explicit and polemical, whereas *Orlando* explores bisexuality more obliquely, via a protagonist whose sex shifts over the centuries. Woolf and Forster both attended the obscenity trial in support of Hall, though he (like many) was not impressed with *The Well of Loneliness* as a work of literature. Hall's dauntlessness contrasts poignantly with Forster's measured self-revelations: Chapter 3 discusses his lifelong fear of exposure as a homosexual, and its effect on his fiction.

Bloomsburians were neither the first nor the last writers for whom the challenge of expressing (and simultaneously disguising) legally or socially proscribed ideas gave rise to cagey, suggestive, and profound art works, whose various audiences understood them in various ways.[24] Though neither Woolf's nor Forster's novels provoked the interest of censors, Lawrence's did. *The Rainbow* was prosecuted in a 1915 obscenity trial, and unavailable in England until 1926. *Lady Chatterley's Lover* was first published in Italy in 1928, and was not published in England until 1960, thirty years after Lawrence's death and one year after a new obscenity Act of Parliament made it possible, on the grounds of "literary merit," to defend works against censorship. Forster was among those who testified to its "merit" in the 1960 case.

While these two novels, with their disregard for sexual proprieties, represent free-speech landmarks, they are conservative in their own way, particularly in the latter's embrace of monogamy as the "quick and central clue to life."[25] Even Russell, given his modest sense of the malleability of human character, and his lack of interest in homosexuality, had less iconoclastic notions than some radicals about the nature of men and women and the best ways to seek intimacy. The members of the "Freudian Left,"[26] for example, from Wilhelm Reich in the 1920s to Herbert Marcuse in the 1970s, articulated anti-essentialist models of human sexual nature (not just questions such as *Women in Love* poses), and rebellious social programs to go with them. They held that the sexes are each polymorphously perverse[27] – not as distinct from one another as Patmore imagined – and that the middle-class Victorian marriage paradigm was inconsistent with this "nature" and should be abolished. This diverse set of multidisciplinary thinkers drew inspiration from Freud's anti-puritanism and his anti-essentialist accounts of human character, but (being to his "left" politically) rejected his accommodations to bourgeois values. *They* were the true foes of middle-class morality for whom Russell was mistaken by his enemies.

Their polemics did not spring from nowhere. Sexologists, discussed further in the chapters on Freud and Woolf, had questioned nineteenth-century notions of sexual essences, defended women's rights, and developed a vocabulary for same-sex love from as far back as the 1860s. Karl Ulrichs, the widely celebrated inspiration for today's LGBT (lesbian, gay, bisexual, and transgender) movements, termed himself an "Urning" (a man who desires men), argued that his desires were natural, and evoked them with the phrase *anima muliebris virili corpore inclusa* (a woman's soul confined in a man's body), in his battle to achieve recognition and acceptance for a previously unnamed population.

Four decades later, Freud would begin his ongoing engagement with the ideas of Havelock Ellis, who between 1897 and 1928 published the seven-volume *Studies in the Psychology of Sex* (the focus of an obscenity trial when first issued in England), and advocated nationalized health care, sex education, sexual equality, and the recognition of "sexual inversion" (the title of the first of the seven volumes to be published). A long-time intimate of Sanger's, who was married to a lesbian and impotent until age 60, Ellis had an outsider's view on sexual mores that served him as it did Ulrichs and Bloomsbury. He hoped, like the Freudian left, that an awareness of the prevalence of what the heroine of *Women in Love* calls "perversions" would foster a more tolerant, liberated society. For him the march of democratic socialism and the march of sexual freedom went hand in hand.[28]

Ellis shared this logically consistent historical meliorism – this conjoined commitment to a *theoretical* rethinking of sexual identity and a *practically oriented* rethinking of human relations – with his contemporary sexual reformer Edward Carpenter. The latter's Whitmanesque poem *Towards Democracy* (1883–1902) gave literary shape to the dream, shared by Ellis and others, of the paired advance of economic justice and sexual liberation. Works such as *Love's Coming of Age* (1912) expressed his feminist convictions, arguing that a just society required female economic independence, that marriage enforced unnecessary celibacy on both sexes and was (*pace* Shaw and others) a form of prostitution. Like Russell, Carpenter wondered whether jealousy is natural to human attachments, or the product of repressive mores. Carpenter influenced many, including Forster, with his ideas about the unique role that the "intermediate sex" (the title of Carpenter's 1908 pamphlet) could play in humanizing society.

Forster was skeptical, however, about society's capacity for tolerance, where Carpenter was more optimistic; thus Forster expressed doubts about the present feasibility of "intermediacy" in several works. In *Maurice*, two men must defy society and escape into the woods to be together; and in *A Passage to India*, the universe itself, from the horses to the temples, is "not yet" ready for love between Fielding and Aziz.[29] Forster's novels, like Woolf's and Lawrence's, made ambivalence key to their depictions of the challenges of modern intimacy; and their internal tensions – even pessimism – contributed to their power. Freud's *Dora*, with its many novelistic qualities, is similarly successful in using a range of aesthetic tools to express a complexly ambivalent attitude toward intimacy.

BLOOMSBURY'S IMPORTANCE FOR MODERNISM

Such an account of Bloomsbury's modernism – as an ambivalent response both to modernity and to Victorianism, informed by Freud – has never been explicitly formulated by the group's many accomplished biographers and exegetes, though they provide a range of valuable interpretive models. Leon Edel's 1979 *Bloomsbury: A House of Lions* conveys the group's vivacity and ambition. In the 1990s, S. P. Rosenbaum documented Bloomsburians' intellectual interrelations, examining what they said about themselves, what contemporaries said about them, and what their writings reveal about their Victorian and modern preoccupations. Raymond Williams's 1978 "The Bloomsbury Fraction" provides a more critical, though balanced, analysis of the group's class allegiances, seeing its commitment to "civilized individualism" as a complex stance both against and in collusion with the dominant values of England's upper class. Finally, Christine Froula's magisterial 2005 *Virginia Woolf and the Bloomsbury Avant-Garde* expands on Williams's examination of Bloomsbury's "civilized" values. Froula situates Bloomsbury in a sweeping post-Enlightenment narrative. For her, modernity consists in the never-completed struggle for human rights, democracy, and peace; and Bloomsburians such as Woolf strive to realize this ideal of "civilization."[30]

My account of Bloomsbury and twentieth-century modernity will, I hope, complement Froula's, and deepen it in several dimensions. First, I treat intimacy rather than geopolitics. Second, by giving other Bloomsburians equal billing with Woolf, I elaborate their shared concerns, as Edel and Rosenbaum do. Finally, the primary historical focus of my six chapters – on the permeable boundaries between Victorian and modern attitudes – is narrower than Froula's.

Admittedly, there is value in integrating Bloomsbury's ideas into a broad historical narrative. Thinkers dating from Mary Wollstonecraft to as far back as Christine di Pizan have seen gender as a social construct, for example. Nor were Bloomsburians confined in their historical curiosity, as demonstrated by Moore's interest in classical Athens (implicitly in its homosexual culture, which he evoked tentatively, wary of Victorian prejudice) and by Lawrence's fascination with the medieval ideal of *Blutbrüderschaft* – a mystical brotherhood between men. But Lawrence and Woolf's strategies for examining gender in combination with sexuality – all in the light of psychoanalytic ideas – could only emerge at a time when thinkers were sorting through the conflicting legacies of conservatives in the mold of Patmore, and of sexologists such as Carpenter. Thus, while Froula celebrates Bloomsbury's continuity with all that she admires in Enlightenment values, my treatment of Bloomsburian ambivalence does not assume the existence of categories (such as "justice," "love," or "womanhood") that have remained stable over the last several centuries and that would enable the group easily to distinguish enlightened from misguided thinking about gender and intimacy.

Nonetheless, despite the "archaeologically" visible differences between Bloomsbury's milieu and ours, the eight decades of cultural history since 1930 illustrate our debt to these post-Victorians, with the proliferation of high and popular literature, television programs and films, magazines, and other media dedicated to grasping the *natures* of women and men; specifying what makes them happy, sexually or emotionally; and deciding whether contemporary shapes of couplehood, family life, and extra-familial friendships answer our needs. Today's debates about gay marriage demonstrate the incomplete evolution, four decades after the Stonewall riots of 1969, in thinking about "sexual orientation" – an identity category vaguely foreshadowed by Freud's term "sexual objects" – but also demonstrate the depth and breadth of change in popular attitudes toward human sexualities, for which the sexologists (and to a lesser extent Bloomsbury) laid groundwork. Nor has academia ignored the topic of intimacy, as attested by a range of multidisciplinary works, such as a special issue of *Critical Inquiry* entitled "Intimacy," published in book form in 2000.

In Bloomsbury's debates and struggles, we can see much of ourselves. When Lauren Berlant, the editor of *Intimacy*, acknowledges in her introduction that "romance and friendship inevitably meet the instabilities of sexuality . . . and exhaustion;" when Laura Kipnis, in "Adultery" – her contribution to Berlant's volume – asks rhetorically, on behalf of a would-be adulterer, "When did sex get so boring [and become something] to 'work at,'"[31] they voice updated versions of Russell's concerns about the deadening effects of monogamy under an economic regime of lingering separate spheres, with overworked husbands divorced from home life, and stultified wives unable to develop (or sometimes even become aware of) their intellectual potential.[32] They echo Lawrence's critique of intimacy as it is actually lived – not merely dreamed of – under the "love-and-marriage ideal."[33] They give voice to feelings of depression and exhaustion in marriage, whereas *Mrs Dalloway* evokes feelings of both resignation and hope, in its picture of a heroine retiring at midday to her attic room, illustrating the importance, to a stable intimacy, of solitary space.

But while feeling the presence of the past can bring Russell's, Lawrence's, and Woolf's concerns to life for us in the early twenty-first century, respecting its past-ness is also salutary for us who approach questions of intimacy after Masters and Johnson – just as Bloomsbury benefited from its uncanny sense of the familiarity *and* unfamiliarity of Victorian predicaments. "Sex and talk," for example – Candace Vogler's contribution to

Intimacy – sees "self-expressive intimacy" (her term for the model of communication recommended by Masters and Johnson) as a frequent sign of "morbid companionate marriage." For her, the "case-study unhappy marriage" suffers not from a dearth but an excess of intimacy, in which partners obsessively check up on the progress of their relationship, analyze each other's motives, and try new sexual positions.[34] Her sense of disillusionment, of exhaustion in intimacy, lies far from the purview of *Mrs Dalloway*, whose protagonist-spouses do not know one another nearly so well. But it may lie equally far from the purview of *Women in Love*: while Birkin and Ursula certainly exhaust themselves with their arguments, the author treats these not as smothering routines, but as signs of the "polarisation"[35] that enlivens the couple's quest for authenticity. Lawrence and Vogler stand on opposite sides of decades of research and popular talk about the promises and perils of intimacy, and at different moments in economic histories that have gradually reduced (though not eliminated) the separateness of male and female spheres, especially for educated classes. Vogler, like Foucault, occupies a retrospective vantage unavailable to Bloomsburians – post-Masters-and-Johnson, post-Kinsey, post-AIDS, and long after divorces have mushroomed to well beyond their rates *l'entre deux guerres* – in the midst of an ongoing discursive explosion concerning sex, intimacy, and the nature of maleness and femaleness. Bloomsbury, with its self-divided ideas about reinventing intimacy in the context of modernist experimentation, bridges the early twentieth and early twenty-first centuries, as it simultaneously marks the distance between them, according to the same dual logic by which the group at once bridges the Victorian and modernist epochs and marks them off against one another with the help of rhetorical attacks such as Strachey's.

After the cyclical returns of conservative family values in the 1920s, 1950s, and 1980s; after the various waves of feminism marking either the differences or the similarities between the sexes, seeking either to celebrate or to question what is "essentially" feminine; and at a time when same-sex marriages are being legally recognized in various nations and American states, Bloomsbury's diverse works enable us to sketch a tale of how the relative stability of late-Victorian ideologies of love led to the ambiguities of modernist ideas about intimacy, and in turn to contemporary ambivalence. (See Table 11 in Appendix for same-sex marriage data.) Bloomsbury records, with exemplary passion and precision, moderns' sense that foundations, essences, and the recent protocols and meanings of intimacy were dissolving, and that for some thinkers, old (Enlightenment, medieval, or classical) protocols might be redeemable.

It is not surprising that Bloomsbury should be sensitive to Victorian–modern continuities, since group members including Moore, Forster, and Strachey had recently been Apostles. The Apostles, discussed further in Chapter 1, were a secret Cambridge undergraduate discussion society that dated to the 1820s, and that, under Moore's leadership in the opening years of the twentieth century, bore the stamp of Victorian reticence. But when Strachey succeeded Moore as the Apostles' leader in February 1902, by force of personality he encouraged the society to embrace the homoeroticism that had long been implicit in its valuation of art and affection. He flouted Victorian prudery, provoking Bloomsburians to question which values they shared with their predecessors and which they did not.

VICTORIANS NO LONGER?

Bloomsburians critically examined a tapestry of Victorian ideas not only about sexual selfhood and intimacy, but also about morality, mental health, and human development. This tapestry had a number of essentialist threads. These included the convictions that the concept "good" is stable, not historically contingent (Moore threatens to unravel, but ends up reinforcing, this conviction); that sanity and insanity are easily distinguishable (Freud and Woolf skillfully blur this distinction); and that children, in their purity, are radically unlike adults (a myth that Freud vigorously rejects). Bloomsbury did not critique these essentialist ideas as loose threads, but as they were interwoven with conservative attitudes toward marriage, monogamy, and family that de-emphasized individual choice, intellectual companionship, and equality, and valued economic sufficiency, stability over time, and social respectability.

At times, Bloomsburians such as Strachey were inclined to rend this Victorian tapestry. But in many instances, Bloomsburians – unlike the Freudian left – labored instead to disentangle what they found useful in the tapestry from what they found outmoded. Often, two works by one writer expressed different attitudes toward Victorianism. "Professions for women" repudiates the idea of the Angel, but in more than one novel Woolf admiringly evokes women who honored the ideal. *To the Lighthouse* pays homage to her mother, much as *Mrs Dalloway* celebrates Kitty Maxse for raising hostessing to an art form.

Critics, too, have recognized Victorian–modern continuities, from the ways literatures of the two eras imagined male–male desire, to their treatments of strident feminists, to their shared conservatism regarding marriage. Eric Haralson sees an undercurrent of "masculine desire" in the work of

Henry James, of which his discerning queer contemporaries were fully aware; and sees James and Wilde as precursors to Gertrude Stein, W. H. Auden, and other modernists who treated same-sex themes more openly.[36] Paul Levy makes a similar case for *Principia Ethica*, using the metaphor of an hourglass to describe how Moore, the funnel of the hourglass, distills the energies of the "English Intellectual Aristocracy" dating back to the 1820s, so that this Cambridge tradition can filter into Bloomsbury and "a great deal of modern philosophy."[37] Ann Ardis discusses how novelists and editorialists of the 1880s and 1890s constructed the "New Woman" – a headstrong feminist who refused the roles of wife and mother – and how modern novels by Woolf, Lawrence, and others respond to this late-Victorian discourse about femininity.[38] Finally, in addition to these continuities between Victorian and modern ideas about what some men can be like (with their gently subversive homoerotic subcultures) and what some women can be like (with their refusal to abide by traditional gender codes), Davida Pines describes a conservative continuity in Victorian and modern thinking about heterosexual monogamy. To Pines it is noteworthy that even as polemical a modernist as Lawrence remains loyal to the "marriage plot";[39] she reminds us that modernists' rupture with their ancestors was not entire. And yet . . .

And yet modernists *did* distinguish themselves from Victorians: George Eliot, W. M. Thackeray, and the Brontë sisters' heteronormative representations of sex belong to a different order of discourse than Woolf's examinations of polymorphous perversity, and the shimmering manner in which she renders Clarissa's conscious and unconscious processes. Both Woolf's fictional and her expository treatments of the Angel record her complex feelings about the transformations she saw taking place in human character – the same transformations that inspired her stylistic experiments.

WOMEN AS "ANGELS," ACTIVISTS, AND "COMPANIONS"

This Angel rose not merely between female authors and their creative originality, but more broadly between women and their public ambitions. Woolf, born in 1882, was not alone in resenting her exclusion from Oxbridge. While conscious of her familial advantages (her father's extensive library, her connections by blood and marriage to English letters), she was also conscious of having been born into a chauvinistic era. The Education Act of 1870 meant that, to a degree, boys and girls across England were educated in tandem and exposed to female authority figures – teachers – outside of their families. This legislation likely played a role, by the twentieth century, in altering the protocols of intimacy, softening the boundaries between male and female spheres. But it took decades for higher education to achieve a comparable equality. Girton College for women had only been established in 1869 (and was not initially recognized by Cambridge University authorities); Newnham College had been established in 1880 (but women were not at first allowed to take degrees, and required special permission to attend lectures). By 1910 over a thousand women attended Oxbridge; but not until 1920 and 1948, respectively, were women admitted to full membership at Oxford and Cambridge.

When the 46-year-old Woolf, therefore, was invited in 1928 to read papers at Girton and Newnham that became *A Room of One's Own*, she felt how changed – though still unfair to women – was the world inhabited by her young audiences. Her fiction attests to this difference between her parents' and her own generation, the latter of which included more examples of the "incandescent," "androgynous" mind[40] extolled in *A Room of One's Own*. Hostesses Mrs Ramsay and Mrs Dalloway bring their artistic visions to bear on social gatherings, but Lily Briscoe realizes her vision on a canvas – a member of Woolf's generation whose abstract materials enable her to transcend gender. In contrast to Lily, Richard Dalloway incarnates his nineteenth-century gender role – that of an upright, public-spirited male – to such a degree that he fumbles to find a common language with his domesticated wife. The Dalloways' marriage indicates that, before the blurring of "spheres," heterosexual intimacies brought together two very different, non-"androgynous" minds.

In the new century's public life, as much as in its private lives, the idea of an angelic female "nature" was contested – by none more forcefully than by militant suffragettes, whose agitations met with both success and failure. Marion Dunlop's 1909 hunger strike may have helped to bring three Conciliation Bills, that would have granted female suffrage, before the House of Commons in 1911, 1912, and 1913, but each bill failed to pass. When WSPU (Women's Social and Political Union) activists burned down Lloyd George's house in 1913, he renounced support for their cause. Nonetheless, in 1918 women over 30 were enfranchised, and a decade later – in the same year as Woolf's lectures at Girton and Newnham – the age was lowered to 21, granting the sexes equal voting rights.

But despite their successes, suffragettes' confrontational tactics led to a backlash. In "Cocksure women and hensure men," Lawrence says that women who fear their own "henny" natures lay votes and ink bottles, not eggs, and thus "miss life altogether."[41] The essay does not say what a henny "nature" implies about a woman's role in an intimate relationship or a family economy. Nor is its image of the female author Lawrence's most original rhetorical gesture. As Ardis discusses, such insults were common currency among opponents of the "New Woman," such as the 1894 *Punch* contributor who opined

> though Foolscap and Ink are the whole of her Diet,
> The nagging New Woman can never be quiet![42]

But although Lawrence could sound like a reactionary Victorian, he had company among modernists – even progressive ones – in regarding activists warily. Katharine Hilbery, the heroine of *Night and Day* (1919) – Woolf's most Victorian novel in style – yearns to escape her family's stuffy drawing room, but does not emulate her suffragette friend, Mary Datchet, whose political commitments damage her personal life. Mary rejects a proposal from Ralph Denham, whom Katharine eventually marries. While far from being antifeminist in a Lawrentian manner – while not insisting that Mary "misses life altogether" – *Night and Day* does blame her headstrong idealism for her fractured life. The stereotype of the New Woman as excessively rational, excessively concerned with social justice, and unfeeling could easily be invoked by an antifeminist such as Lawrence, but also by Woolf, who differs from feminist predecessors such as Mary Wollstonecraft, Harriet Taylor, and John Stuart Mill in her determination to treat erotic life frankly, to value it, and even to be critical of female characters who do not.

Night and Day implies that Katharine and Ralph might find erotic fulfillment as part of a "companionate marriage,"[43] a model of domestic democracy – treated in Chapter 4 in this book – that stresses bonds of friendship and intellect over those of fleeting passions; that values spousal equality; and that sees economically sound partnerships as bulwarks of a middle-class social order.

Women in Love, on the other hand, broadens the Bloomsburian discussion, questioning whether the rationalistic ideal of companionate marriage is healthy, or whether it exalts selfhood, equality, and heterosexual normalcy at the expense of passion, self-transcendence, and bisexual fulfillment. When does a same-sex friendship, such as Rupert and Gerald's, assume erotic significance? What kind of love-partner(s) should a man or woman choose? Should such partnerships be permanent and exclusive of other amorous experiences? Does either the Enlightenment vocabulary of equality or the chivalric vocabulary of love provide modern men and women an authentic way to cultivate their feelings? From *Principia Ethica* to *Dora* to the novels, Bloomsburian texts pose such historically informed questions; blur disciplinary divides; and build up, each in their own dialect, a shared language of modern intimacy put to the test.

THE DEMOGRAPHICS OF MODERN HUMAN CHARACTER

In developing such a language, Bloomsburians give philosophical shape to demographic developments that distinguish nearly a century of British social life from what preceded and followed it.[44] The latter decades of the nineteenth century inaugurated the aforementioned "era of mandatory marriage," when rates of people "married but not churched" dropped, as did common-law and other "irregular" marriages. As the twentieth century neared, matrimony sanctioned both by state and ecclesiastical authorities became socially obligatory, especially in the lower and middle classes. Merely civil marriages were reserved largely for pregnant brides and run-away couples, potential outcasts preserving what respectability they could. Illegitimacy rates dropped and (aside from wartime "bumps") did not rise again to mid-nineteenth-century levels until the 1960s (see Table 12 of Appendix). When the Brangwen sisters, at the opening of *Women in Love*, question whether marriage constitutes the "end of experience,"[45] they question a far-reaching norm.

Despite late-Victorian and modern citizens' shared "compulsion to marry," however, moderns redefined matrimonial conventions, for example in their less crowded households. In the final decades of the nineteenth century, as middle-class families amassed disposable incomes and mimicked the aristocracy, they also faced requirements of maintaining appearances: entertaining in fine style, and keeping multiple domestics.[46] After World War One, however, middle-class communities developed separate stand-ards of respectability, and even wealthier ones often maintained more modest staffs. By the mid-twentieth century, live-in servants were mostly an institution of the past. As more wives and mothers found time (however limited) in private spaces, new patterns of contemplative self-fashioning developed – a process that had been under way since the Victorian years.[47] In *Howards End*, the open, well-lit spaces of the titular dwelling are instrumental in helping the Schlegel sisters repair their relationship at a time of crisis: Helen is far from arbitrary in wanting to sleep in a particular house – not a hotel. With the smaller populations of middle-class twentieth-century households, and young adults' increased freedom from familial supervision, such breathing space became available to a wider section of the population.

Perhaps most crucially to their freedom in their intimate lives, twentieth-century parents had fewer children than their parents. Whereas women married in 1871 averaged 5.9 offspring, their counterparts married between 1925 and 1929 – beneficiaries of the contraception and family planning advocated by Stopes and Sanger – averaged 2.1. In the late-nineteenth century, middle-class family sizes decreased at a disproportionately accelerated rate, but in the twentieth century working-class families benefited comparably from contraception, and shrank numerically at rates nearly identical to those of their middle-class peers (Tables 6–7 in Appendix). This development, of course, did not guarantee that parents and children of any class would be confidantes, nor that family members would have rooms of their own.[48] Nonetheless, when modernists asked new theoretical questions about maleness and femaleness, and new practical questions about intimacy, the smaller family formed part of the background against which such questions were framed. Whereas Victorians from the Brontës to Dickens to Eliot to Hardy depicted households with multiple children, often including orphans, Clarissa Dalloway has a single daughter to whom she is not close; the protagonists of *Women in Love* are childless (Ursula muses that "perhaps one doesn't want [children] in one's soul – only superficially"); and Margaret Schlegel says that she "does not love children" and "is happy to have none," though she encourages her widowed sister to love her illegitimate son.[49]

Notwithstanding the lessened burden of smaller households, the ideal of companionship could itself be burdensome, as Russell and Lawrence intuited in their time, and as Berlant and others have analyzed in light of additional evidence in ours. But modern companionate-marriage experiments, with all their trials and errors, did not follow after a golden past. Victorian compulsory marriage contained the seeds of its own dissolution. As more mid-nineteenth-century couples wed – not necessarily happily, as happiness was not necessarily their main goal in marrying[50] – the institution came under unavoidable strain. The 1857 Matrimonial Causes Act established the Divorce Court, which gave middle-class couples access to civil divorce. (Parliamentary dissolutions of marriage were reserved de facto for the wealthy and well connected.) *The Times* called the establishment of this civil court, and the paradigm of marriage based on contract rather than sacrament, "one of the great social revolutions of our time," although this "revolution" needed decades to unfold – as, for example, subsequent divorce legislation added protections for women's property.

Liberal English thinkers prided themselves on these advances, which distinguished their country from Ireland, and from continental Catholic nations, whose more restrictive divorce laws they considered medieval. But at the same time, liberal Victorians prided themselves on not being Americans, whose higher divorce rates they saw as a sign of social dissolution. In the latter nineteenth century the "democratization of divorce" swept all Western nations, but at different paces. England found a middle pace, with which many thinkers felt some comfort. Even Evangelicals and other respectables, who had stigmatized divorce earlier in the nineteenth century, grew less antagonistic as it was woven into the social fabric.[51]

But a spike in divorces after World War One made it more difficult to remain equanimous about this "revolution." The year 1911 saw fewer than 600 English and Welsh divorces; 1918, the last year of the war, saw over 1,100; and 1920 saw over 3,000. "By the 1920s," says sociologist E. J. Graff, "every third magazine article seemed to be entitled 'Will Modern Marriage Survive?'"[52]

In retrospect, however, threats to its survival during Bloomsbury's years seem less cataclysmic than they did at the time. Roderick Phillips argues that there have been three major phases of increase in the history of English divorce. The first "phase of take off" lasted from the establishment of the Divorce Court in 1857 through World War One; the second phase – still modest, though larger than the first – lasted through 1960; and only in the post-'sixties phase has "mass divorce" been institutionalized.[53] What seemed ominous in Bloomsbury's time can seem in hindsight like manageable (though not negligible) dislocations, as testified to by the liberalization of divorce laws since World War One, and by the high rates of divorce in recent decades – over 50 percent for marriages performed in 1991, for example (see Tables 13–14 in Appendix).

Despite their legal freedom, then, Bloomsbury's contemporaries lacked the social freedom to terminate marriages, on anything like the scale that men and especially women have known since 1960. Early-twentieth-century spouses needed to find freedom *within* marriage. The mandate to wed meant that modern couplehood could feel like an iron cage, as Birkin complains. But the stigma of remaining single, especially for women, meant that bachelorhood and spinsterhood could also be cages. Helen Schlegel is fortunate enough, though single, to raise her child on an idyllic rural property. Good luck saves her from wandering throughout Europe, unable to show her face in respectable England. Being an unwed mother, of course, exacerbates her risk of alienation, but being unwed in itself brands her as unusual, as the contrasting examples of Margaret and Henry, Leonard and Jacky Bast, and the various married Wilcox progeny all illustrate.

THE LOVE THAT DARED TO SPEAK

Taken together, patterns of early-twentieth-century marriage (given its frequency) and divorce (given what hindsight reveals to be its modest rate of increase) illustrate the power of social norms to contain crises, as much as they suggest – in combination with other data – that intimacy was being reinvented. But those desires that lurked beyond the borders of the law – a man's for a man, a woman's for a woman – are among the most threatening and potentially the most liberating forces in this era of cultural history.

To early-twenty-first-century readers, the identity categories "gay" and "lesbian" are relatively sharp, but a century and more ago they were still emerging, in what Foucault calls a "reverse" discourse against the prejudice with which sodomy and other non-normative sexual practices were regarded.[54] Nineteenth-century English law simultaneously expanded the range of prosecutable homosexual offenses and reduced the sentences for such offenses. This process culminated with the 1885 Labouchère Amendment, which subjected acts of "gross indecency" to punishments of up to two years in prison, and which enabled Wilde's 1895 conviction. Because "gross indecency" could apply to an unspecified variety of behaviors, it broadened suspicions among police and judges, and heightened fear among homosexuals. Not until 1967 did the English legal code reverse this dynamic, gradually bringing laws about homosexual and heterosexual behavior into parity (see Table 15 in Appendix). It is little wonder, therefore, that Forster feared exposure, only showing *Maurice* to select friends and lamenting his "weariness of the subject that I both can and may treat – the love of men for women and vice versa."[55] And it is little wonder – although men were more likely to be targeted as sexual criminals than women – that *A Room of One's Own* imagines the sentence "Chloe liked Olivia" as possible only in a future literature,[56] and that a life-partnership between Clarissa and Sally is never entertained in *Mrs Dalloway*, even as an abstract possibility.

Thus, although an 1892 translation of Krafft-Ebing first brought the words "homosexuality" and "heterosexuality" into English, they would not be frequently used for the better part of a century. Sexology, however, spoke the names of a range of non-normative loves,[57] and challenged intolerance with the scientific scrupulousness – the careful definitions, the rational acceptance of human sexuality in all its variety – absent from much public discourse.

While the Bloomsburian texts I examine do not plead for tolerance, nonetheless the controversies regarding modern intimacy – marriage and divorce, roles and opportunities for the sexes, attitudes toward same-sex desire in particular and erotic life in general – thoroughly inform them, thematically and stylistically. Clouds of sexual oppression loom over the marriages of Margaret Schlegel (before her husband's emasculation) and Sackville-West's heroine Lady Slane (as long as her marriage lasts). Specters of heteronormativity motivate silences in *Principia Ethica.* Didacts Freud and Lawrence argue, under the guise of narratives, that psychic health or spiritual vitality is damaged when males and females as young as 14 repress their incestuous, homosexual, morbid, or aggressive desires. How moderns might allow such desires their proper scope, while maintaining the exclusive intimacies that Birkin craves with his chosen woman and man, or while accommodating social customs as Freud advises, is a problem that neither didact – to his credit – claims to solve. Bloomsbury's various ambivalent contributions to the reinvention of intimacy share a resistance to simple resolutions.

THE BLOOMSBURIAN COHORT

The following chapters will trace these ambivalent reactions, to see how, having unwoven the Victorian tapestry, Bloomsburians weave modern texts into being. The chapters move chronologically through three decades of Bloomsburian history, beginning with *Principia*, which functioned like a bible for the group.[58] Previous commentators have debated whom to count as members of Bloomsbury. I see Moore, Forster, and Woolf as essential to the group, though Edel's house of lions excludes the two men. Chapter 1, on Moore, and Chapter 3, on Forster, will explain my reasons.

Freud belongs for many reasons in this study of why Bloomsbury matters to modernism, and how this group changed modern notions of selfhood and love. He analyzed several group members including James and Alix Strachey (Lytton's brother and sister-in-law), whose monumental, twenty-four-volume *Complete Psychological Works of Sigmund Freud* not only disseminated Freud to the English-speaking world, but also – because of its scrupulous editorial apparatus of introductory notes, indexes, appendices, etc. – served as the basis for scholarship on Freud's work in other languages, including his native German.[59] Freud also trained Bloomsburian associates as psychoanalysts, including Adrian and Karen Stephen (Virginia Woolf's brother and sister-in-law), who helped the profession to establish its foothold in England. After Leonard and Virginia Woolf's Hogarth Press took over the publication of the papers of the International Psychoanalytic Institute in 1924, Hogarth became Freud's authorized publisher in England. Leonard Woolf said that "the greatest pleasure I ever got from publishing *The Psycho-Analytical Library* was the relationship which it established between us and Freud."[60] Beyond Freud's personal and professional relations with Bloomsbury, a Freudian intellectual climate after World War One gained his works wider readerships, and the treatment of delayed shell shock won medical respectability for psychoanalysis. Whether sympathetic or resistant to these developments, Bloomsburians could not ignore them.

Lawrence, by contrast, was hostile to Bloomsbury. In a 1915 letter to David Garnett, he applies the label "beetles" to John Maynard Keynes, Francis Birrell and Duncan Grant, whose sexuality he found repulsive.[61] He portrays Grant unflatteringly in *Lady Chatterley's Lover*. But his antipathy belies his connections to the group. He collaborated with Leonard Woolf and S. S. Koteliansky on Hogarth's translation of I. A. Bunin's *The Gentleman from San Francisco and Other Stories* (1922). Like Virginia Woolf and other Bloomsburians, Lawrence was a frequent guest at Garsington, Ottoline Morrell's country property that housed conscientious objectors during World War One.[62] Morrell is satirized mercilessly as Hermione in *Women in Love*, which is no friendlier to London's Bohemia (a possible swipe at Bloomsbury) than it is to Hermione's set. But Lawrence's repulsion for Grant and Morrell indicates the important roles that Bloomsburian culture, including its unconventional masculinities, played in his imagination. Just as Bloomsburians (whatever their mixed feelings) could not ignore Freud, neither could Lawrence ignore Bloomsbury. A profoundly original thinker and artist, he was also a satellite in the group's orbit, obsessed by similar questions and aware of its importance to England's literary and philosophical scene.

Vita Sackville-West's connection to Bloomsbury is detailed in Chapter 6, in particular her love for Virginia Woolf and her envious emulation of Woolf as a writer. Like Freud and Lawrence, she too was connected to Hogarth. In 1931 she and her cousin Edward Sackville-West published a translation of Rainer Maria Rilke's *Duineser Elegien* through the Woolfs' Press.

By virtue of these connections to other aspects of British and European culture – via Hogarth; psychoanalysis; its patron, Morrell; its aristocratic admirer, Sackville-West; and its working-class critic and self-styled enemy, Lawrence – Bloomsbury insinuates itself into modernity and modernism. I follow previous scholars including Rosenbaum in examining the group's dynamic interactions with the larger culture. But my six chapters do one new thing: build this story of interaction around the reinvention of intimacy.

Part I, entitled "Philosophical backgrounds," examines the anti-essentialist accommodations of two very different texts. In Chapter 1, "Yellowy goodness in Bloomsbury's bible," I see the "linguistic turn"[63] of *Principia Ethica*'s opening chapter and the (coded) celebration of homoerotic affection in its final chapter as philosophical moves with far-reaching anti-essentialist potential. Moore changed English ethical philosophy by making the language in which it is conducted a central object of its own study. However, having specified that "good" and "bad" are "predicates" (linguistic atoms), Moore's first chapter squanders this anti-essentialist insight, and his opportunity to destabilize their meaning, by insisting that they refer to unchanging (Platonic) ideals. Then, having asserted that personal affection is life's greatest good, and having implied that male–male affection is the model under discussion, Moore's final chapter examines this affection from an aesthetic angle, replacing a question about eros with one that might as well be about art appreciation. These are pointed criticisms, to be sure, and my own Chapter 1 poses them more complexly, in part by exploring how Moore's analogy of "good" and "yellow" invokes the 1890s sexual counter-culture. But the accommodations that balance Moore's flashes of anti-essentialism are one of *Principia*'s defining gestures.

Chapter 2, "Freud's denial of innocence," explains how, in contrast to Moore's timidity before the topic of sex, the founder of psychoanalysis denies that the object of his case study, even when she was only 14, could have reacted to Herr K.'s advances – at the crucial unconscious level – with "innocent" modesty. Not only must, and should, Dora feel sexually aroused by Herr K., but erotic currents also pass between her and numerous other people, including Freud, her father, and Frau K. Various strictures are breached by these erotic feelings: the incest taboo, proscriptions against same-sex and doctor–patient couplings, and a code of femininity according to which no woman should be filled with such varied desires. Freud's anti-essentialist attack on the Angel in the House is at least as far-reaching, and certainly less ambivalent, than Woolf's critiques in *Mrs Dalloway* and *To the Lighthouse*. The essence ascribed to angelic Victorian women – self-sacrificing innocence – is thoroughly dissolved in Freud's depiction of his polymorphously perverse, tough, vulnerable, selfish protagonist. But just as Moore accommodates social proprieties despite his homoerotic themes, so too the pragmatic Freud seeks for ways that "Dora" and others may integrate their polymorphous energies into the "middle-class social order."[64]

Part II, entitled "Defeated husbands," carries my analyses of battles between the sexes into Bloomsburian novels. Both *Howards End* and *Women in Love* depict wives' victories, but in each case the victory is ambiguous. Chapter 3, "Forster's missing figures," discusses how the essentialism of *Howards End* in two ways compromises its rejection of marriage on a Wilcoxian model. First, its heroine Margaret begins the novel as a single New Woman and ends it as a married angel, as naïve and incurious as Henry Wilcox's first wife, Ruth. Henry's physical crippling is more than counterbalanced by Margaret's intellectual devolution. The Margaret of the early chapters goes *missing* in the later ones. The second missing figure in *Howards End* is the male "intermediate" whose feminine traits make him a potential moral example. Intermediates appear in other Forster novels, so their absence from this one is conspicuous, and it partly inspires my critique of how *Howards End* projects masculine and feminine "Soul-material" – Carpenter's term for gender-driven psychologies – into the new century.

Chapter 4, "The love that cannot be escaped," returns my study to the dominant form of Bloomsbury's ambivalence – the anti-foundational accommodationism of *Women in Love*. Birkin is the novel's anti-foundationalist, desiring to move beyond the concept of "love" into an impersonal plane where he and Ursula might balance one another like stars.[65] This quest is consistent with the novel's critique of selfhood as a foundation on which love might be built. *Women in Love* would seem to agree with Birkin that the notion of a self-knowing subject telling a knowable object "I love you" is problematic on both ontological and ethical grounds. Nonetheless Birkin and the novel make substantial concessions to the "love-and-marriage ideal"[66] for which Ursula is an ambivalent spokeswoman. Imperfectly as heterosexual monogamy and companionate marriage answer to Birkin's mystical spirit of rebellion, he must live – and to a large degree, think – according to their logic, both because Gerald dies, and because Ursula makes a compelling case for the value of "love."

Part III, entitled "Domestic Angels," examines how Woolf and her acolyte Sackville-West weigh their heroines' marriages against the lives these marriages prevent them from living. Chapter 5, "Woolf's sane woman in the attic," argues that *Mrs Dalloway* makes anti-essentialist accommodations in a roughly Freudian vein, finding Clarissa's marriage, on balance, a wise and healthy arrangement. Thirty-three years into this union, admittedly, she continues to love Peter and to treasure her adolescent kiss with Sally as "the most exquisite moment" of her life.[67] She remains polyamorous and, at least in the past, seems to have been bisexual. Nonetheless, marriage gives her a husband who – notwithstanding his limitations – is kind to his wife and daughter. Richard provides Clarissa a home with an attic room of her own in which she can mend her frayed psyche, and a common area in which she can practice her artistry as a hostess. Her marriage may cost her opportunities for intimacy, but it gives her a safe environment that a life with Peter would have been unlikely to include.

Sackville-West's novel, on the other hand, critiques marriage in a way unlike *Mrs Dalloway* and more like *Howards End.* Its essentialist pictures of gender – particularly of its elderly heroine, a remnant of the Victorian era – undermine this critique, or at least render it deeply ambivalent. The novel's aesthetic conservatism, moreover, reinforces its unadventurous treatments of sexuality. Thus, notwithstanding its accomplishments, *All Passion Spent* serves as a bookend of my study of Bloomsbury and modernism. As I argue in my concluding chapter, "A return to essences," *All Passion Spent* emulates *Mrs Dalloway* without the precursor text's avant-gardism. The absence of such modernist experiments – which are also epistemological roadmaps – entails a conceptual as well as a technical loss.

When the modernism is drained from a work by Woolf's ardent devotee, it is on its way to being drained from Bloomsbury. Lawrence died the year before *All Passion Spent* appeared; Forster published his last novel six years prior to that; and Moore had long since become a defender of common sense, discarding the Platonism that makes *Principia* philosophically schizophrenic – which is its great strength. Woolf and Freud remained productive through the 1930s, though arguably their best work was past them, and Freud was largely codifying and consolidating – into the protocols of a profession dedicated to shoring up the middle-class social order – the dazzling metaphors that, not long earlier, had seemed so threatening to this order.

Of course, Freudian metaphors did not lose their power to unsettle, once James and Alix Strachey had compiled the *Complete Psychological Works.* And the anti-foundational ideas of Woolf and Lawrence did not lose their capacity to provoke – but instead served as inspirations for subsequent writers – after Bloomsburian modernism became (more or less) a closed chapter in cultural history. Just as the line between Victorian and Bloomsburian sensibilities is blurry, so too is the line between the age *of* Woolf and Freud and the age *after* Woolf and Freud. Nonetheless, it is on a note of some nostalgia that I conclude my reading of *All Passion Spent*, Bloomsbury's sixth ambivalent text, in which Sackville-West only begins to examine Victorian *assumptions* about sexual selfhood, though – like Strachey's "Glass Case" comment – it sharply criticizes Victorians for *practicing* intimacy with little passion or creative skill.

PART I

Philosophical backgrounds

CHAPTER I

Yellowy goodness in Bloomsbury's bible

> Good is good, and that is the end of the matter.
> "Good" is a simple notion, just as "yellow" is a simple notion.
> Personal affection and the appreciation of . . . Art or Nature, are good in themselves.[1]

G. E. Moore's 1903 treatise *Principia Ethica* has been widely admired, criticized, and mobilized in the century since its publication by readers with a variety of agendas. But none yet has given a full account of its modernist, and therefore quintessentially Bloomsburian, qualities: its *anti-essentialist* theoretical ideas and its *accommodationist* social attitudes. Yet it is largely because of these two qualities, and the tensions between them, that *Principia* continues to provoke readers, and to confuse them in productive ways.

At times in his opening, middle, and final chapters, Moore seems prepared to leap away from Victorian assumptions and inhibitions, into a brave new century. His opening chapter anticipates twentieth-century philosophy's "linguistic turn"[2] by asserting that the predicate "good" and its corollary "bad" constitute the primary subject matter of ethics, a maneuver with far-reaching anti-essentialist potential.[3] His middle four chapters, which explore the divide in nineteenth-century ethics between Kant's categorical imperative and Mill's utilitarianism, develop Moore's anti-essentialist themes even further. Kant represents duty and self-restraint, an implicit check on sexual libertinism, even when sex is not explicitly mentioned, whereas Mill implicitly endorses the pursuit of victimless pleasures. Moore responds to Kantian precedents by exposing the constructedness of social mores, refuting appeals to the "natural" and "normal" as ethical guides, and critiquing the ways in which conservative moralists invoke "duty."[4] Finally, his sixth and concluding chapter proposes a set of ethical values – friendship and art are among life's greatest goods, he says – without offering foundational support for them in nature, God, or reason. Furthermore, the model of friendship he examines is coded as homoerotic.

This is a risky theme to develop, even obliquely, less than a decade after Oscar Wilde's imprisonment. And it is a sly way of raising questions pertaining to the new century's reexamination of intimacy in a document seemingly unconcerned with social issues. It suggests that, having regarded essences and foundations warily, Moore may be prepared to propose new social paradigms as part of a new philosophy.

But almost as frequently as he steps forward, Moore falls back into respectable or essentialist attitudes. His linguistic turn lacks an historical sense, and therefore relies on Platonic (essentialist) assumptions in ways that other linguistically oriented philosophers from the late-nineteenth and early-twentieth centuries – such as Nietzsche and Wittgenstein – do not. Despite the skepticism with which they regard the "normal," Moore's middle chapters largely defer to the scarcely distinguishable standard of "custom" – society's stand-in for Kantian imperatives – as a moral arbiter.[5] Moore's anti-essentialism, in addition to informing his critique of duty, makes him an equal-opportunity critic of Mill as well. Therefore he attacks what he sees as the essentialist mistakes of utilitarian thinkers,[6] both in chapter 2, on "naturalistic ethics," and in chapter 3, on "hedonism." Moore says that thinkers commit a "naturalistic fallacy" (a term of his coining) when they equate good – which is non-natural – with something, such as happiness or pleasure, which is "natural," and therefore open to "empirical observation."[7] The critique in chapter 3 also serves as a vehicle for the middle chapters' conservative themes: Moore fully intends for "hedonism" to carry its popular, negative connotation – not the only time that he aligns himself rhetorically with respectability. His middle chapters articulate a troubled compromise between Kantianism and utilitarianism that tilts in favor of the former. His anti-essentialism, which hypothetically could be the basis of a socially radical argument, instead provides the framework for his accommodationist attitude.

Along similar lines, Moore's concluding chapter treats same-sex affection in so attenuated a manner as to take the sting out of this potentially subversive topic. His exaltation of friendship and art reveals Moore's debt to the Apostles, for whom "friendship" carried homoerotic suggestions. The chapter participates in an ongoing Bloomsburian discussion of "higher sodomy"[8] – spiritualized, rather than embodied, male–male attachment – but defers to the taboo that landed Wilde in prison by never daring to speak the name of what it celebrates, even in its spiritualized ("higher") version. It is precisely this ambivalence – the tensions between Moore's bold premises and his capitulations, his anti-essentialism and his accommodations, his modern and Victorian attitudes – that makes *Principia* such a rich symbol of the new century's struggle to reinvent intimacy.

Critics with literary and cultural interests, as well as those with technical philosophical concerns, have noted various aspects of these ambivalences, though not in the context of the reinvention of intimacy, and not with the assumption that *Principia*'s self-divisions are assets. On the philosophical front, Moore's technical contributions have been detailed and disputed. Linguistic philosophers including Richard Rorty, Norman Malcolm, and Gustav Bergmann[9] discuss his role in shifting twentieth-century philosophy's focus to the ways in which language is used. A. J. Ayer and John Coates, among others, examine Moore's claims to pursue philosophy according to the methods of science and common sense, the latter especially in the post-*Principia* years. Tom Regan, W. K. Frankena, R. M. Hare, and George Nakhnikian are among those who criticize or defend *Principia*'s attack on the "naturalistic fallacy."[10] Many of these philosophical engagements with *Principia* are dazzling in their attention to its discipline-specific details, but ignore its qualities of aesthetic and broader cultural import.

Iris Murdoch gives a rich account of Moore as a Platonically influenced thinker.[11] She sees beauty as a route to truth for both Moore and Plato, as I explain further below. She sees aesthetic forms of cognition – the ability to *picture* ideas – as crucial methodological skills for philosophers. Her insights into Moore's Platonism are astute, but she passes over one theme that further betrays the treatise's indebtedness to ancient Athens: its homoeroticism. Like Socrates, Moore saw beauty not only in aesthetic objects, but also in other men. Were it not for this fact, *Principia* would be less complex and interesting, and its audience over the last century would have been smaller.

Other commentators have also illuminated *Principia*'s aesthetic qualities and range of cultural ramifications. S. P. Rosenbaum has shown how subsequent Bloomsburian texts play variations on the Moorean themes of art and affection.[12] Regan argues that *Principia* did not merely suggest themes to Bloomsburians, but functioned as "Bloomsbury's bible," expressing the group's core aesthetic and moral values. Paul Levy's work complements Regan's, claiming that Moore's personal charm, especially his innocence – more than *Principia*'s doctrinal content – was an inspiration for the group.[13] Levy is also sensitive to how *Principia* balances sympathy to same-sex intimacy with deference to social custom, and alert to how its production and reception shed light on the Apostles and Bloomsbury's evolving mores. Even these critics, though, fail to go as far as they might in situating *Principia*'s ambivalences – its forays out of essentialism and its accommodations of respectable values – within a larger sociological matrix of modern*ity*, including the reinvention of intimacy, and a larger intellectual matrix of modern*ism*.

Principia appeared during a complex cultural moment marked both by skepticism and the building of new intellectual paradigms. A post-Wildean queer sensibility emerged, with both philosophical and social implications. Sexology was broadening conceptions of human desire, as groups such as Bloomsbury and Gertrude Stein's Paris salon came into being. Anti-essentialist ideas also informed Freud's theory of polymorphous perversity and his picture of a divided psyche – a far cry from the unified, reason-driven Kantian subject. Einstein's theory of relativity drained the stable, objective, essential content that Newton's paradigm had attributed to time and space. And a range of philosophical and linguistic works, including Nietzsche's *On the Genealogy of Morals* (1887), drained from words and concepts the essential content that previous philosophers had attributed to them. According to Nietzsche (in contrast to Moore), the word "good" refers to no immutable Platonic essence, but to one thing in a classical context, when its binary opposite is "bad," and to something different in a Judeo-Christian context, when its binary opposite is "evil."

Principia intervenes, therefore, in multiple discussions about essentialist modes of thought, the relation between nineteenth-century assumptions and modern beliefs, and the relation between philosophy and daily life. It was largely in the parlance of the Yellow Nineties – the 1890s sexual counter-culture of which the Apostles partook, even in the opening years of the new century – that these discussions overlapped and enriched one another.

Of course, Apostles including Moore and Lytton Strachey were not the first writers to express unconventional erotic sentiments in indirect ways. Henry James simultaneously divulged and disguised loves that dared not speak their names, in ways that escaped the censure of some readers and excited the special interest of others. Wilde joked about "Bunburying," bringing sodomy dangerously close to literary explicitness.[14] *Principia*'s coded endorsement of homoeroticism, from its first to its final chapter, had wide precedent in the Yellow Nineties.

As Moore's readers in 1903 could hardly have forgotten, the 1890s prized the new, the bizarre, the shocking, the modern – from teacups embroidered with willow patterns to Aubrey Beardsley's mannered illustrations to Wilde's irreverent witticisms. Colors, including green and purple, enjoyed vogues on garments and buildings in London and its radii. A connoisseur of sensory stimulation, Wilde wrote of "rose-colored joy," "nacre-colored air," and "apricot-colored light."[15]

But no color captured the time-spirit as thoroughly as yellow, as Richard Le Gallienne's 1896 prose fancy "The Boom in Yellow" attested. Yellow clothing became a sign in mid-1990s London that its wearer was modern, yellow bill posters signaled what sort of plays they advertised, and sunflowers bloomed as decorative carvings and paintings across England's capital. *The Yellow Book*, a hardback magazine with a dazzling yellow cover, for three years represented the cutting edge of decadent aesthetics.[16] The Henry-James disciple Henry Harland was its literary editor, and Beardsley its artistic editor; Beardsley women graced its pages in cascading dresses, thick and elegant coats. Its color conveyed "all that was bizarre and queer in art and life [and] outrageously modern."[17] Wilde carried a yellow-backed French novel, Pierre Louÿs's *Aphrodite*, on his trip to jail.[18]

In mentioning "yellow" (see the second epigraph above), *Principia* invokes the 1890s' broad revolt against Victorian sexual normalcy. Until the Wilde trials of 1895, cultured men enjoyed considerable latitude in dandyism – as long as they were not known sodomites. All of these precedents notwithstanding, however, *Principia* carried an authority for Bloomsburians that Wilde and James did not. Moore was the leading philosopher at turn-of-the-century Cambridge, respected for his "scientific" reasoning[19] and editorship of the journal *Mind*, and loved by Apostles for his charisma in discussions. For many public school and Oxbridge graduates of E. M. Forster's generation (Forster was born in 1879), Plato's texts provided the fullest picture of reputable male–male eros. When an accomplished neo-Platonic philosopher of their time lent his approval to Greek love, the effect was intoxicating. But it is not until its final chapter that *Principia* delivers the payoff – where the topic of intimacy is concerned – on the deposit constituted by the mention of yellow. Along the way, the treatise makes other innovative philosophical contributions.

A SOFT LINGUISTIC TURN

Good is good, and that is the end of the matter.[20]

Principia's opening chapter threatens to break decisively from the metaphysical ideas of Moore's contemporaries, but it largely reinforces them. Moore anticipates philosophy's linguistic turn by placing two words – "good" and "bad" – at the center of the discipline of ethics. This "turn" promised both a methodology and a set of conclusions sharply at odds with the "British Hegelians" – F. H. Bradley at Oxford and J. M. E. McTaggart at Cambridge – whose metaphysical assumptions included a belief in the "Absolute," a denial of the reality of space and time, and a claim that the material world was mere "appearance."[21] Indeed, in spite of its conservative elements, *Principia* did shatter the notion of a moral Absolute.

Nonetheless, *Principia*'s conservatism is made evident by a comparison to Nietzsche's *Genealogy*, published sixteen years earlier. Nietzsche not only examines ethical predicates *as* predicates (as Moore does), but he also treats them as elements in a system (not as linguistic atoms, as Moore and Bertrand Russell do), and he sees this system in historical terms (which Moore does not). These maneuvers enable Nietzsche to portray "good" as a changing concept, and thereby to challenge the assumption that language represents an eternal Platonic (or Christian) order.

Because Moore lacks Nietzsche's historical sense, his linguistic turn is oblique: it angles him only slightly away from Plato. Moore claims that words are much less important than the (presumably unchanging, non-linguistic) ideas to which they refer. Hypothetically, he says, people might employ a word other than "good," but still refer to the same idea. "By what name we call this object is a matter of indifference," he says, "so long as we clearly recognize what it is."[22] Moore was too savvy not to recognize that different cultures have different ethical priorities. He acknowledges that "certain periods in the world's history" and a "particular age and state of society" are bound to have different ideas of what constitutes "good effects" of human action.[23] But "good effects" do not mean the same thing to him as "good" itself. Unlike Nietzsche, he maintains that the "object" denoted by the word "good" would not change, even if social customs and values did.[24]

Moore is of two minds, in other words: both that of a modern – anti-essentialist – thinker, and that of one who seeks for certainties that transcend history. He is committed to examining words, but not their "usage" – to a linguistic focus, but also (illogically) to one that would exclude social issues, such as "custom." Entitled "The subject matter of ethics," *Principia*'s first chapter aims to define the discipline. What, asks Moore, is common and peculiar to all ethical judgments? Not, he answers, that they pertain to conduct – which non-ethical judgments might also do – but that they employ the predicates "good" and "bad." These predicates are among the building blocks of thought: they are "simple,"[25] "indefinable," "unanalyzable" (three synonymous terms). They cannot be broken down into component parts as "horse" can be analyzed into "head, tail, hoofs, etc." "Good" and "bad" mean nothing more than themselves; they are "unique simple object(s) of thought."[26] Moore insists on a firm distinction between "proper usage" (a messy, empirical process) and "objects of thought." "Good is good, and that is the end of the matter," he asserts.[27]

But he recognizes that "simple-ness," or "indefinability," itself requires elucidation. Thus he introduces his famous method of "inspection" – wherein readers are encouraged to take inventory of their minds – and his thinking assumes both a metaphysical and an aesthetic dimension.[28] Unlike a horse, with its legs, head, etc., "good" has no "parts," Moore says. In this way, "good" is like "innumerable *objects* of thought" that also resist analysis. The infinitude of such objects is important enough to warrant repeating, though Moore is inconsistent in describing their nature. "There must," he says, "be an indefinite number of such *terms*," and adds that "there are many instances of such *qualities*."[29] That these "simples" are described, within the space of a single paragraph, once as "objects," once as "terms," and once as "qualities" reveals that Moore's imagination is prone to slip between categories. It is difficult to ascertain, for example, whether Moore's "objects of thought" always correspond to linguistic "terms," or whether he believes that some such "objects" escape expression in language. His imagination becomes especially slippery, moving between abstract definitions and aesthetic qualities, when he expands, from one to two items, his list of these "innumerable" simple objects by comparing "good" to yellow.

Other Cambridge thinkers including Wittgenstein weighed the importance of concepts and pictures as building blocks of cognition. But the sly manner in which *Principia* elides these two categories – and threatens to commit its own naturalistic fallacy – suggests that their elision is an important thematic hinge. Moore claims that innumerable "indefinables" such as "good" exist, but offers only one example. "Consider yellow," he says. His phrasing ("Consider . . .") makes yellow seem like an innocent choice, selected arbitrarily upon "inspection" of his mental warehouse. But given that *Principia*'s next chapters critique Bentham and Mill precisely for equating "good" with felt qualities, it is problematic for Moore to analogize it with a color. Regardless of the analogy's logical dubiousness, however, the combined aesthetic and political resonances of yellow, a few short years after the Wilde trials, suggest that it is far from an arbitrary selection. This analogy is a prime example of how *Principia* can be productively confusing; of how, in blending disparate inquiries – linguistic, erotic, aesthetic, metaphysical – Moore concocts a rich brew of ideas redolent at once of the reinvention of intimacy and of other turn-of-the-century concerns.

MOORE'S SENSUOUS PLATONIC GOD

"Good" is a simple notion, just as "yellow" is a simple notion . . . just as you cannot . . . explain to anyone who does not already know it, what yellow is, so you cannot explain what good is.[30]

In his preface, Moore downplays the importance of aesthetics to *Principia*'s ethical methodology. Many commentators who criticize flaws in his reasoning accept his self-characterization as a non-aesthetic thinker.[31] While Moore's recourse to aesthetics does not erase the flaws they notice, it does draw *Principia* away from strictly logical concerns, and thus renders logic only one of several standards by which the argument may be judged. Moore's preface credits Franz Brentano's 1902 *Origin of the Knowledge of Right and Wrong* with anticipating many of his volume's premises. But Moore says that Brentano's "fundamental ethical concept" is "beautiful," whereas his own is "good."[32] Moore specifies that his ethics does not rest on an aesthetic foundation.

This protestation notwithstanding, the good–yellow comparison – a fulcrum at which Moore's logic is dubious – is laden with aesthetic significance. Moore's explanation of the simple-ness of one term by way of the simple-ness of the other raises two troublesome questions, one ontological and one epistemological. First, his use of scare quotes suggests that "good" might exist only as a mental "notion." But when the scare quotes vanish – when "good" becomes good in the above epigraph – the "notion" threatens to assume extra-linguistic reality. Such a process of incarnation was not foreign to his imagination. John Maynard Keynes wrote that Moore "had a nightmare once in which he could not distinguish propositions from tables. But even when he was awake he could not distinguish love and beauty and truth from the furniture. They took on the same . . . stable, solid, objective qualities."[33] What might be a "nightmare" for Moore – the confusion of concrete and conceptual material, a naturalistic fallacy hounding his sleep – was, for the half-facetious Keynes, a sign of Moore's poetic gift.

The good–yellow analogy also raises an epistemological question. Is sensuous knowledge (of "simple" qualities such as yellow) as trustworthy as conceptual knowledge (of "simple" qualities/terms/objects such as good); are the senses better guides to understanding than reason? Moore's failure to answer these questions leads some commentators to mistrust his analogy. The comparison "can only confuse us," says Constantine Cavarnos.[34] His complaint is valid on the ontological and epistemological grounds mentioned above. Moore asserts that good is "a simple notion" just "as" yellow is, yet his own distinction between natural and non-natural entities calls the meaning of "as" into question. The epigraph to *Principia* – Bishop Butler's "Everything is what it is, and not another thing" – conveys Moore's Wittgensteinian appreciation for clear distinctions, his mistrust of false analogies. The challenge that Moore frequently issued to fellow Apostles in philosophical discussion – "Do you really mean exactly that?"[35] – could apply to his own analogy. Does Moore really mean that "good" is simple *as* "yellow" is simple, and not that "good" is simple *in a different way than* yellow? Cavarnos is keen to spot this logical slippage. But he fails to extend his examination from logic into aesthetics, and thus to recognize the productive (Platonic) qualities of the confusion, as Keynes recognizes the use of conflating beauty and truth with "furniture."

In Moore's writings, as in Plato's, aesthetic and metaphysical perceptions reinforce one another; beauty serves as a route to truth, as Murdoch recognizes.[36] If *Principia* does not endow good with the solidity of a table, it nonetheless hints that this cardinal predicate – with its yellow-like simpleness – is as luminous as the sun. In Plato's analogy of the cave, the sun symbolizes the good, an unknowable quality (the Platonic equivalent of a Moorean "indefinable") toward which other ethical ideals – even love – can only lead the moral pilgrim. Plato's good, as Nietzsche saw, is a dehumanized god term, and Moore invokes good in much the same vein. Although Plato's sun stands for an abstract principle, it is luminously sensuous, laden with aesthetic value: a picture of good. It stands at the top of his ethical pyramid, with the more definable virtues of wisdom, courage, and temperance expanding downward from it. Likewise, the quality/term/object good floats in *Principia*'s sky, with particular intrinsic goods (friendship and art) billowing down from it, and with general routes toward right conduct raining downward from them. The *Republic*, like *Principia*, combines aesthetic sensitivity with philosophical wisdom, using the former to enrich the latter. It was a short step for Moore also to blend the Greek love of aesthetic beauty with the Greek love of male beauty; nonetheless *Principia*'s restraint – its accommodation of Victorian mores – leads its treatment of homoerotic themes to be so oblique as to lose its human element.

Such aestheticism (including such sexual restraint) was endemic to the Apostles, not just to *Principia*, nor to the dreams that Moore shared with Keynes. Goldsworthy Lowes Dickinson, a warm-hearted homosexual don and Apostle, wrote the neo-Platonic dialogue *A Modern Symposium* (1905), about "The Seekers" – a club Dickinson attempted to found[37] – whose thirteen members spend a calm English summer night delivering philosophical speeches in a poetic vein. Forster wrote a loving 1934 biography of Dickinson, which criticizes his tendency to mystical dreaminess, just as Dickinson had criticized this tendency in McTaggart. When Moore strove to improve upon McTaggart with *Principia*'s clear argumentation,[38] he took up an old Apostolic challenge. It is fitting that Bloomsbury – a colloquy of intellectual, aesthetic, and erotic seekers – should take inspiration from Moore's thematically overdetermined treatise.

BLOOMSBURIAN RECEPTIONS

Although these Bloomsburian seekers may not have been as discerning as Murdoch of the methodological value that Moore finds in aesthetic cognition, many of them were alert to homoerotic themes – subtly woven into his examinations of non-sexual matters – that they recognized from their group's discussions. Strachey admires the support for male–male affection in *Principia*'s final chapter to such a degree that he overlooks how Moore subordinates the theme to aesthetic ones. Russell, on the other hand, is tone-deaf to the chapter's sexual–aesthetic politics. He mistakenly blames Strachey for imposing an escapist ethic upon *Principia*, when in fact Strachey – an outspoken public figure – was less deserving of such criticism than Moore.[39]

Like literary Bloomsbury, Strachey viewed philosophy with respect, but also with a sense of its foreignness. He thunders with praise for *Principia*'s anti-Victorian themes, in fact its freedom from all constraining moral codes, in a letter written days after its publication. "I have read your book, excited and impressed," he tells Moore.

> I'm afraid I must mainly be classed among "writers of Dictionaries, and other persons interested in literature," so I feel a sort of essential vanity hovering about all my "judgments of fact." But on this occasion I am carried away. I think your book has not only wrecked and shattered all writers on Ethics from Aristotle and Christ to Herbert Spencer and Mr Bradley, it has not only laid the true foundations of Ethics, it has not only left all modern philosophy bafouée – these seem to me small achievements compared to the establishment of that Method which shines like a sword between the lines. It is the scientific method, deliberately applied, for the first time, to Reasoning. Is that true? . . .
>
> The last chapters interested me most . . . Your grand conclusion [that friendship and art are life's two greatest goods] made me gasp – it was so violently definite. Lord! I can't yet altogether agree. I think with some horror of a universe deprived forever of real slaughters and tortures and lusts. Isn't it possible that the real Ideal may be an organic unity so large [as] the Universe itself?[40]

This playful letter illustrates how amenable *Principia* is to a reader's interpretive desires. While Russell does not imagine that it "wrecks" or "shatters" anything, Strachey half-jokingly says that it shatters foundational figures of Western philosophy and religion. He is genuine in his admiration for Moore's "grand conclusion" in favor of the Apostolic and Bloomsburian values of friendship and art, even as he teases Moore's vision of a universe without "tortures and lusts" by saying that such a vision inspires "horror." Strachey maintains a small degree of ironic distance from *Principia* in a letter that largely fawns over it. He reads *Principia* in the light of his own desires, which are a source of both blindness and insight, and his interpretation matters. It inaugurates a tradition, freshly invigorated by Levy over a half century later, of understanding Moore's work in the context of sexual prejudice, Victorian prudery, and Wilde's legacy.

Russell, however, thought that Strachey and Keynes did the philosopher a disservice by reading him in light of their own sexual and aesthetic values, and underestimating his moral seriousness. "The generation of Keynes and Lytton aimed," Russell recalls in his autobiography:

> at a life of retirement among fine shades and nice feelings, and conceived of the good as consisting in the passionate mutual admirations of a clique of the élite. This doctrine, quite unfairly, they fathered upon G. E. Moore, whose disciples they professed to be . . . Moore gave due weight to morals and by his doctrine of organic unities avoided the view that the good consists in a series of isolated passionate moments.[41]

Although "retirement" is not Strachey's word, but one that Russell uses in denigrating Strachey's interpretation of Moore, it does capture an important limitation of *Principia*'s final chapter. Therefore, although Russell is correct in attributing elitism and aestheticism to Strachey's "generation," he is incorrect in implying Strachey to be more inward-looking (given to "retirement") than Moore. In fact the opposite was the case.

Moore had been the Apostles' leader when he "took wings" (resigned his official membership) in January 1901 to work on *Principia*. While it bore his stamp, the society tended toward reasonableness in tone, restraint in its banter (though homoerotic humor had long been its trademark), and a limited interest in politics. All this changed in February 1902, when Strachey assumed leadership, transforming Apostles' "naughty verbal mannerisms and Whitmanesque feelings of comradeship into overt full-blooded – almost aggressive – homosexuality."[42] Even when Strachey was not among intimates, his outlandish personal style posed a deliberate challenge to prudery and prejudice. Contrary to Russell's accusation that Strachey "fathered" a "doctrine" of "retirement" upon Moore, when Moore relinquished his stewardship, the society became less, not more, inward-looking.

"Fine shades and nice feelings," in particular feelings between men, had in fact been among the society's primary fascinations since its inception in the 1820s. Long before Russell, Moore, and Strachey were elected, unconsummated attractions between its members were among its trademarks. Russell, in other words, is correct to see "nice feelings" as Stracheyan and

Keynesian values. But he is historically forgetful to imagine that those two men introduced them to the society. Moore himself had been an acolyte of such values; *Principia*'s opening chapter puts the "fine shade" of yellow to extensive work. But it was Moore's personal crisis of intimacy that led "nice feelings" to become an explicit topic of philosophical inquiry, and that led *Principia* to develop aesthetic and erotic themes both in conjunction with and in opposition to one another.

THE GENESIS OF CHAPTER 6

The composition history of *Principia*'s final chapter suggests why its erotic themes waver between expression and repression, and why the playful speculations of Strachey – with his personal knowledge of the author – should not be discounted. As Moore struggles to figure himself out, he cannot keep this struggle out of a chapter entitled "The ideal," despite *Principia*'s generally impersonal tenor. *Principia*'s first five chapters were years in the making. While teaching a course on Ethics in 1899, Moore "developed the main outline" of the book. But between conception and delivery lay strenuous labor. "I found this an extremely troublesome business. I write very slowly and with great difficulty," Moore says, "and I constantly found . . . something wrong with [my drafts]."[43] Yet chapter 6 flowed from Moore's pen in mere weeks. Why?

In 1899, Moore was a 25-year-old Trinity Prize Fellow. Like many Apostles, he entered adulthood as a virgin of uncertain sexual orientation. But when Alfred Ainsworth was elected an Apostle, Moore grew close to him. Strachey loved the thought of his philosophical mentor being gay, and encouraged the friends to see themselves as lovers. Strachey was successful enough in this endeavor that in 1904 – when Moore's fellowship expired shortly after *Principia*'s publication – Moore moved to Edinburgh to live with Ainsworth. Their romance, however, never progressed beyond hand-holding.[44] Ainsworth eventually married Moore's younger sister, and Moore married and had two sons by Dorothy Ely.

Despite the limitations of this romance – its "fine shades" that never broke into full sunlight – it may well have inspired Moore's final chapter, "The ideal."[45] Even a mere shade of an ideal, however, must often be articulated cautiously if a text is released beyond its author's intimates, to a wider, "respectable" community. Such tactical considerations may account for the strange absence of sensuous specificity – even anything on the order of hand-holding – in a chapter supposedly committed to the defense of embodied affection. For whatever reason, Moore's third greatest good (art) usurps the place of his greatest good (friendship), in part because aesthetics provide the paradigm for his examination of intimacy. His hierarchy of values deconstructs, as the aesthete in Moore gets the better of the humanist in him – a confusion of priorities that subsequent Bloomsburian texts would rectify.

THE DEHUMANIZATION OF MOORE'S ART

Personal affection and the appreciation of ... Art or Nature, are good in themselves.[46]

In *Principia*'s final chapter, Bloomsbury's first anti-foundationalist proposes a system of earthly values to replace the heaven in which he does not believe. Having debunked "Naturalistic Ethics," "Hedonism," and "Metaphysical Ethics,"[47] – whether or not he has "shattered" Aristotle and Christ – Moore faces the problem of nihilism. How shall he justify his chosen values? He offers no first principles; instead he names his preferred "goods," and hopes that readers who "inspect" their minds will find the same contents, ranked in the same order.

Moore's hierarchy of values is infused with intellectualized–aestheticized love. He ranks loving people first; the chapter's intimations of same-sex attraction contain its radical potential. Loving nature comes second, since nature exists, says Moore, whereas art works – the love of which ranks third – are fictional. Love of god ranks below the love of art, since it is based on a likely mistaken assumption that god exists. (Moore is too diplomatic to assert his atheism, though it is implied in his rankings.) Throughout this system, Moore conveys his preference for the human and the physical over the abstract and the mystical. He criticizes thinkers – McTaggart in specific, but implicitly Victorian puritans in general – who denigrate "corporeal" qualities.

But Moore compromises this preference by stepping back from same-sex attraction into aesthetic cognition, where dangers of "corporeal" encounters are reduced, if not eliminated. Thus, *Principia* provides a less politically tendentious solution than it might to the problem of nihilism. Having debunked Mill and Kant, Moore proposes nothing so shocking in their place as a homoerotic utopia. Instead, he offers a philosophized picture of Apostolic culture, short on concrete examples, though laden with all of the unexplored sexual possibilities that marked this culture during his tenure as leader.

Admittedly, the final chapter's insistence on embodied love, its opening salvos against utopianism, establish its anti-puritanical credentials. Just as chapter 1, entitled "The subject matter of ethics," begins with a meticulous statement of its purpose, so too chapter 6 begins by specifying what kind of "ideal" it will examine. Moore says that he is not concerned with (1) "the *best* state of things *conceivable*," nor with (2) "the best *possible* state of things in this world," but with (3) what is "good in itself in a high degree."[48] This statement of purpose comprises a gesture against (1) the Absolute of McTaggart and the Heaven of Christians, and (2) the Utopia of political dreamers; on behalf of (3) the known world of a happy Edwardian man.

Moore thinks that the problem with heavens is that they omit much we know to be of value, on the mistaken assumption that a universe comprised only of the best goods is preferable to one comprised also of lesser goods. McTaggart's "Reality," for example, is "an eternally perfect harmony of pure spirits united by Love."[49] But "pure spirits" do not include bodies, and *Principia*'s concluding chapter – in its ambivalent way – attempts to justify corporeal existence. According to Moore's anti-essentialist principle of "organic unities," a great good is not vitiated by being combined with a lesser good (nor even, necessarily, with a positive evil): the value of such a "whole" need not equal the value of the sum of its parts. Spirits, therefore (such as Cambridge aesthetes seeking truth and beauty), are not defiled merely because they are materially incarnated.

Moore includes, among the various mistakes of Utopian thinkers, their tendency to count as actual "goods" things which are in fact "mere means to good," such as freedom.[50] He thinks that a universe containing only this quality would be valueless – not an unusual thing for a Bloomsburian liberal to believe. Forster hoped that he would have the courage to betray his country rather than his friend.[51] Bloomsburians did fight for large political ideals, but the test of such ideals was how they told on the personal life. Until freedom could be instantiated within the context of a friendship, it was an empty concept, as far as Moore was concerned.

Having disposed of heavens and utopias, Moore turns to the question of what is "good in itself in a high degree" – with the help of the method of isolation. What, if we picture it by itself, would we most like to have (more even than the freedom to pursue it)?

> No one, probably, who has asked himself the question, has ever doubted that personal affection and the appreciation of what is beautiful in Art or Nature, are good in themselves; nor, if we consider strictly what things are worth having *purely for their own sakes*, does it appear probable that any one will think that anything else has *nearly* so great a value as the things which are included under these two heads.[52]

Moore offers no foundational support for his preferences; the methods of isolation and inspection are meant to render such support unnecessary.

Moore appeals directly to readers' intuitive sense of what matters most in life. Such an appeal is most likely to fall on sympathetic ears when the audience is limited to the author's intimates.

But from the start, *Principia*'s audience was larger than this, which may explain why its argument is restrained even at the level of its sentences. We have seen how chapter 1 turns toward language – at a safely oblique angle – by treating "good" in a quasi-metaphysical manner. We have seen how the middle chapters both defend freedom on utilitarian grounds and defer to "social custom." Despite Strachey's enthusiasm, chapter 6 anaesthetizes its homoerotic turn by aestheticizing it. It is restrained even when announcing its greatest goods: Moore embeds qualifications ("No one, *probably* . . ."; "nor does it appear *probable* . . .") within his assertion ("No one . . . has ever doubted"). Moore seems aware that, while Apostles may share his values, the more *Principia*'s audience expands, the more its certainties are likely to dissolve.

Thus he articulates his ideal of a friendship trembling on the edge of romance, which must stand for readers on the basis of its immediate and largely aesthetic appeal. The final chapter's discussion of aesthetics introduces its treatment of human relations, but remains too vague to endow those relations – even indirectly – with an embodied quality. Aesthetic appreciation, Moore says, is an organic whole made up of three main components: *emotional* and *cognitive* states, and *beliefs*. Among the several virtues of this complex definition, it avoids the shortcut of ascribing a simple essence to such appreciation. Moore is also skillful in his Platonic definition of beauty – as a means toward reaching good – which connects major inquiries in *Principia*'s first and final chapters. Moore returns to the priority that distinguishes him from Brentano, by ranking beauty below good. But this hierarchy is undermined by Moore's pictures of affection, despite their prudish lack of sensuality.

His depiction of aesthetic appreciation remains vague even when he treats the three parts of the organic whole. Moore spends less time discussing actual art works (e.g., Beethoven's Fifth Symphony) than discussing how hypothetical works should be encountered. Moore becomes a connoisseur not of his own sensuous responses to art, but of imaginary people's mental activities. Rather than "seeing the object in itself" – with Matthew Arnold – Moore sees the seeing of a non-specific object.

Regarding the *emotional* component of aesthetic appreciation, Moore's ideal viewer should not "merely see the beautiful qualities in a picture," but also "appreciate" them; he should "feel and see" the picture's beauty.[53] When the speaker of Coleridge's "Dejection" ode bemoans his inability to respond to the beauties of the clouds, stars, and moon – "I see them all so excellently fair, / I see, not feel, how beautiful they are!"[54] – he describes the incomplete response that Moore would prefer to avoid. Coleridge's speaker *cognizes* beauty (the second of Moore's three components of aesthetic appreciation) without a concomitant *emotion*.

Conversely, Moore's ideal subject would avoid a second kind of emotional error: that of "bad taste," of cognizing qualities accurately but appreciating them inappropriately, of experiencing positive "feelings toward qualities, which the object does possess but which are in reality not beautiful."[55] Moore says that errors of taste, however intense or exalted the emotion to which they give rise, are "in most, if not all, cases . . . a considerable positive evil."[56] In *Women in Love*, Birkin's attraction to the sadomasochistic qualities in Hermione, and Gerald's attraction to the same qualities in Minette and Gudrun, constitute what Moore might call "bad taste" in women. The men would be better off, Moore's reasoning implies, if they cultivated positive "feelings toward qualities . . . which are in reality . . . beautiful." In leaving Hermione for Ursula, Birkin demonstrates a capacity for good taste in women that Gerald, to his mortal detriment, never learns.

As the errors of failed "appreciation" and "bad taste" illustrate, "nice feelings" are not the sole ingredient in Moore's aesthetic morality. The "real" qualities of the "object" in question – aesthetic or human – matter also. An exalted emotion by itself, or one inspired by a fantasy, comprises a less satisfying organic whole, according to Moore, than an appropriate emotional response to extant qualities in an extant art work. This is why Russell admires Moore's ethics, in spite of their aesthetic basis. Moore does not, thinks Russell, exalt "isolated passionate moments" – individual Apostles lost in solipsistic reverie – but values intelligent engagement with external material, over time.

Regarding the *cognitive* component of aesthetic enjoyment, Moore defines carefully what he means by "object." His ideal viewer should not merely cognize that Picture X is beautiful, but that qualities Q, R, and S are the reasons for its beauty. The relevant qualities, not the picture itself, constitute the "object." Here Moore's account of seeing might appear akin to Arnold's "seeing the object in itself" – or even to improve upon Arnold, given Moore's conscientious definition of "object." But no example fortifies Moore's account. Which qualities in which painting illustrate his distinction between the aesthetic "object" as commonly (mis)understood, and as properly understood by him? At the threshold of specificity, Moore stalls.

Concerning the *belief* component of aesthetic cognition, Moore treats several erroneous attributions that a viewer might make, and his discussion blends the aesthetic and the human. The first genre of error involves "the attribution to an object of really beautiful qualities which it does not possess"[57] – a possibility that haunts Forster's *Longest Journey*. The protagonist Rickie (Forster's alter ego) falls in love with a crass suburbanite named Agnes, though his best friend Ansell (partially based on Moore)[58] immediately recognizes the danger she poses. Rickie errs in attributing to her "really beautiful qualities [e.g., warmth, generosity] which [she] does not possess,"[59] and Ansell warns him against "the subjective product of a diseased imagination ... which, to our destruction, we invest with a semblance of reality."[60] Thus *The Longest Journey*, perhaps Bloomsbury's most Moorean novel, dramatically realizes the theme that Russell admires in *Principia* – its mistrust of "passionate moments" of reverie.

Moore treats the *belief* component of aesthetic cognition (and other moral situations) for many pages. He warns against a second kind of erroneous attribution – loving belief in a god that may not exist – and wonders what the consequences of such a mistake might be, though he does not assert that they are "in most ... cases ... evil." He develops elaborate hierarchies – complete with categories and subcategories – of how true and false beliefs positively or adversely affect encounters with people, landscapes, art works, and hypothetical deities:

> Where both the cognition of beautiful qualities and the appropriate emotion are present we may *also* have either (1) a belief in the existence of these qualities, of which the object, i.e., that they exist, is true: or (2) a mere cognition, without belief, when it is (a) true, (b) false, that the object of the cognition, i.e., the beautiful qualities, exists: or (3) a belief in the existence of the beautiful qualities, when they do not exist.[61]

Few readers could navigate such a maze of distinctions. But the final chapter's main purpose remains to privilege human relations as the "greatest good." When such relations entail a lover correctly cognizing beautiful qualities that exist in the beloved, and feeling an appropriate emotion toward those qualities, then the ideal of ideals has been instantiated.

But Moore only begins to examine this greatest good after an elaborate prelude; the structure of his argument suggests that intimacy is a subcategory of aesthetics. His discussion of a viewer's emotion, cognition, and belief – specifically the belief in a picture's qualities Q, R, and S – gives way to a discussion of belief in the existence of a person, landscape, or god. Friendship enters the concluding chapter's discussion of proper cognition through a back door, much as yellow (and by implication aesthetics) slyly enters the opening chapter's analysis of language.

Eventually, albeit briefly, Moore turns to what Forster terms "personal relations."[62] He evaluates the importance of corporeal and mental qualities in a beloved. His attempt to value the physical leaves him at a distance from the emotions – and bodies – that he would celebrate. Corporeal qualities can be "beautiful," he says, but only mental qualities can be "good."[63] The link between these attributes concerns both ethics and aesthetics. Moore defines the beautiful as "that of which the admiring contemplation is good in itself."[64] A philosopher who imagines a patron viewing a beautiful painting, and appreciating its beauty, would describe the patron-viewing-painting "organic whole" as "good." If "beauty" is correctly attributed to the painting by the viewer, then "good" can appropriately be assigned to the attribution by the philosopher. By logical extension – though Moore never draws this parallel – the same philosopher imagining a lover viewing a worthy beloved could describe this organic whole as "good." The ethical philosopher affixes the predicate "good" to organic wholes comprising two human beings, or comprising a man and an art work, much as the aesthetic thinker affixes the predicate "beautiful" to the organic whole of a single complex art work. Ethical and aesthetic judgments are structured similarly. Both require the attribution of a predicate to an organic whole; both are described by Moore without being concretely exemplified.

The shadow of political strife lies nowhere near either attribution. Hence Strachey feigns "horror" at the thought of a universe without "slaughters and tortures and lusts," but his mock horror contains genuine criticism of Moore's placid "ideal" universe. It took Keynes longer to recognize the limitations of Moore's vision.[65] After two world wars, no longer confident that "human nature is reasonable," Keynes worried that the tranquility of *Principia*'s last chapter could lead to "thinness, superficiality, not only of judgment, but also of feeling." He was one of *Principia*'s warmest early admirers, and continued to extol Moore's thinking into their old age, but also looked back critically on their youthful Apostolic idealism. "We were not aware," he reminisces, "that civilization was a thin and precarious crust erected by the personality and will of a very few, and only maintained by rules and conventions skillfully put across and guilefully preserved."[66] Late-Victorian Cambridge provided its Apostles an extended taste of a guilefully preserved civilization.[67]

It is impossible to know how much, if at all, Moore worried about his tendency to "retire" from a world of "slaughters, tortures, and lusts," or about the "thinness of judgment" that might result from his treatment of the human mind as a "reasonable" organ. Certainly his treatment of affection adds dimensions to *Principia* that have been crucial to its afterlife. But the differences between how he and – for example – Lawrence handle corporeal life reveal that Bloomsburians contributed to the reinvention of intimacy in greatly varied ways, from Lawrence's identification of a "crisis"[68] to *Principia*'s expression of Apostolic tranquility, which only hints at crisis by virtue of what it does not say.

In a moment of attention to the body, if not to its "lusts," Moore says that their mutual admiration of each other's mental qualities, above all else, enables two lovers to comprise the ideal organic unity. But how could they gain access to each other's minds except through their bodies (facial expressions, gestures, etc.)? "It is, indeed," Moore explains, "very difficult to imagine what the cognition of mental qualities *alone*, unaccompanied by *any* corporeal expression, would be like; and, in so far as we succeed in making this abstraction, the whole considered certainly appears to have less value" than a whole which includes mental *and* corporeal qualities.[69] McTaggart's picture of "pure spirits united by love" – spirits without bodies – is less deserving of the appellative "good," thinks Moore, than his own picture of embodied spirits in love. The body is the necessary gateway to the mind, beauty our most effective route to the good. When Plato equates beauty and truth, he expresses a similar intuition – that an intellectually and ethically rich life requires a developed aesthetic apparatus. For Moore, in fact, the body isn't merely a gateway; but is also part of the terminus of proper affection: "bodily expressions . . . do form a part of the object toward which the affection is felt."[70] Moore implies that we should not be ashamed of this. McTaggart's Idealism is a useful target for Moore's larger salvo against Victorian prudery.

Moore's valuation of accurate belief in aesthetic enjoyment leads, like a long prelude, to his discussion of reciprocal affection. The spectacle of such affection (in a healthy relationship) greatly pleases the viewing philosopher – even more than the spectacle of a knowledgeable patron in an art gallery. The loving couple entails two people not merely *cognizing* and *appreciating*, but accurately *believing* in the *real existence* of one another's admirable mental qualities – all because the mind shows through the body. Love is the ultimate work of art. The aesthetic turn of the final chapter desexualizes, and thus to a degree dehumanizes, its treatment of love.

In literary terms, *Principia*'s speaker is a painfully timid character who does not participate in the affections he admires. "The most valuable appreciation of persons," he says, "appears to be that which consists in *the appreciation of their appreciation of other persons*."[71] The speaker admires the way lovers appreciate each other, though the author lacked experience of such a dynamic at the time of *Principia*'s composition. A moment earlier in the text, this would-be materialist praises "the contemplation of such contemplation" as lovers engage in. And a moment later, he asserts that "the love of love, is far the most valuable good we know." Appreciation of appreciation, contemplation of contemplation, and love of love! Where is love itself in this hierarchy of values? It remained for Bloomsburians to enact what *Principia* suggested, to fall in love not just with love, but with one another, as individuals.

However mitigated *Principia*'s rebellion against Victorian prudery, however dehumanized its celebration of corporeal affection, many Bloomsburians took inspiration from it, and Strachey found it liberating. It is doubtful, to be fair, that *Principia* achieves the degree of "penetration" implied in Strachey's playful 1903 letter, with Moore's "scientific method" shining "like a sword" – or phallus – "between the lines," and Strachey being made to "gasp" by Moore's "violently definite" "grand conclusion" in praise of affection. But Strachey's mock-sexual excitement is as historically important as *Principia*'s restraint. Even if Moore did not intend the final chapter's homoerotic frisson, he was comfortable enough with it that he never disputed Strachey's reading.[72]

But Strachey was only one of *Principia*'s progeny. Moore's subtly blended discussions of language, art, ethics, and affection helped usher Bloomsbury into the new century, with the group's variegated and ambivalent attitudes toward the theoretical essentialism and social conservatism common in their parents' generation. Like Freud, Lawrence, and Woolf, Moore gave shape to this ambivalence with *anti-essentialist accommodations*: a suspicion, at once, of essentialism, Kantian conservatism, and heteronormativity,[73] that ends up making pragmatic compromises with each of these three belief systems. In fact, so intricate is *Principia*'s ambivalence that it could be better labeled as *anti-essentialist with a lingering dependence on Plato* and *accommodationist despite its sympathy for the counter-culture.* Freud's corpus, as we will see in the following chapter, is enriched by similarly serpentine ambivalence.

CHAPTER 2

Freud's denial of innocence

The early-twentieth century's reinvention of intimacy tested the skills of theorists and storytellers – from Freud and G. E. Moore to D. H. Lawrence, Virginia Woolf, and others – as cultural diagnosticians. In England, on the continent, and across the Atlantic, thinkers probed the psychological question *What are children, men, and women like?* and the ethical question *How should we conduct our intimate lives, within and between families?* Modernist authors designed state-of-the-art instruments for examining consciousness and the unconscious. More fully than anywhere, Freud displays his own modernist skills in *Dora*,[1] where his cagey depictions of the protagonist (Dora) and antagonist (himself) help him to develop his *anti-essentialist* answers to the theoretical question above, and his *accommodationist* answers to the ethical question.[2] In the following pages we will see how subsequent Freudian texts play variations on these answers, and how the tensions between Freud's theoretical radicalism and ethical conservatism anticipate the tensions in Bloomsburian novels. We will also see how the absence of the category "adolescent" (developed early in the twentieth century by G. Stanley Hall)[3] limits Freud's options in theoretically imagining Dora, and thus also his options for advising her about how to navigate the challenges of her intimate life – although Freud gropes his way, at various points in *Dora*, toward something like Hall's idea.

FREUD THE THEORIST VS. FREUD THE THERAPIST

The locus of *Dora*'s anti-essentialist themes is Dora herself. She is as far from an angelic woman or an innocent child as possible – as far as possible, that is, from two essentialist stock characters of some Victorian imaginations.[4] Freud the theorist is responsible for this invaluable contribution to modernism, this innovative depiction of a selfish, amorous, petty, highly intelligent, and in many other ways self-contradictory, mature female character, who may lack any essence, whether conceived in Victorian or other terms. Moreover,

Dora's provocative qualities, and the text's subversive energies, are intensified because she is the protagonist – the heroine who resists the imposing interpretations and sordid advice of the antagonist, Freud the therapist.

But Freud's anti-Victorian assumptions about Dora's sexuality cut two ways. On the one hand, his non-judgmental discussion of her desires – in fact his implicit celebration of such desires as sparks for her curiosity and insight – secure Dora's place in a gallery of multidimensional nineteenth- and twentieth-century heroines, such as Emma Bovary, and link her to an emergent field of twentieth-century study. In his groundbreaking *Adolescence* (1904), Hall sees "psychic adolescence" as a time of storm and stress; of wildly fluctuating emotions; and cruel, antisocial behaviors. It is marked by the emergence of adolescent instincts, chiefly sex consciousness. Hall says that puberty broadens people's horizons, emotionally and morally: they learn to revere nature; and pubic rites in tribes across the world mark conversions from "autocentric" to "heterocentric" ways of being.[5] On Hall's account, psychic adolescence is a mixed blessing, though one to be celebrated: it can be a source of pain and conflict for the adolescent, family, and community, but it is also a necessary and beautiful awakening into adult consciousness. Hall's thinking, over the coming decades, would owe much to Freud,[6] and *Dora* anticipates – thanks in part to Freud's literary skills in depicting his heroine's shrewdness, her cruelty and generosity, her autocentric fragility and heterocentric awareness of the psychosexual matrix in which she lives – themes that Hall would develop in more sociological and anthropological ways.

Whatever Freud's insight, however, as a critic of Victorian Puritanism, and whatever his proficiency in constructing a character, as a theorist he is so spiteful of myths of feminine purity that he imputes sexual desire to Dora – and therefore her complicity in the tale's erotic intrigue – at every opportunity. He is something of an essentialist in spite of himself, imagining that he has unlocked the secrets of Dora's personality and neuroses. He refuses to entertain the possibility that her unconscious could say "No,"[7] that she might be without desire for Herr K. (or her father, or himself as an object of transference), and this theoretical narrow-mindedness limits the range of practical advice he can give. Among the numerous commentators who call Freud to task, Erik Erikson wonders if Freud overlooks "developmental considerations" in assuming that a healthy girl of 14 would consider Herr K.'s advances "neither tactless nor offensive." Erikson asserts that Dora's neurosis is "rooted in the crisis of adolescence," and that Freud's effort to help her understand her own unconscious (as he imagines it!) would only be appropriate in the case of a "mature ego."[8]

Freud the therapist, therefore, is dubious in both intellectual and moral terms when he proffers one strain of the case history's pragmatism. His answer to the ethical question, *Given that young females are nothing like Victorian mythology allows, how should our heroine pursue intimacy and erotic pleasure?* is his advice that Dora take Herr K. as a lover. Her justifications for resisting this advice, on both theoretical and ethical grounds, will be discussed in further detail. When Dora not only resists this advice, but undermines the therapist's authority by withdrawing from treatment, the text's quagmire becomes more pronounced: it ends without any answer to the above question.

That the tale is so open-ended, that the answer to this question is *not* clear, that the blind spots of Freud's theoretical assumptions (which are not limited to the question of adolescence) and the domineering quality of his advice *are* both so clear – all this signifies that *Dora* is no epistemologically straightforward study. And Freud the therapist is not merely a less-than-trustworthy character; he is also the narrator! The reader's only source of the therapist–patient agon is thoroughly unreliable: the ironies in Conrad, Ford, and other modernists sow no greater perplexity in readers' minds than does the brilliant, snide, partly blind narrator of this case history. It is doubtful that Freud the theorist-author intended to subject Freud the therapist-narrator to dramatic irony, but regardless of intention, *Dora*'s unreliable narrator enables its distinctive and ambiguous version of anti-essentialist accommodationism.

A high-altitude survey renders this basic fault line running throughout Freud's work – between his anti-essentialism and his accommodationism – clearly visible.[9] But Freud is a complex enough thinker that additional layers of paradox enrich his diagnoses of modern intimacy. For example, although he is an anti-essentialist in many regards, he strays occasionally into essentialist lines of thought, into the notion given more decisive expression in texts such as *Howards End* – that men and women are innately and insuperably different.

Furthermore, while he is an ethical pragmatist in many ways, he frequently strays from a socially respectable line of thought into one more befitting a libertine. We are all familiar with the conservative Freud who insists that "psychoanalysis has not said a word in favor of unfettering instincts that would injure our community; on the contrary it has issued a warning and an exhortation to us to mend our ways."[10] But he is balanced by the Freud, prominent in *Dora*, who finds Victorian mores oppressive, and whose accommodationism has definite limits. Which of these two Freuds advises Dora to couple with the husband of her father's paramour?

In one sense, as Madelon Sprengnether argues, Dora's therapist "enforces Oedipus": he prods Dora into assuming her role in a play rigged by the patriarchy.[11] Far from "injuring" the community, embarking on an affair could be Dora's way of accommodating the community's conventional hypocrisies. Yet Stephen Marcus arrives at a different ethical valuation, though his analysis of the therapist's advice shares much with Sprengnether's. Marcus argues, in the lingo of the 1970s, that Freud proposes a "swinging solution" to Dora.[12] What Marcus sees as a risqué counter-cultural idea, Sprengnether sees as an all-too-familiar reinforcement of male interests. Tensions in Freud's ethical thought, punctuated by such instances of ethical undecidability, extend throughout his corpus, which blends conservative pragmatism with a reformist's zeal and a hatred of Puritanism.

At a finer level of resolution, then, Freud the anti-essentialist accommodationist can usefully be relabeled as an anti-essentialist who makes strategic forays into essentialism and an accommodationist with anti-puritanical passions. It remains to tease out these salutary tensions in various Freudian writings, especially *Dora*, which bears strong resemblances to Bloomsburian diagnoses of modern intimacy.

Broadly speaking, essentialist ideologies dominant in Victorian culture held that children are sexually innocent (biological education was designed accordingly); that men and women are distinct (public and domestic spheres were ordered accordingly); that normal and pathological individuals differ in kind, not merely in degree (mental illness was treated accordingly); and that gender roles reflect a biological and moral necessity.[13] These complexly interwoven, conservative attitudes were critiqued by Freud and his fellow sexologists, including Krafft-Ebing and Edward Carpenter, as well as by Lawrence and Bloomsbury. Admittedly, Moore's *Principia Ethica* (published in 1903, two years prior to *Dora*), Lawrence's *Women in Love* (1920), and Woolf's *Mrs Dalloway* (1925) each reimagine intimacy in different ways. But their similarities with *Dora* are compelling, especially their shared antipathy for Victorian conceptions of sexuality.

Notwithstanding the absence of "adolescents" from his rich taxonomy of human types, Freud examines sexuality more broadly than any Bloomsburian. He holds that children are sexually curious (though destined to form misguided theories); that young adults such as Dora are sexually sophisticated, even when repressed; that men and women, beginning in infancy, are "polymorphously perverse," each containing traits of the other sex, and likely to be unhappy and unproductive if they cannot satisfy their desires; that normal sexual and psychic life contains many pathological elements; and that people assume adult sexual roles as part of a social contract, not in accordance with moral or biological laws. Together, these assumptions constitute a radically anti-essentialist vision of *what children, men, and women are like* that could not fail to shock a significant portion of the bourgeoisie whose Puritanism he so detested.[14]

Despite their radical anti-essentialism, however, neither Freud nor Bloomsbury generally prescribes equally daring strategies for pursuing sexual intimacy and pleasure. To the dismay of his followers on the "Freudian Left,"[15] Freud prescribes an ever-shifting balance between instinctual satisfaction and renunciation, with the latter often asserting the stronger claim. Our polymorphous perversity notwithstanding, Freud's prescription generally runs, we should endeavor to grow into the roles that bourgeois society has shaped for us – including the role of spouse – so that we can transcend "hysterical misery" and experience "common unhappiness."[16]

Dora endures an anomalous unhappiness at the thought of the "swinging" role that her therapist suggests. She does not dread the thought of lifelong monogamy, and the self-denial it entails, but the thought of an unwanted, premature sexual adventure. Her dread is no less acute than that of more typical neurotics, who are unable to satisfy their sexual appetites – a discontent that Freud sees as endemic to life in civilization, and often worth the price.

Given his emphasis on the inevitability of unhappiness, Freud's accommodationism has a tragic element, particularly where "masculine," or "active," sexuality is concerned – in both sexes. Girls must endure a "wave of repression,"[17] renouncing their masculinity on their way to womanhood, and boys' Oedipus complexes must be "smashed to pieces" before the father's erotic claim on the mother. The formation of mature, normal – often discontented – adults depends upon such harsh rites. The "race" gains collectively, while each of its members suffers individually.[18]

But while Freud's accommodationism has a tragic dimension – favoring repression and accepting discontent for the sake of civilization – it also leads him to stress liberatory themes. Since children are sexually curious, Freud advises adults to treat the topic of sexual life without "mystery-making," like any other matter that children don't yet understand. This strategy will lessen the mistrust children feel when adults equivocate, and also – by virtue of satisfying curiosity – help it to pass off, rather than dam up in hazardous ways. Parents should not deliver "all sexual knowledge" to their children on one occasion, in "solemn and turgid language," but should largely leave to schools the job of teaching the child – before he is 10 years old – about his place in the animal kingdom.[19] After the age of 20, Freud says, sexual abstinence is a terrible idea; men and women should gain (hetero)sexual experience.[20] These opinions express the counter-cultural sub-current in Freud's answer to the ethical question *How shall we conduct our intimate lives?* and demonstrate that he did not always repress his reformist instincts, despite his claim that "it is certainly not a physician's business to come forward with proposals for reform."[21] Sometimes, for Freud, the pragmatic thing to do was to challenge the prevailing system.

But not usually. His advocacy of *hetero*sexual experience indicates his broadly conservative attitude. It is a good idea to marry, Freud (sometimes) says, for marriage offers protection against one of life's greatest miseries – loneliness. Whether married or not, it is wise to refrain from masturbation, which vitiates the character and accustoms one to easy pleasures; from homosexuality, a "side channel" for the libido, not where its "main stream" should run;[22] and even from "perverse forms of [marital] intercourse," such as oral sex, which degrade love "from a serious matter to a convenient game." When people eschew these perversions in favor of what Freud, with clinical precision, calls "the union of the genitals of the two opposite sexes," they are more likely to remain brave, happy, and curious in many aspects of life. For "normal intercourse," far from being a threat to extra-familial accomplishments, "lays down the pattern for other modes of reacting to life. If a man is energetic in pursuing the object of his love ... he will pursue his other aims with an equally unswerving energy."[23] At times Freud sounds as orthodox – as fearful of perverse "swerving" and faithful in the "pattern" of normative institutions – as the respectable society he disparages.[24]

But his orthodoxy only goes so far: he sees limited value in monogamous marriage. Spouses will likely grow bored with one another after their initial euphoria, at which point it is good (perhaps for men especially) to seek extra-marital pleasure. If women attempt to live up to wifely and motherly ideals, or men to ideals of non-cruelty, they will likely bring more misery than joy to themselves and their loved ones, for such ideals are at odds with our natures.[25]

These orthodox and heterodox opinions do not give a complete picture of the competing impulses behind Freud's answers to practical questions concerning intimate conduct. But they give a good general picture of the direction in which *Dora* tacks, of the choppy theoretical and ethical waters it navigates, of what happens when Freud elaborates the principles behind the case history – with its sensuous specificity – in the form of more general observations about how moderns were reinventing intimacy.

RESPECTABILITY AND THE MODERN FAMILY

Freud is not out of step with his time, in his combination of conservative and liberatory impulses, of respect for the value of repression and hatred of Puritanism. Rather, these tensions in his thought evoke the many paradoxes of the reinvention of intimacy, which saw one status quo burn away and another (not wholly different) arise in its place. On the one hand, increased rates of matrimony suggest a triumph of conformism and respectability in the new century.[26] On the other hand, emerging ideals of companionate marriage and spousal equality altered the domestic sphere, just as women's larger roles in the workforce and higher education altered the public sphere. Did these developments signal triumphs of respectability or its undoing? Admittedly, they betokened a comprehensive rethinking of femaleness. The increased frequency of divorce after the passing of Queen Victoria in 1901 suggests that female emancipation and sexual equality posed a threat to marriage – at least to its Victorian paradigm – and explains the anxiety of many early-twentieth-century popular writings on the subject.[27]

Nonetheless, women's prominence in the public sphere merely enlarged the parameters of respectability, without compromising its importance as a social ideal. In fact, the spread of English schools after the 1870 Education Act, the development of middle-class suburbs (in conjunction with schools), and the turn-of-the-century increase in state-recognized marriages (especially in the lower classes, where marriage had often been de facto but not de jure) together meant that, with the new century, respectability had asserted itself not merely as an ideal, but had expanded in various directions as an institutional reality. Even Freud, the frequent anti-puritan, informs readers that Dora regards his "treatment," despite its "openness about sexual matters," as "far more respectable than Mr. X's conversation!" This self-defense, however wry, reminds readers of Freud's concern over his reputation as a corrupting influence, even as he scoffs at "the respectability of these gentry" while resisting "the temptation of writing a satire upon them."[28]

The structure of modern families – the main loci of respectability in the new century – profoundly altered parent–child relations. Early- to mid-Victorian households often had five to ten children and (depending on their class) many servants. Primogeniture laws meant that a wealthy family's eldest son stood in a different relation to the inheritance than his siblings. Due in part to improved contraception, post-World-War-One households often had two or three children (who divided the family fortune more equitably) and few servants, conditions that afforded opportunities for greater privacy and new kinds of familial intimacy.[29] Ida Bauer, the historical basis of "Dora," came from a transitional but largely modern middle-class family. Servants played a role in her upbringing, but did not usurp the functions of her parents,[30] whom she knew well, perhaps too well. She had only one sibling dividing their attention from her (or from their other pursuits); the family led a mobile existence, depending on the father's erotic adventures and his professional and health needs, and they visited specialists, including Freud. In the conventionally decadent lifestyles of the families depicted in *Dora*, we see antecedents both of the modern nuclear family as a normative institution, and of the sexual daring that led Bloomsburians to stretch the definitions of family as they did.[31]

As nuclear families were altering the cultural landscape of the new century, so too were same-sex passions.[32] From Bloomsbury to continental and American salons, man-loving men and women-loving women spoke in a range of voices of their "perverse" desires,[33] and the crises that such desires provoked – though they often paid homage to respectability in other ways. Given Freud's belief in a universal bisexual disposition, it is not surprising that James and Alix Strachey – who despite their shared bisexuality found happiness in marriage and in their psychoanalytic labors – became his primary English translators. They were drawn to Freud's diagnosis of the challenges of intimacy, which specified permanent causes (human perversity) and contemporary ones (crumbling Victorian mores). Freud, like his translators, held jaded attitudes toward these mores and toward marriage, even as he geared his labors largely on behalf of "normal" sexual life and the "middle class social order."[34]

DORA'S ASSAULT ON THE IDEA OF THE HAPPY FAMILY

Although *Dora* tells the story of two respectable, accomplished families who share their author's bourgeois background, Freud does not need to venture far beneath the surface of their lives to diagnose their dissatisfaction. Dora's father is "a man of rather unusual activity and talents, a large manufacturer in very comfortable circumstances."[35] His success might stem from his "perspicacity" and "shrewdness"[36] – traits that run in his family.[37] Dora herself possesses "critical powers which developed early;"[38] Freud describes her more than once as "sharp-sighted";[39] even her sexual neurosis stems from her "high level of intellectual and moral upbringing."[40] Despite the adverse "circumstances" of infectious diseases and fruitless treatments, Dora "developed into a mature young woman of very independent judgment."[41] To complement these intellectual strengths, she is "in the first bloom of youth – a girl of intelligent and engaging looks"[42] – a flattering description that does not linger unduly on her external traits, as the need for identity protection proscribes Freud from doing. Nor is she the only character presented with this combination of admiration and tact. Herr K., says a footnote, is "still quite young and of prepossessing appearance."[43] Dora praises Frau K's "adorable white body" as well as her taste in gifts.[44] Dora's parents and the K's, with whom they have formed an "intimate friendship,"[45] comprise two marriages that Freud's therapeutic interventions may help to keep intact – though on complex terms – and the families possess enough admirable qualities to make such an effort seem worthwhile.

But beneath their estimable appearance, and their perspicacity notwithstanding, their intimate lives are far from enviable. Dora's mother is "uncultivated" and "foolish," the picture of "housewife's psychosis," a label that denies dignity to her suffering and suggests that many marriages echo her own.[46] Dora's symptoms are also labeled condescendingly, as "merely a case of *petite hystérie*,"[47] though Marcus suggests that Freud is disingenuous to aver that "more interesting cases of hysteria have no doubt been published."[48] However false this fit of Freud's modesty may be, his dislike for the subject of his prize case history[49] shows in his frustration with the "wearisome monotony" of her grievances,[50] and their "incessant repetition."[51] Her tendency to repeat complaints infects Freud's complaints about her. At once a "mature woman" and a "girl," at once "sharp" and "monotonous," Dora – or her analyst's attitude toward her – embraces contradictions and eludes stable categories, a theme to which I will return.

While *Dora*'s female figures are repressed and perhaps frigid, its male subjects are instinctually unsatisfied. Dora's father protests that he gets "nothing out of my own wife."[52] Herr K. seems to get nothing from his wife. The socially prescribed erotic channels for these men, each still driven by desire, have run dry. Such fates for men and women strike Freud as common. Often within one family, he writes (in one of his more essentialist moments), siblings illustrate the active–passive sex distinction: "a brother is a sexual pervert, while his sister, who, being a woman, possesses a weaker sexual instinct, is a neurotic."[53] The crises that these siblings will later suffer, when they reach the ages of Dora and her parents – the likelihood of their being at cross purposes with their heterosexual partners – have roots deep in their psychosexual development.

It is no surprise, then, that the individuals in *Dora*, though joined in intimate friendship, should so often complain about one another, and take elaborate risks to reanimate their passions. Dora's father and Frau K. carry on a longstanding affair, to which their spouses acquiesce, and Herr K. propositions Dora. Sexual boundaries are violated multiply: two adults break marital vows, and a third proposes to do so with a "girl," to recall Freud's epithet. Social mores would seem to be flouted, unless such extra-legal erotic satisfaction is built into the mores. Of course, the heroine's decision to terminate treatment undermines the authority of Freud's recommendation, whatever ideological label we may affix to it.

Whatever Freud's political leanings, his jaded rendition of contemporary bourgeois sexual culture may appear to suggest that the quandaries of intimacy fall far short of the "crisis" that Lawrence perceived, given the opportunities that social conventions afford for infidelity and remarriage.[54] These options enable people to reconcile the competing demands of civilization and instinct – or at least seem to. But Freud's evocation of widespread dissatisfaction, even misery, suggests that there is a crisis (stemming from both perennial and permanent causes), that even while fashioning complex moral compromises, families and individuals remain desperate. Frau K. hopes to "escape the conjugal duties she so much detested,"[55] Dora's mother reports (perhaps dubiously) that her husband is suicidal,[56] and Dora (perhaps without serious intent) threatens to kill herself.[57] Desperation animates Dora's "reproach of malingering" against her father and Frau K., as Freud demonstrates when he turns the reproach back on Dora: however inauthentic an illness, malingering amounts to a plea for attention that cannot be won by less surreptitious means.[58] In a sociological vein, Freud describes a generic family crisis in a female child who discovers that "falling ill" is a "means of enticing out its parents' love," and who, later in life, as the wife of an "inconsiderate husband," sees again that "ill health" is "her one weapon [to] procure the care she longs for."[59] This "child" is a theoretical generalization of processes represented concretely in Dora, her father, and Frau K., each of whom gains attention from illness. Freud's sense of such frequent suffering, some of it disingenuous, explains his modest hope for the curative potential of therapy – merely to lift patients into "common unhappiness" by attacking the psychic sources of hysterical symptoms.

These jaded evocations of the private lives behind two families' estimable appearances begin to reveal why Freud's conception of *what men and women are like* was so tendentious. But nothing was calculated to shock the bourgeoisie like his assault on the idea of "innocence." In part because he did not imagine Dora on a continuum between childhood and sexual maturity, and in part because he was determined to deny psychological innocence even to children, Dora becomes an explosive test case for his anti-puritanical themes. But as a survey of Freud's cultural milieu reveals, other thinkers went further than he – and with more determination to provoke controversy and outrage – in their salvos against Victorian attitudes toward women and children.

MODERNISM MEETS "INNOCENCE"

Particularly after his abandonment of the seduction theory in 1897, Freud contributed to a break in Anglo-European attitudes toward youth, in particular the nineteenth-century "cult of the child." Historians of childhood frequently note that, as the Industrial Revolution exploited child labor (particularly poor children) with unprecedented scope and efficiency, Romantic writers developed a new character – "the child." Children had appeared in literature and visual arts previously, to be sure, but the differences emphasized between, for example, poor and wealthy ones mitigated against the emergence of an archetypal "child." More specifically, pre-Romantic theologies that emphasized original sin further blocked the emergence of an archetypally "innocent child" in the popular imagination. Freud's theories represent a post-Romantic return to this darker view of human nature, with their emphasis on infantile capacities for sexual attachment, jealousy, and hatred.

Between seventeenth-century Protestantism and twentieth-century Freudianism, numerous literary and philosophical works contributed to the cult of the innocent child. Rousseau's *Emile* (1762) links youth and nature as sites of innate goodness. Dickens represents children as orphans and as victims of adult machinations and economic oppression.[60] Freud's seduction theory works roughly in this vein, conceiving of children as objects – both physical and psychic – of adult cruelty. Much now-obscure popular fiction, such as the stories of Mary Louise Molesworth in the 1880s and 1890s, and Victorian "Sunday" literature – tales of moral edification – mythologizes youth even more than Dickens, depicting children as instruments of parents' salvation.[61]

But the nineteenth century was not monolithic in its attitudes toward children; in some ways it anticipated modernist transgressions. From Victoria's England to Freud's Vienna, various artists flouted proprieties, exploring liminal zones between childhood, puberty, adolescence (as we now know this developmental stage), and adulthood. Lewis Carroll's 1858 photograph *Alice Liddell as "The Beggar Maid"* depicts its 6-year-old subject – the inspiration for *Alice's Adventures in Wonderland* – with a hint of allure, one arm bare, one nipple exposed by a dress that seems arranged particularly for this effect, and a gaze in which viewers could read a knowledge beyond her years.[62] (See Figure 1.) On the continent, Egon Schiele's 1911 drawing *Standing Female Nude* depicts a model who appears well

Figure 1 Lewis Carroll, *Alice Liddell as "The Beggar Maid"*

over 6, but – judging from her hairless genitalia and undeveloped breasts – still prepubescent. Her youth is belied by her hair, flowing onto one shoulder in abundant curls; her painted lips, pursed in an arguably inviting way; and her gaze, which, as Alessandra Comini comments, conveys a "disturbing innuendo of [the subject's] complicity" in the viewing.[63] (See Figure 2.) (Such assaults on propriety led to Schiele's brief imprisonment for "immorality" and seducing a minor.)[64] A few years older than Schiele's *Nude* appears to be,

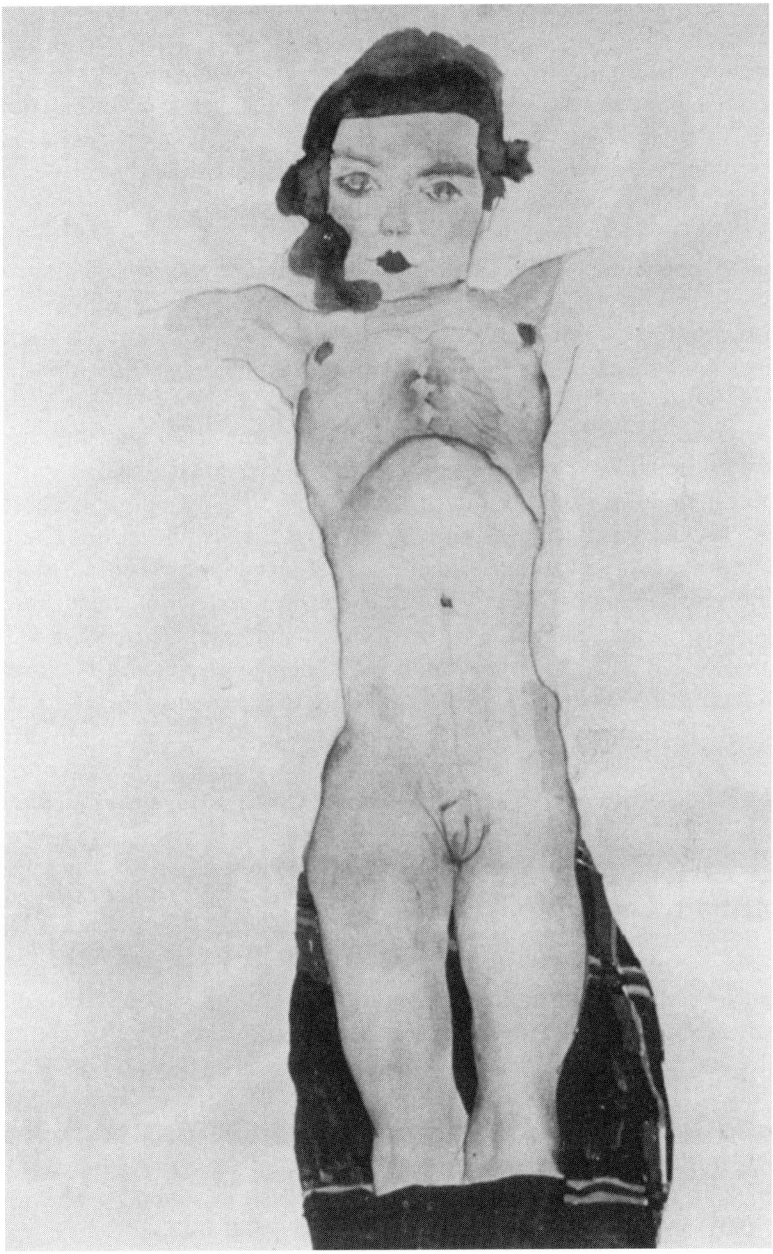

Figure 2 Egon Schiele, *Standing Female Nude*, 1911

Dora – 14 when kissed by Herr K., 16 when introduced to Freud, 18 when she enters psychoanalysis – also occupies an ill-defined developmental area, illustrates the fluidity of female sexual development, and pushes to the breaking point the late-Victorian conceptual scheme that, as Freud and others saw it, infantilized women.[65]

Moving to a developmental stage that overlaps with and stretches past Dora's, Oskar Kokoschka was 21 when he produced *Dreaming Youths*, a 1908 sequence of eight color lithographs, for the Klimt Group's "Art for the Child" display. To public dismay, he represented sexual awakenings rife with melancholy, anxiety, and confusion. His avant-garde technique – a lyrical, stream-of-consciousness prose poem runs beside his images – recalls that of modernists including Freud, whose *Interpretation of Dreams* influenced *Dreaming Youths*. *Eros*, the penultimate lithograph, shows three dynamically posed female youths nude under a magical night sky, one in a pool of deep blue water, and a posture of what could be sexual or spiritual supplication. A fourth, seemingly masturbating female figure hovers on a grassy background in what could be the sky or a dream space. The text (spoken by a lover, perhaps Kokoschka) seems addressed to a vision or memory of a beloved.[66] He identifies with her, reiterating their "resemblance," and links her both with nature (woods stand around her "like amazed boys") and with "the working of all being." In spite (or because) of these exalted sentiments, he implores her not to "come any closer," for their story would "cease to exist" if "touched" – a poignant comment on unconfessed adolescent sexual desire, conveyed (to the envisioned beloved only) as intensely in words as in the image with which they are ambiguously juxtaposed. (See Figure 3.)

Kokoschka described *Dreaming Youths* as a "love letter" to Lilith Lang, who appears with him in the final lithograph, *The Girl Li and I* (Figure 4, and on the jacket of this book), which refigures Adam and Eve's expulsion in its image of two gangly adolescents. Though clearly sexually demarcated by their genitalia, the figures are androgynous in other ways. The male, diminutive compared to his counterpart, has an expression that could be read as sad, shy, or self-conscious; he crosses his legs with feminine delicacy and covers his chest as if with breasts to hide. The female, reminiscent of Donatello's *David* with her *contrapposto* stance and long hair, has no breasts to reveal. Each figure's facial features could belong to either gender. Their ambiguous sexuality and physical separation – neither looking at the other, each encased in his or her white background – could account for the male's melancholic expression. The speaker, like that of the previous lithograph, suffers from ecstatic confusion – passion in a double sense.[67] At one

Figure 3 Oskar Kokoschka, *The Dreaming Youths – Eros*, 1907, 1917

Figure 4 Oskar Kokoschka, *The Dreaming Youths – The Girl Li and I*, 1907, 1917

moment he feels himself "in the love of all being," an oceanic sense carried over from the previous lithograph's text, though one that this image does not clearly convey, and arguably undercuts. Soon later he can find no one to "respond to [his] calls," another poignant evocation of pubescent loneliness. Each of Kokoschka's lithographs, both the image and the text – not to mention their sometimes confluent, sometimes divergent drifts – begs for fuller comment than I can give here. Whatever the book's full import, *Dreaming Youths* reveals – like Schiele's *Nude* – that Freud's sense of childhood as postlapsarian is far from modernist Vienna's most radical assault on the Romantic cult of asexual childhood.

Vienna assaulted this Romantic creed so forcefully that it gave birth to its own more briefly lived cult of the "child woman," with its own protocols for sexual intimacy. The satirist Karl Kraus, editor of the newspaper *Die Fackel* (The Torch), published an inflammatory article, "In praise of the whore" at a time when child prostitution was common in the Austrian capital.[68]

Kraus considered himself a defender of women's liberty and championed the reclamation of mythic female sexual power. He encouraged his protégée, the uncultivated 17-year-old actress Irma Karczewska, to be carefree and promiscuous. He shared her tutoring with male acquaintances including Fritz Wittels, Freud's early colleague and first biographer, and published Wittels's 1907 paper "The child woman," which attempted to lend a psychoanalytic imprimatur to the cult, by invoking Freud's theory of polymorphous perversity in its analysis of history's misunderstood and sexually charismatic women.[69] Whereas Freud suggests that Dora indulge in an affair with Herr K., Kraus and Wittels fashioned a "late-born Greek," a "hetaera" (courtesan) as a test of the editor's theories.[70] Unfortunately, Wittels acknowledges in his memoirs, the experiment met with poor results. "Irma" – to revive her *nom de célèbre* – became so sated with the experiences imposed upon her that this supposed "primeval woman" soon had "no sex urge left at all," and later felt she had been exploited by Kraus.[71] She committed suicide after four failed marriages. In a more sensational way, her unhappiness, in marriage and in general, recalls that of Ida Bauer, who remained bitter and resentful of men decades after Freud's ineffectual treatment.[72]

Kraus's experiment with Irma, though tragically misguided, emerged from genuine reformist tendencies in Vienna. Kraus championed persecuted women in court, and defended women's right to privacy. Like Freud, he wrestled simultaneously with practical questions, including legal ones, related to Vienna's sexual and moral crises, and with theoretical questions about the nature of women – including so-called "child-women." During a period of high levels of STDs, such as the syphilis contracted by Dora's father,[73] cultural attitudes toward women and sexuality were polarized, and Kraus aroused conservative opposition with his 1907 publication of a pseudonymous Wittels essay advocating legalized abortion.[74] Freud, aware of its true author, told Wittels he subscribed to "every word of it."

But Freud's social radicalism was limited and tactical, while his philosophical radicalism was more far-ranging and more a source of his personal pride. While he was quietly sympathetic to some legal reforms; while he believed that women as young as Irma at 17 and even Dora at 14 were sexually mature; and while he advocates limited sexual adventures for Dora at 18, his aims were in many respects the opposite of Kraus's. Freud disapproved of the "child-woman" and "child-man" cults with which psychoanalytic figures, including Wittels, were connected.

Nonetheless, Freud was as far from Rousseau's exaltation of childhood innocence as from the Victorian celebration of feminine purity – the worship of the Angel in the House. Freud saw the defeat of the notion of "innocence" as one of the great achievements of psychoanalysis. He attacked the idea repeatedly and directly. He sometimes put the term in scare quotes, with derisive intent: "there are . . . no 'innocent' dreams," he says, and he expresses similar skepticism about "innocent" jokes.[75] He sometimes attributes the idea to a straw man whom he proceeds to blow over. "A doctor," argues one such straw man, "has no right to intrude upon his patients' sexual secrets and grossly injure their modesty (especially with women patients) . . . which can only . . . offend the innocence of young people and encroach upon the authority of parents." Freud accuses this imaginary opponent of "a prudery which is unworthy of a physician and which inadequately conceals its weakness behind bad arguments." Freud terms other hypothetical opponents "clever men, who call themselves child psychologists [and speak] in terms of reproach of a 'desecration of the innocence of childhood,'" and accuses these opponents of "sentiment instead of argument."[76]

Many icons are smashed in these passages: "sexual secrets" in general (Freudian analysis leaves little room for such secrets), the "modesty" of women in particular, the "innocence" of the young, the "authority" of parents, and the notion that innocence might be "desecrated." Such religiously coded notions – what Lawrence, with equal impatience, would call "old hat"[77] – the families whose authority rests on them, and the limited roles such families allow for women and children: Freud treats these all as byproducts of a prudish "sentiment" that cannot withstand his science and logic. His professional rivals who "call themselves child psychologists" have succumbed to such sentiment.

Freud pursues this offensive not only at the hypothetical level, but also with individual case studies. In his "Postscript" to the "little Hans" paper, he alludes to the "indignation" that greeted its publication over a decade earlier: "a most evil future had been foretold for the poor little boy, because he had been 'robbed of his innocence' at such a tender age" (5). But none of these apprehensions had come true," Freud assures his readers. "Hans was now a strapping youth of nineteen [who] was perfectly well, and suffered from no troubles or inhibitions."[78] Freud's honesty in reporting the therapeutic results of his case studies has been challenged:[79] unlike Wittels, he is not apt to admit that his charges have met with unhappy ends.

His motives for such obfuscation are easy to infer. Many of his theoretical campaigns stand to suffer in the face of contrary empirical evidence, including his diatribes against innocence. Do pre- and post-pubescent youth possess it? When is it dangerous for an analyst to violate it? In

Dora, Freud, as a theorist, stops short of asserting a universal lack of innocence, but is confident that psychoanalysis poses no threat to this psychological state, should it exist. His justification for exculpating psychoanalysis lies in his theory of the unconscious as a source of hysteria. "There is never any danger of corrupting an inexperienced girl," he asserts. "For where there is no knowledge of sexual processes even in the unconscious, no hysterical symptom will arise." In the absence of such symptoms, this passage suggests, therapy would likely be unnecessary in the first place. Conversely, Freud continues, "where hysteria is found there can no longer be any question of 'innocence of mind' in the sense in which parents and educators use the phrase."[80] With some rhetorical wizardry, Freud constructs "parents and educators" – pillars of respectability – as unwitting villains in their efforts to protect and prolong "innocence," and psychoanalysis as a largely risk-free endeavor.

But this logic is slippery. It is one thing to attribute "knowledge of sexual processes" to a patient such as Dora, particularly to her "unconscious," where the attribution cannot be falsified. It is something different to imply, as Freud does, that "unconscious knowledge" functionally amounts to "experience" and thus to immunity from "corruption" at the hands of an analyst who reads her "No" as "Yes."[81] At such moments, when Dora's protestation is not taken literally, Freud the theorist (constructing her as sexually knowing but unself-aware) becomes difficult to distinguish from Freud the therapist (whose method of treatment is predicated on this questionable construction).

Admittedly, Kraus's approach to Irma, as her mentor, differs markedly from Freud's approach to Dora, both theoretically and therapeutically. Kraus uses Irma as his foot soldier in his battle against prudery and feminine sexual propriety. The arena of the battle is the wide public, and Irma is thus subject to potential scorn. Freud, by contrast, does not plunge his patient into varied sexual experiences, but merely suggests that (what he infers to be) a single object of her desire should not be rebuffed. He and Dora struggle in a private arena – the therapist's office – and as long as Ida Bauer's identity remains hidden, she risks no public scorn.[82] Even if she follows Freud's advice, and takes Herr K. as a lover, this need not tarnish her reputation with the far-from-guiltless "middle-class social order" into which Freud aims to integrate her.

In theoretical terms, polymorphous perversity does not, for Freud the theorist, equate to the "wildness" that Kraus and Wittels saw as basic to Irma and aimed to unleash. Instead, it entails a combination of diverse tendencies that need to be channeled in socially accepted ways. Hence

Freud does not plunge deeply into an *essentialist* assumption about Dora's sexuality. That she has desires (and should probably act on them), Freud is confident. But their precise nature – to what degree they are conscious or unconscious, hetero- or homosexual, exogamous or endogamous, extra-therapeutic or enmeshed in transference – Freud leaves strategically vague. By contrast, Kraus's project is predicated on a more precisely defined (though crudely imagined) essence.

Freud's theories of sexuality, furthermore, are sensitive to developmental stages, even if his scheme may not perfectly match today's conventional wisdom about adolescence. The last of the *Three Essays*, entitled "The transformations of puberty," treats this stage – following the latency period – as one in which crucial metamorphoses occur. The sexes differentiate from one another, the genital zones achieve primacy, and individuals find objects for their desire, rather than the desire remaining undifferentiated or auto-erotic.[83] While Freud's and Hall's accounts are similar – each links somatic to psychic change – Freud's *Three Essays* focus on the somatic processes of puberty, whereas Hall's primary agenda is to define a period of psychic adolescence that is distinct from adulthood. In *Dora*, on the other hand – as Erikson discusses – it is not clear whether the innovative modernist author means to categorize his patient (if he means to categorize her at all) as an adult. At fourteen, she is sexually developed enough to arouse the interest – and kiss – of Herr K., a potential "object" for her desire. She experiences a "violent feeling of disgust" due to "the pressure of his erect member against her body," we may infer, because her genital zone is her primary zone, though she is not yet psychically equipped (as Freud believes she should be) to embrace the "distinct feeling of sexual excitement" that "a healthy girl in such circumstances" would enjoy.[84] Both the *Three Essays* and the case study mark the first years of puberty as a period of difficult psychological transitions: one text describes them generically, the other dramatizes the transitions as a "neurotic" undergoes them, wavering (largely unconsciously) between homo- and heterosexual object choices, fearing the contact of a male genital.

The temporally imprecise nature of these transitions may explain some instabilities in Freud's terminology. At 14, Dora is described only as a "girl" (not a "woman"), despite her having been physiologically mature enough to react – potentially – with a "healthy ... genital sensation."[85] At 18, on the other hand, she is – as mentioned – in one context a "mature young woman" and in another a "girl ... in the first bloom of youth." If, even at 18, she is not consistently classified as an adult, then as a 14-year-old girl, she may well have needed protection from, not incitement to, sexual experience with a married man. At the very least, Erikson argues, the 18-year-old patient might have benefited, had her therapist sympathetically acknowledged her feeling of violation by Herr K., rather than doubting the feeling as psychologically dishonest. But Freud is definitive that hysterical symptoms preclude the possibility of "innocence of mind." "With children of ten, of twelve, of fourteen, with boys and girls alike," he states, he is certain of this fact.[86]

In Freud's denial that even the hysterics of a 10-year-old can be "innocent," one element of his theoretical radicalism – his picture of *what children are like* – recalls Kraus. In spite of their different ways of handling Dora and Irma, each thinker was motivated by deep opposition to ideas about youthful purity running through such major figures as Rousseau, Wordsworth, Blake, Dickens, Hugo, and Baudelaire.[87]

THE CONTENT OF DORA'S CHARACTER

Freud's myth busting, however, is not limited to the topic of youthful innocence. Children are not innocent, he maintains; families are not happy (at least not in the ways that respectable appearances would suggest); and women are not innocent. This latter conviction – Freud's picture of *what women are like* – even as it eschews Kraus's cult of female sexuality, reacts just as strongly against a nineteenth-century cult of female asexuality and moral perfection. Lord Acton is cited as a representative Victorian for saying that "the majority of women (happily for them) are not very much troubled with sexual feeling of any kind . . . The best mothers, wives, and managers of households, know little or nothing of sexual indulgences. Love of home, children, and domestic duties, are the only passions they feel."[88] With even science supporting such an exalted (though also condescending) view of women, it is not surprising that Charles Kingsley should see the "woman," conceptually speaking, as "the natural and therefore divine guide, purifier, inspirer of the man,"[89] nor that as committed a reformer as Beatrice Webb (herself childless) should echo countless contemporaries in praising "the holiness of motherhood."[90] Although Bloomsburians viewed this Victorian ideal of femininity with great suspicion, nonetheless Forster (in the figures of Ruth Wilcox of *Howards End* and Mrs Moore of *A Passage to India*) and Woolf (in Clarissa Dalloway and Mrs Ramsay) each sketch their own admiring, though ambivalent, variations on it.

Freud, on the other hand, was never tempted to embrace this ideal, even in Forster's and Woolf's limited and ambivalent ways. One route assumed by Freud's skepticism is a rigorous anti-essentialism that denies any deep content to femininity. In "Femininity," he reiterates his frequent assertion of bisexuality, even at the physiological level, and asks whether psychology can "lay hold of" the masculine–feminine distinction as anatomy cannot. He answers his own question in the negative, acknowledging that psychology often resorts to the active–passive binary, which the animal kingdom doesn't even always support as a sex distinction.[91]

Dora does not pursue an anti-essentialist argument as resolutely as "Femininity": the case history, for example, depicts Dora's mother and father as so thoroughly enmeshed in their gender roles that the masculine–feminine distinction is fully intact, as far as their psyches are rendered knowable. Instead, the case history brings into the Bloomsburian discussion an idea of *what women are like* that echoes philosophical and literary traditions very different from Patmore's. Victorian England had its woman worshippers, to be sure, but it also had passionate critics of this attitude, including male ones. T. H. Huxley scorned the "philogynists," as he called them, who saw females as "the higher type of humanity," arguing instead that the sexes had the same "senses, perceptions, feelings, reasoning powers," that "the female type of character is no better nor worse than the male," and that women should be neither "men's guides nor their playthings, but their comrades, their fellows, and their equals."[92] J. S. Mill supported the female franchise with arguments that anticipate Margaret and Helen Schlegel. Liberty and equality should apply to both sexes, says Mill, and he critiques the separate spheres, and the chivalric values he sees implicit in them, by saying that women deserve "equal rights, equal admission to all social privileges; not a position apart, a sort of sentimental priesthood."[93]

When its heroine defies the therapist, *Dora* shares with these liberal Victorian writings a picture of a leveled sexual playing field. It raises the idea of *what women are like* in one sense by lowering it in another. Employing the Enlightenment value of reason as a standard, Huxley and Mill deny female moral superiority but also deny male intellectual superiority – at least as an innate endowment. These thinkers doubt the existence of sexual differences, where the capacities for feeling, reason, and civic responsibility are concerned. (Mill lamented that men, at present, were more inclined than women to see public duty as honorable, and wrestled with the question of whether this resulted from correctible inequalities in the educational system or from a something inherently masculine about public life.)[94]

In its admiration of its heroine's reasoning powers, *Dora* belongs to an international discourse, spanning the late-Victorian and Edwardian years, of female characters who confront the "Woman Question" and in some cases defy male authority. Canonical figures such as Ibsen's Nora and Forster's Schlegel sisters share the stage with popular figures such as the heroine of Elizabeth Robins's 1907 play *Votes for Women!* Dora's defiant streak does not, like Nora's, lead her to champion a particular cause, but it does earn Freud's admiration. He cites, as evidence of her "independent judgment," her ability to "laugh at the efforts of doctors and . . . renounce their help."[95] His contempt for "those who call themselves child psychologists" indicates his sympathy for her mistrust of ordinary practitioners. Dora's ability to see through the pretenses of male authority figures, and to challenge them, contrasts with the timidity of Frau K. and especially of Dora's mother – and this ability does not spare the father to whom Dora is "tenderly attached." Precisely because of this attachment, she notices and takes "offense at many of his actions and peculiarities."[96] Of course, Freud the therapist is also subject to her "pitilessly" critical eye, and she denies him the opportunity to complete treatment. But this does not stop Freud the author and theorist from admiring the many traits, including the independent judgment, of his half-documented, half-imagined protagonist.

Admittedly, Freud does not have the didactic and reformist agendas of Robins and Ibsen, and *Dora* has even – for good reasons – been the target of much feminist criticism.[97] But its lack of a didactic agenda and its interest in irrationality enable *Dora* to pursue themes beyond the reach of Robins and Ibsen. Its refusal of sentimentality links it to another international tradition, spanning the nineteenth century, that focuses on the complex imperfections – including the selfishness and unreason – of its heroines, including Emma Woodhouse, Gwendolen Harleth, Isabel Archer, Anna Karenina, and Emma Bovary. These are neither perfectly reasonable nor unselfish women, though Austen, Eliot, and Tolstoy value reason and unselfishness as ethical ideals. Nor is any of these heroines without blind spots, especially concerning herself, though each is also perspicacious. Emma and Gwendolen, for example, can be cruel and driven by unconscious urges despite their mental adroitness. Dora's limitations, too, contribute to her complex humanness. "She might be blind in one direction," says Freud, "but she was sharp-sighted enough in the other."[98] Reason and unreason, selfishness and unselfishness are difficult to disentangle in these subtly drawn heroines. *Emma* tells a hopeful tale – hearkening back to the chivalric values that Mill and Freud despise – of the heroine's self-knowledge increasing under the influence of her older male mentor, Knightley (whose name suggests medieval virtue). In *Dora*, by contrast, the older male mentor – Freud – is highly fallible. The title character may gain more by rebelling against Freud than by following his intellectual example.

Whether or not Dora achieves any meaningful liberation from Freud, her intellectual strengths and weaknesses fold into one another in complex ways. In her temporary "blindness," she senses nothing amiss in Frau K.'s relations with her father, despite the "advanced" and "well-read" governess's discomfort with this extra-marital "intimacy." But at the same time, in her sharp-sightedness, Dora perceives the governess's love for her father – because she recognizes that the governess's attentions to *her* had been indirect attempts to win his attention. Nonetheless, Dora is blind to the parallel between this stratagem of the governess's and her own stratagem (as Freud reads it) to win Herr K.'s affection by attending to his children.[99] How different a world she inhabits than Vaughan and his wife, each of whom perceives all that there is to see in the other! The one character in *Dora* who might occupy the role of domestic angel is the heroine's mother, but her "housewife's psychosis" illustrates how different Freud's categories are from Patmore's.

Finally, in addition to belonging to an Ibsenian tradition of heroines who defy male authority, and arguably culminating a nineteenth-century tradition of complexly selfish heroines, Dora stands at the forefront of a modernist lineage of perverse heroines. Both Clarissa Dalloway and the Ursula Brangwen of *The Rainbow* (with her attraction to Winifred Inger) are kindred figures. Molly Bloom and her vibrant monologue bring to its fullest bloom this radical modernist project of representing female sexuality as multifarious and beyond inherited categories – without a trace of moral judgment. Admittedly, such texts do not refuse to entertain judgments about their characters' choices: for example, in *Women in Love* – a loose sequel to *The Rainbow* – Ursula speaks harshly of "perversion." But such judgments express the authors' (or their characters') willingness to accommodate social norms. The modernists' theoretical convictions, on the other hand, link them to the sexologists' emancipatory project of cataloging – without condemning – human desire in all its forms. Molly (and especially Leo) Bloom are like sexological case studies projected into avant-garde literature. Dora – the incest-minded daughter with lesbian tendencies, perpetually jealous and mistrustful – links the sexologists and novelists by inhabiting a text at once medical and literary in orientation.

Each of these philosophical and literary traditions from which Dora draws, or culminates, or helps to inaugurate, enriches the *content* of her femininity. How essential is this content? Too much, according to critics including Jacqueline Rose,[100] who suggests that Freud, at times, betrays his salutary mistrust of sexual categories and equates "femininity" – as a natural category – with a lack of sexual aim and an impossibility of satisfaction. While Rose's critique is well taken (Freud does make forays into essentialism), *Dora*'s contribution to the Bloomsburian discussion of *what women are like* is largely emancipatory and anti-essentialist. Freud mercilessly unravels myths about women and children – and especially about innocence. Whereas Forster and Woolf express some (uneasy) nostalgia for decades gone by, and for a way of life that dignified Ruth Wilcox in her angelic role, Freud has no admiration for Victorian efforts to maintain a child in a naïveté with which her own unconscious is unsatisfied, nor for Victorian efforts to erect a psychological *cordon sanitaire* around the concept of "woman."

Whatever Freud's attitudes toward the practical aspects of marriage and other social institutions – where he was loath to unfetter instincts that could damage the community – at the theoretical level he was determined to defeat myths with what he saw as the scientific truths of psychoanalysis. In conjunction with these anti-Victorian impulses, Freud's modernist skills enable his morally ambiguous depiction of a possibly essence-less heroine. Far less incendiary than Kraus's glorified "whore," Dora is more usefully provocative: she opens a twentieth-century literary path that other writers would both follow and alter.

With greater breadth and depth than *Principia*, *Dora* interrogates the new ways that middle-class English and European men and women were imagining, forming, and dissolving erotic bonds. Subsequent Bloomsburian texts, notably *Mrs Dalloway*, would draw on Freud's insights and echo his savvy combination of skepticism concerning sexual essences with his reluctance to defy social norms as brazenly as Kraus. Having deprived its protagonist the protection of innocence, *Dora* is left with the difficult narrative question of what this deprivation means in practical terms. The difficulty of answering this question perhaps explains *Dora*'s open ending. It may also explain why the conclusion of *Howards End* – as the next chapter discusses – retracts the question and restores Margaret's innocence, after the bulk of Forster's novel frames the question in broad and thoughtful ways.

PART II

Defeated husbands

CHAPTER 3

Forster's missing figures

As both practitioner and theorist, E. M. Forster brought subtle attention to various aspects of the novelist's craft, from story and plot to pattern and rhythm. His most famous theoretical contribution may be his distinction between "round" (complex) and "flat" (one-dimensional) characters, and his analysis of the uses to which each can be put.[1] Pursuing a related line of inquiry, this chapter examines characterizations, or figures, of masculinity and femininity in *Howards End*, specifically how Forster uses, revises, and rejects New Womanliness and sexual intermediacy as philosophical vehicles. By virtue of the richness or poverty with which he imagines them, and of the attitudes that Forster's narrator expresses toward them, these psychosexual paradigms enable *Howards End* to address the questions *What are men and women like, or what should they be like, if they can redefine themselves?* and *Should they seek intimacy according to a Victorian or post-Victorian model?*

Broadly speaking, *Howards End* answers with an essentialist rejection of patriarchal marriage. This approach to intimacy distinguishes the novel both from *Principia Ethica* and *Dora*, with their anti-essentialist accommodations, and from Forster's other five novels, which examine male sexuality, including male effeminacy, in radically different ways. In opposition to critics who see the novel hoping to synthesize Wilcoxism and Schlegelism,[2] I argue that *Howards End* spurns patriarchal marriage primarily by depicting the brutish paternal and filial personality types that it enables. With fathers and husbands as insensitive as Henry Wilcox, sons (Charles and Paul) as emotionally stunted as their father, and wives largely restricted to the family sphere, something has to give: men and women need to negotiate new ways of being masculine and feminine. The novel's rejection of the Wilcoxian matrimonial model, in conjunction with its author's sexual orientation, and thus his strong personal interest in rethinking gender, virtually obliges *Howards End* to pursue anti-essentialist strategies for characterizing sexuality.

So it might seem. But this pessimistic – or perhaps simply reactionary – novel confounds such expectations. This tension in its treatments of selfhood and intimacy has received too little critical comment. In arguing that two key figures are missing in *Howards End*, I follow Roland Barthes and Ann Ardis in using the term "figure" to denote something supplementary to social reality, without denying Forster's skills as a documentarian.[3] While neither Margaret, Ruth, Leonard, nor Tibby necessarily corresponds to a particular Edwardian person, Forster uses them as symbols, albeit complex ones, to celebrate or criticize types of people who populated cultural discourses as well as society.

With this sense of Forster's characters as vehicles, I pose two queries to *Howards End*. First, *what happened to the New Woman* that Margaret once was? Through the bulk of the novel, the elder Schlegel sister fulfills this role: she is independent minded, concerned with social – including sexual – equality, and possessed of a formidable capacity for reason. But in the final chapters, this Margaret disappears, replaced by a domestic Angel reminiscent of Ruth Wilcox. The novel's well-known embrace of rural beauty against the spread of "grey" cosmopolitanism is, in many instances, beautifully articulated. But it comes at a price. Cosmopolitanism and socialism offer models of femininity beyond those with which Ruth was familiar, and thus opportunities for the author to signal his sympathy with reformist attitudes toward gender. The rural-matron role entails a different moral investment for Forster, one that associates virtuous womanliness with quietism and a mystical connection to the land. In investing a reactionary model of femininity with moral authority, perhaps *Howards End* expresses doubt that New Womanliness is likely to be efficacious in the twentieth century – or a sense that, if it were efficacious, this would not be worth the price of a vanished rural England.

Second, I ask *Why is male intermediacy treated so obliquely and disapprovingly, given its more direct and in some cases celebratory treatment, in other Forster novels*? "Intermediates," as theorized by Edward Carpenter, are distinguished by several features. Through today's lens of identity politics, their love for other men appears crucial, as it was for Carpenter and Forster. Carpenter also shared with contemporary sexologists an interest in what he called masculine and feminine "Soul-material," and in the ways it overlaps with – but does not correspond to – sex and sexual orientation. Because intermediates bring issues of Soul-material to the fore, Carpenter credits them with playing an avant-garde role in historical change. Extending a discourse developed in Whitman's poetry, he argues that intermediates' psychic hermaphrodism makes them "guides" toward a freer, more humane future. Their ability to form cross-class intimacies is a particular source of his enthusiasm.

This optimism distinguishes Carpenter sharply from Forster, whose sense of intermediates' place in present and future society, across all his novels, ranges from skeptical to cynical. *Howards End* is unusual in this œuvre for its lack of a gay protagonist, but its depictions of Leonard Bast and Tibby perform as thoroughgoing an analysis of male Soul-material as any of Forster's novels. Admittedly, Leonard and Tibby are not linked to one another sexually, and Leonard's heterosexuality is never in question. However, because one hails from the working class and the other from a privileged class, and because they both lack robust Wilcoxian virility, these two figures enable *Howards End* to depict different kinds of masculinity from across the socioeconomic spectrum, and thus to broaden its examination of gender and patriarchy. Critics have underemphasized the degree to which *Howards End* punishes their heterodox masculine Soul-material, in Leonard's case by virtue of plot machinery and in Tibby's case by virtue of narrative tone. Thus these characters reveal the possible anti-essentialist routes for maleness that – even as it evokes them – the novel proscribes as viable ways out of impasses in Victorian and Edwardian social relations.

Since the posthumous revelation of Forster's homosexuality, critics have left no stone unturned in their examinations of how his works engage with queer themes, or with what this project broadly construes as anti-essentialist approaches to sexuality. Paul Armstrong argues that the narrator of *Howards End*, both an insider and an outsider with regard to Edwardian mores, is the locus of its queer energies. Armstrong's claim is provocative for several reasons, among them its reminder that Forster's narrator is not a transparent medium, but continually intrudes with jokes, social observations, etc. Nonetheless, Armstrong fails, in my reading, to account for the harsh treatment accorded to Leonard and Tibby, and relies instead upon a too-flexible use of the concept "queerness," according to which virtually any ambivalence toward dominant cultural values contributes to the novel's gender critique.[4] I reverse Armstrong's strategy: where he emphasizes how the novel incorporates queer values, I focus on how it excludes or condemns them, using its missing figures and expressions of hostility as signs of its troubled response to the challenges of modern intimacy, its lack of a hopeful answer to the question *What should men be like, if not like Wilcoxes?*

VICTORIAN "NEW WOMEN," THEIR MODERN PROGENY, AND FORSTER

Because Victorian and modern New-Woman fiction has been treated thoroughly by Ann Ardis,[5] my treatment is brisk. A number of its key characteristics, however, bear directly upon *Howards End*. The "New Woman" was a figure constructed – as heroine or straw woman – for specific rhetorical purposes. Rational (like Margaret can be) or passionate (like Helen), impelled by her belief in sexual equality or (more likely) her lust for freedom, the New Woman refused to be angelic: she pursued non-marital love, sometimes outside of England, and even bore illegitimate children. (Helen belongs to this tradition in several ways and Forster's narrator treats her harshly for it.) In terms of plot machinery, some rebel heroines meet with tragic ends, such as suicide, which either entails a cautionary warning to would-be rebellious readers, or a comment on oppressive social conventions.

But *Howards End* plays its subtlest variations on Margaret's, not Helen's, New-Woman precursors. Ardis writes of other heroines who don't meet with sensational ends, but instead "boomerang"[6] back from rebellions into traditional roles – another ending that could convey a reactionary message (an endorsement of said roles) or a social critique (the heroine's domestication entailing a quiet tragedy). Expanding from Ardis's texts, I read Margaret in a line of New Womanly heroines including Isabel Archer and Dorothea Brooke, whose sense of confinement in marriage is key to their novels' arguments. I borrow the metaphor of the boomerang to describe not the plot of *Howards End*, but Margaret's psychological arc, the locus of the novel's pessimism concerning the new century's chances for a renaissance of gender.

Regardless of their ideological bent, Victorian New-Woman texts explicitly posed questions about *what women are, can, or should not be like*, and about *how to seek sexual and marital intimacy*. Bloomsburians' originality lay not in their posing such questions, but in their complexly self-divided approaches to them. While some Bloomsburian characters do have large symbolic resonances (Mrs Dalloway, Mrs Ramsay, Ruth Wilcox, and Mrs Moore all signify a passing era of femininity, while Margaret Schlegel, Lily Briscoe, and Ursula Brangwen signify an emerging one),[7] such characterizations never carry unambiguous messages. Whether old or "new," these women compel readers to sort through the contradictions of an era's gender roles, intimacy regimes, and spiritual inclinations.

But New-Woman novels did not necessarily lack complexity. In contrast to the more "pulse-less" conventions of other popular literature, they aimed to depict sexual desire frankly. They were praised in their time for improving upon moribund Victorian realism – fit only for drawing rooms and censorious circulating libraries – by capturing the inconsistencies of human character.[8] They often made sexual desire a source of a character's unpredictability. In the twentieth century, Freud and Woolf carried this aesthetic principle further; and the "round" heroines of *Howards End* also have conflicting tendencies – sexual and otherwise.

New-Woman novels further demonstrate their capacity for subtlety in the close relations they depict between female characters which, while not necessarily sexual, nonetheless suggest alternatives to a social order built on patriarchy and separate spheres, in which a woman's main intimacies lay with her husband and children. The concluding chapters of Forster's novel, wherein Henry is crippled and the Schlegel sisters inherit Howards End, play a variation on this lesbian-inflected New-Woman tradition.

Finally, Victorian New-Woman fiction bears on *Howards End* because it frequently explored the compatibility of feminism and socialism – the question of whether reforming the economic and sexual orders were interconnected projects. *Howards End* is less Manichean in thinking about socialism and philanthropy (Schlegelian values) and about hard-headed capitalism (a Wilcoxian *modus operandi*) than in thinking about other traits associated with these two gendered families. Nonetheless, the association of Schlegels with softness and Wilcoxes with hardness links *Howards End* to the New-Woman novel tradition of treating issues of economic and sexual justice in dynamic interplay.

Such interplay was exceptionally dynamic in the writings of Carpenter, who championed workers, women, and intermediate men, all of whom he saw as victims of the values summed up by Forster in the figures of Henry and Charles Wilcox. Though Forster considered Carpenter less than a genius, he admired Carpenter's social activism and intellectual courage. The ways that *Howards End* diverges from Carpenter's models of male sexuality – and also from the models in Forster's other novels – illuminate its unique and ideologically troubling diagnosis of Edwardian intimacy.

CARPENTER ON "INTERMEDIACY"

Maurice, Forster's only explicitly gay novel, was composed during 1913 and 1914 (following the 1910 publication of *Howards End*), circulated only among Forster's friends during his lifetime, and published posthumously in 1971. It was written, Forster explains, "as a direct result" of his 1912 visit to Millthorpe, where Carpenter – whom Forster approached "as one approaches a savior" – had a farm. There Forster met George Merrill, Carpenter's working-class "comrade," a term for male companionship that Forster borrows from Carpenter, who borrowed it from Whitman. Merrill, says Forster, "touched my backside – gently and just above the buttocks,"[9] an anatomically vague account of a revelatory moment. Whether Forster describes sodomy is unclear, but Merrill expanded his sexual imagination beyond the model of "higher sodomy" (spiritual male companionship) popular among Moore's Apostles, to include physical comradeship rooted in working-class passions. (The title character Maurice and his lover, the gardener Alec Scudder, evoke Carpenter and Merrill. These characters are mirrored in a heterosexual vein by Constance and the gamekeeper Oliver Mellors in Lawrence's *Lady Chatterley's Lover*.)[10] That Tibby and Leonard are *not* paired sexually indicates an important difference in the architecture of *Howards End*, from that in *Maurice* and other Forster novels.

Carpenter's theories about intermediate character types suggested to Bloomsburians and other moderns one way of understanding *what men and women are like*. His advocacy of intermediate culture offered a non-patriarchal, non-monogamic *model of intimacy*. Havelock Ellis credits Carpenter with "an original voice . . . that made a direct appeal to me," much the same language in which Forster praises Whitman.[11] Ellis says that his friends cherished Carpenter's Whitmanesque book of verse *Toward Democracy* (1883–1902) "as a kind of Bible." Writing with characteristic skepticism, Forster says that Carpenter "*may* have a message for the future, for the generations unborn" (my emphasis).

This "message" was conveyed in multi-generic writings, including the 1908 pamphlet *The Intermediate Sex*, which alternates between using Karl Ulrichs's term "Uranians" and Carpenter's own term "intermediates" to describe gay men (primarily) and women (who play a smaller but significant part in his discussion). Carpenter says that intermediates are misunderstood; but that ascertainable facts capture what they are like; that they have a rich history; that attitudes toward them are improving; that their place in modern society is a major issue that cannot be ignored; and that they have unique things to offer the world.

With regards to their being misunderstood, Carpenter says that their valuable social work goes unrecognized because they are not recognized, being compelled to "conceal [their] temperament from the public."[12] Society suffers from failing to see how comrade-love liberates people "from the responsibilities and impediments of family life" to perform "audacious" and heroic "social and mental activities." Thus, while "close affectional ties" are necessary to a complete life, society would do well to recognize that such "ties" take different forms, and yield different benefits.[13] Just as Christians, socialists, the women's movement, and other reformers have been misrepresented – but eventually vindicated by history, Carpenter says – so too he sees a bright future for intermediates.[14]

Given current ignorance about them, though, he is intent upon rebutting stereotypes and clarifying definitions. He anticipates – contingent upon empirical study – that this population, like any other, will be found to include "good and bad, high and low, worthy and unworthy."[15] Moreover, says Carpenter, "individuals affected with inversion" do not differ from the general population in any "physical or mental particular,"[16] a claim to which he does not consistently hold.

Being like other people, intermediates are not many things that they have been labeled: they are neither "licentious" nor "nervous,"[17] though even some of their champions, including Krafft-Ebing, cling to this latter label. Sensitive to how terminology can both stigmatize a population and contribute to forming its character, Carpenter anticipates "that the epithet 'morbid' will probably before long be abandoned" with regard to "homogenic" people,[18] and his 1912 book *Love's Coming of Age* makes a similar prediction with regard to "angel" and "lady" as labels for women, adding that the "lady" (a woman who conforms to a false Victorian ideal) "has man's covert contempt."[19] Thus Carpenter's feminism and his advocacy of intermediate men reinforce one another.

But in addition to being like other people, Carpenter's intermediates are also unlike others. *The Intermediate Sex* refers to them as a "race,"[20] diction echoed in *Howards End* when Margaret worries that the sexes are "really [separate] races, each with its own code of morality."[21] When Carpenter refers to a "race," however, he does not describe a narrow and impermeable essence, but a range on a continuum of human traits. Complicating Ulrichs's notion that Uranians have female souls in male bodies,[22] Carpenter says that "there are distinctions and gradations of Soul-material in relation to Sex" shading off "most subtly from male to female, and not always in obvious correspondence with outer bodily sex."[23] A similar notion of a continuum informs his thinking about love and friendship: intermediates, he says, can improve society by bringing to light the subtle gradations between these forms of attachment, increasing the chances for all attachments between the two pure (sexual and non-sexual) forms to thrive.[24]

Given that the intermediate race has "good and bad" elements, Carpenter is careful – in his effort to win wider acceptance for the group – to distance himself from its "extreme specimens," the males of which are "distinctly effeminate . . . sentimental, lackadaisical," etc., and the females of which are "markedly aggressive," with "masculine manners and movements, practical in the conduct of life, sensuous rather than sentimental in love," their rooms "decorated with sporting scenes, pistols, etc.," and rife with "fragrant weed."[25] Many of these "unattractive" signs of "extreme" masculinity in homogenic women are also apparent in Wilcox men: Carpenter and Forster share an aversion to hyper-masculine values.

But *The Intermediate Sex* supplies the missing figure that *Howards End* omits: Carpenter celebrates the virtues, as he sees them, of homogenic men, who include many artists and scholars; are unusually sensitive, owing to the "constant interaction between [their] masculine and feminine elements;"[26] and are to be admired for "putting Love before everything else," including "money-making, business, success, [and] fame, which occupy so much space in most people's careers."[27] These men's feminine traits can be humanizing examples for heterosexual men, from whom they differ, after all, only by gradations. Chapter 2 of *Love's Coming of Age*, entitled "Man, the ungrown," explains why normal men would need role models, for they are "in matters of Love for the most part a child."[28] Worse yet, in affairs of state (which have analogs in the home), a "half-grown man" is a "tyrant." Thus patriarchal rule "has for many ages meant the serfdom of Woman," says Carpenter.[29]

Forster shares Carpenter's contempt for the "ungrown" sides of the normal male. His essay "Notes on English character" says that British public-school men – many of whom administer the British empire – "go forth" into a world far more diverse than they can imagine "with well-developed bodies, fairly developed minds, and undeveloped hearts."[30] Wilcox men such as Henry – physically robust, intellectually able concerning practical matters such as his management of the Imperial and West African Rubber Company, and emotionally "undeveloped" – argue the same point as Forster's essay, and reinforce Carpenter's argument about the spiritual dangers to men of narrowly "masculine" roles.

Yet Carpenter was optimistic in ways that *Howards End* is not, about alternative roles open to Edwardian men. How different is his "intermediate" title figure from Tibby and Leonard! Despite his aesthetic and scholarly inclinations, Tibby is neither creative nor sensitive to others' feelings, in an ideally hermaphroditic way. Leonard may struggle, as he peruses Ruskin, to achieve the heights of refinement that Carpenter values, but his fine feelings never come to fruition, and in their embryonic form they set no example for other men to emulate. Woolf, more optimistic in some writings than Forster is in *Howards End*, admired Shakespeare's "androgynous mind" and hoped that more such minds could flourish in the new century. Carpenter, more optimistic yet, was confident as early as the late-Victorian years that they already were flourishing.

In fact, he argues in various works that they have long flourished (albeit often in unacknowledged ways), that their history stretches through past centuries.[31] Carpenter answers the question *What are men like?* not merely by claiming *They* ***can*** *be like this*, but by asserting that *They* ***long have been*** *like this* – society just doesn't know it. *The Intermediate Sex* notes homogenic bonds in African blood rites (reminiscent of the *Blutbrüderschaft* entertained by Birkin); commends history's remarkable intermediates, including Michelangelo; and catalogs writing on male–male affection from Plato to Shakespeare, Melville, Tennyson, Whitman, and Pater. Forster and other Cambridge students had taken inspiration from the classical Greek model of male–male love, with the help of such instructors as Goldsworthy Lowes Dickinson. With the 1889 publication in *Blackwood's* magazine of Wilde's "Portrait of Mr W H," Shakespeare's sonnets had been claimed for an emerging canon of homogenic literature.[32] Through his scholarship, Carpenter aimed to expand this canon geographically and temporally.

Buoyed by his sense of the universality of homogenic passions, Carpenter asserts that, thanks to elite European sexologists, popular opinion is changing for the better. Inversion is coming to be seen as "instinctive and congenital," "twined in the very roots of individual life," and perfectly healthy in most cases.[33] *Maurice* recapitulates this tale of prejudice overcome, but on an individual, not a social level. The hero visits a hypnotist in hopes of conquering his sexual "problem" – not an uncommon effort for men of Forster's time and class – but by novel's end embraces his natural feelings and flees into the woods with Scudder. The fairy-tale ending, with its merely superficial happiness, cannot disguise the novel's pessimism: Maurice and Scudder must escape from society to live as lovers. Carpenter, by contrast, sees many successful homogenic "alliances and friendships ... formed and carried on beneath the surface of society," "beyond the inquisitions ... of Mrs. Grundy," even in Edwardian England.[34]

Thanks to the momentum of the homogenic movement, the subject of intermediacy is "pressing upon us from all sides" as the large number of people "occupying an intermediate position between the two sexes" becomes harder and harder to deny. Such people have always existed, of course, and their increasing recognition could merely be a product of social enlightenment. But Carpenter is intrigued enough at the human capacity to evolve to wonder whether "some important change [is] actually in progress,"[35] i.e., whether Uranians could be growing in number. The narrator of *Howards End* claims that men and women are "evolving" in immeasurable ways[36] – themes echoed in Woolf's comment that "on or about December 1910, human character changed."[37] But whereas Carpenter takes hope from the evolutionary transformations that might *currently* be in progress, Margaret and Forster's narrator project such possibilities into a vague distant future.

From Carpenter's point of view, Uranians have lessons for society not only concerning *what men and women should be like* – namely, that each sex contains psychic and physical traits of the other and can draw on its hermaphrodism to be more sensitive and less competitive in men's case; more active, athletic, and leader-like in women's case. Uranians also offer models of *how to seek intimacy*. Their habits of free love – unfettered by compulsory marriage and Mrs Grundy's respectability – make them less possessive than heterosexual lovers, and Carpenter's anti-capitalist values lead him to decry any form of possession of one human being by another. Forster develops his critique of Victorian marriage and patriarchy in Henry's possessive attitude toward Margaret. Carpenter shares Margaret's contempt for the sexual double standard, embraced by Henry, that leaves him fit for society despite his affair with Jackie (while he was wed to Ruth), but casts out Helen for her indiscretion, though – as Margaret tells Henry – "You have betrayed Mrs. Wilcox, Helen only herself."[38]

But in addition to despising double standards, Carpenter also questions the value of jealousy under any circumstances. Margaret may be admirable for struggling to overcome her jealousy and "forgive" Henry, when she tells herself that Ruth's "wrong" was for Ruth, not herself, to suffer.[39] But the mention of "forgiveness" implies that Henry has transgressed against a monogamic code. For Carpenter, by contrast – to switch from a literary–critical to a biographical observation – there was no question of Merrill transgressing when he "touched" Forster on the backside. Uranian mores led Carpenter to suspect that jealousy is as much the product of an ownership society as of human nature.

Carpenter's critical attitude toward some social mores does not amount to a rejection of "institutions and forms" per se, he is at pains to clarify. *Howards End* rejects marriage more forcefully than *The Intermediate Sex*, for the novel's positive (Schlegelized) picture of matrimony in the final chapters requires Henry to be crippled, whereas the pamphlet says that because Uranian experience forms itself "freely," it "comes as a guide . . . towards the future." Such experience suggests that all people tend toward long-term, even lifelong, partnerships, such as that between Carpenter and Merrill. Of course, these partnerships need not be sexually exclusive: they entail a different form of commitment than the heterosexual world generally preaches, though not so different than it generally practices. Carpenter values "fixed standards and ideals," and thinks Uranians would benefit from having more of them, but prefers them to be less rooted in Christian and capitalist traditions, and more consistent with human nature as he understands and values it – creative, hermaphroditic, polyamorous.[40]

In all six novels (*Howards End* least explicitly), Forster brings both his reservations about, and his admiration for, Carpenter and the homogenic movement – its idealism, its avant-garde examinations of gender, and its sympathy with many feminist principles[41] – to his depictions of the sexes and of the relations between them. Forster also brings his literary sensibility, enriched by the Anglo-American and French canons as well as by classical culture, to the overlapping Bloomsburian and modernist discussions about *what men and women are like* and *how to seek intimacy.*

FORSTER'S "DOUBLE NARRATIVES"

Forster's first novel, *Where Angels Fear to Tread* (1905), deploys a "double narrative,"[42] a form he would refine throughout his career. One half conforms to the conventions of straight literature, and the other tells a subterranean tale of same-sex desire. The protagonist Philip Herriton is attracted both to Caroline Abbot (he thinks, consciously) and to Gino Carella (unconsciously), in a male–male–female erotic triangle. At a climactic moment, she seems poised to tell Philip "I love you," and he to respond "I love you too." Instead she tells Philip "I love him," meaning Gino, the coarse Italian peasant whose child they had conspired to steal. Philip surprises himself by remarking "Rather! I love him too!"[43] and this twist suggests that Philip's awkward desire for Caroline and sterile ironic attitude toward life stem from the homoerotic desires he has been too cowardly to acknowledge. But in proclaiming "I love him too," Philip gains more insight into his violent affection for Gino – with whom he has engaged in a near-fatal brawl – than Margaret ever gains, concerning her unconscious aggression toward, and ultimate triumph over, Henry. Though not specifying its treatment of Philip's sexuality as a source of its success, Woolf compares *Where Angels Fear to Tread* favorably to *Howards End.*[44]

Forster's second novel, *The Longest Journey* (1907), employs a *triple* psychosexual narrative: the hero Rickie must choose not only between a male and female sexual object, but between two different types of same-sex intimacy. Early in this gay *Bildungsroman*, Rickie and his Cambridge friend Stuart wrestle on the grass, swim naked, and read Plato together – activities that stop just short of full physical intimacy and that evoke Apostolic "higher sodomy." Nude swimming scenes form a homoerotic motif in Forster's fiction – including *A Room with a View* – recalling the nude bathing scene in Whitman's "Song of Myself." But Rickie leaves Stuart to enter a doomed marriage with a manipulative woman.[45] Eventually he leaves her to pursue fuller physical intimacy with his coarse half-brother

Stephen ("brother," like "friend," being a sexually loaded term).[46] Like Maurice and Alec, Rickie and Stephen illustrate Carpenter's hope that homogenic love can transcend class divisions. Rickie even sacrifices his life to save Stephen's, an illustration of Carpenter's idea that comrade-love inspires "audacious" acts. Legal necessity compelled Forster to represent Rickie's homoerotic tendencies in this coded manner.[47]

Because his third novel, *A Room with a View* (1908), employs a female protagonist, its treatment of homoeroticism is displaced and its double structure hard to discern. The surface plot – a romantic comedy – unites young lovers (Lucy and George), despite an elderly blocking figure (Aunt Charlotte). Reverend Beebe functions at first as a foil to Charlotte: an enabling figure who hopes that Lucy will live her life with the same passion she brings to the piano. But later these elderly figures switch roles. Once the lovers are united, George says that Charlotte had always, "far down in her heart,"[48] wanted them together. By contrast, Lucy says that Beebe "will never forgive us – I mean, he will never be interested in us again."[49] Beebe, indeed, tells Mr Emerson that George "no longer interests" him.[50]

What accounts for Beebe's resentment of the marriage? The answer lies in his repressed homoerotic desire, evident in the Sacred Lake scene. The naked Freddy, George, and Beebe frolic in the lake and swap clothing. George is radiant. His library includes volumes by Butler and Housman that were seminal in the development of Forster's homosexual awareness.[51] Beebe's attraction to George unleashed at the lake, the Reverend transforms – in the novel's subterranean, homosexual plot – from Lucy's ally to her jealous (albeit unconscious) rival for George's affection. Through the figure of Beebe, a detached bachelor like Forster,[52] *A Room with a View* expresses distrust of marriage, beneath its surface celebration of young, heterosexual love, and anticipates the ambivalent attitude toward marriage in *Howards End.* Forster's only two novels to employ female protagonists terminate with their marriages, on apparently happy notes: Lucy wins her man and Margaret wins her property. But each text encodes its author's sexual frustrations.

By contrast, since Forster shared *Maurice* only with friends, it celebrates same-sex desire explicitly.[53] It omits a female love interest for its protagonist, but recapitulates the rest of Rickie's dilemma. The hero first pursues intimacy in the "higher sodomy" vein with his Cambridge friend Clive Durham, then, rejected by Durham, pursues a physical bond with Scudder. Like *The Longest Journey*, *Maurice* revolves around the question: *Which form of intimacy shall a man seek with his male partner: a merely spiritual, or an embodied one?* Though cognizant of the risks involved, each novel endorses the latter option, and its risk-taking hero contrasts with the cowardly Tibby.

A Passage to India (1924), no less than the aforementioned novels, probes its protagonist's sexual inclinations. The concluding verdict of the earth and sky – "No, not yet . . . no, not there" – conveys Forster's pessimism about cross-national and same-sex intimacies. The novel disguises Fielding's sexual dilemmas from "respectable" eyes, but includes numerous intimations of queerness. Aziz's love of poetry and intoxicants marks him as sensually overdetermined. Fielding's employment in a colony distant from England, combined with his sympathy for Indians, marks him as a queer outsider. These details, admittedly, could suggest a non-sexual "queerness." But Aziz's loan of a "back collar stud" to Fielding,[54] while the latter showers, carries unmistakably sexual overtones. Fielding travels in both a geographical and a spiritual sense: eventually he relocates to England and integrates himself into the heterosexual order, but his sojourn on the subcontinent indicates that alternatives were imaginable, if not socially acceptable.

Each of Forster's four intermediate male protagonists, in conclusion, struggles to live an emotionally authentic life. Each is haunted by the questions *Shall I seek intimacy with a man or a woman?* and *If with a man, what form of intimacy – Platonic or sexual?* Each novel sees destructive as well as productive forces immanent in sexual desire. Each novel prizes the overcoming of innocence, whereas *Howards End* prizes its heroine's recovery of this quality, and in so doing, revises canonical depictions of female protagonists in profound ways.

MARGARET'S ANTECEDENTS

The Schlegel sisters draw on a rich Anglo-American literary tradition of examining the strengths and limitations of female consciousness in a world controlled largely by men. Jane Austen's Elinor and Marianne supply prototypes for the comparatively rational Margaret and passionate Helen,[55] whereas George Eliot uses Dorothea and Henry James uses Isabel to explore what happens when an intelligent and independent-minded woman engages to marry a domineering or dishonest man. That Margaret is flawed – as both the narrator and Margaret herself repeatedly mention – contributes to her usefulness as a vehicle for examining the association of female virtue with purity. The Bloomsbury-style discussion group to which she belongs proposes – to itself – abstract solutions to complex social ills. But Margaret is abashed enough to recognize that "independent thoughts" depend upon "independent means,"[56] and to submit her group's philanthropic notions to Henry's (potentially better-informed) judgment. This impatience with liberal foolishness could not speak better for her character. She demonstrates the ability that Henry lacks: to see herself from the outside. To the degree that her discussion group embodies feminine compassion, whereas Henry represents masculine competitiveness, her interest in his opinion suggests her desire to "queer" her own gender-bound habits of thought, to use Armstrong's term, or to occupy what Carpenter calls an "intermediate" zone, where "masculine and feminine elements" constantly "interact." (Sadly, it is precisely this desire – perhaps Margaret's most admirable quality – that gets jettisoned in the conclusion.)

Her intellectual limitations, perhaps attributable to her social class and family culture, are not her only flaws, though none of her flaws is damning. The narrator describes her variously as "a hateful little girl," the "less charming of the sisters" as a result of her inferior physical attractions, and as possessed of a "Londoner's impatience."[57] Margaret criticizes her own tendency to make "speeches," her proclivity for cant, her impractical nature.[58] This introspective ability elicits our complex sympathies. Before her reversion to innocence, Margaret is a more effective example of a round, admirable, non-angelic Edwardian woman for these humanizing imperfections. She is a triumph of her author's imagination, including his feminist-inflected (if not quite feminist) twentieth-century values.[59]

But can a woman with these flaws and strengths make a success of marriage to a man such as Henry? Margaret's literary antecedents do not give cause for hope. Only Casaubon's death releases Dorothea to pair off with a more worthy man. From entrapment in Osmond's castle, no escape seems acceptable to Isabel. In one sense, Forster reiterates Eliot's and James's moral that a heavy price will be exacted when a broad-minded woman marries a small-minded man. But Forster reverses the moral by depicting a different kind of price. Unlike Margaret, neither previous heroine loses her mental clarity after marriage; if anything, they gain sharper understandings of their chosen fates. Margaret has the good fortune to be dealt, by fate, a crippled and submissive husband, but her intelligence is dulled in the bucolic Howards-End setting.

FORSTER'S CONTEMPORARIES ON MARRIAGE

If Forster's literary forebears were so skeptical about marriage, could he find signs elsewhere of a sexual lingua franca? Among his contemporaries, including men, were committed critics of sexism and Victorian sexual essentialism. Lytton Strachey, a passionate advocate for gay causes, also supported feminist ones,[60] and flaunted his dandyism, particularly in wartime.[61] Woolf hoped for a novel about "Chloe's" affection for "Olivia" and wrote a novel – *Orlando* – in which the heroine's sex morphs over time.[62] In representing Leo Bloom, a "womanly man,"[63] with boundless affection, *Ulysses* raises the ante of Freud's *Three Essays*. Freud links polymorphous perversity to immaturity; Joyce's everyman is still polymorphously perverse – lovably so – in adulthood.

But for all their excitement about androgyny, these contemporaries often viewed opposite-sex intimacies dubiously. Leo Bloom's womanly traits bring him no closer to his wife, who cavorts with the manly Blazes Boylan. *Mrs Dalloway*, published fifteen years subsequent to *Howards End*, expresses a common Bloomsburian concern about the sacrifices exacted from wives: the villainous Dr Bradshaw subjects his spouse – likely without even realizing he does so – to "the slow sinking, water-logged, of her will into his."[64] Strachey worried that both sexes are prone to such sinking: his 1904 Apostles paper entitled "Does absence make the heart grow fonder?" calls boredom the "Scylla" of Marriage and bemoans that marriage "necessarily implies that a large number of hours of the twenty-four should be spent nose to nose; the two persons will almost certainly come to an agreement upon every point."[65]

Howards End, however, was only the first Bloomsburian novel to probe the hours spent "nose to nose," and others reach hopeful conclusions, even as they ponder a husband's limitations or a spouse's lost autonomy, including his or her chances for same-sex love. Clarissa treasures her kiss from Sally even as she values the stability of her life with Richard. Birkin concludes *Women in Love* by maintaining that "another kind of love" was possible, despite his wife's disagreement. Nonetheless, his marriage, like Clarissa's, brings rewards that outweigh the sacrifices, according to a difficult calculation that each protagonist continually revisits.

Even Margaret, notwithstanding her lack of same-sex passion, seems to anticipate Birkin and Clarissa when she enters marriage with open eyes. She ponders the historical and natural differences between the sexes; she is fully aware of Henry's peremptory attitudes toward female independence; yet she determines that marrying him will bring her more happiness than suffering.[66] With her curiosity, ambivalence, and ultimate optimism, she figures *what a woman can be like* who lives on the cusp of two eras and cultures: that of a disappearing traditional England and that of a transforming modern nation. She is confident enough, both in the decency of her values and in Henry's capacity for change, that she forms presumptuous designs: "all her deeper being" yearns to "help him," to effect the "conversion of Henry" to her way of thinking.[67] She projects her own capacity for patience and the cultivation of fine emotions onto him: "the more she let herself love him," she ruminates, "the more chance was there that he would set his soul in order."[68] Nonetheless, if her situation seems to anticipate that of Birkin and Clarissa, or to offer hope for a marriage of minds with Henry, this is a false lead.

By novel's end, her hope for Henry's "conversion" is exposed as misguided: the barriers between a Wilcox and a Schlegel attempting intimacy are too massive. *Howards End* rejects the possibility that a marriage formed in the Wilcoxian image can work, if it includes a woman with a modicum of Schlegelian intellectualism, liberalism, or individualism. The force of events and the pain of humiliation, not the art of "conversion," compel Henry's submission. And the limitations of his and Margaret's union are no surprise, given the novel's well-elaborated gender schema. From its opening pages, *Howards End* associates the worst of maleness with Wilcoxism and the best of femaleness with Schlegelism. Wilcox sons follow their patriarch's example, interacting brusquely, even forcefully, with one another, with visitors such as Helen, and with "admiring" station porters.[69] By contrast, the Schlegel sisters exalt "personal relations" and "affection" as life's supreme gifts. In biblical terms, Wilcoxes incline toward Old Testament morality – revenge and punishment – and Schlegels toward the New Testament dispensation: "pity was at the bottom of [Margaret's] actions."[70] It is no accident that Ruth, whose name is synonymous with Margaret's Christian virtue, is the one Wilcox who dies. Other Wilcoxes see life as a "battle" and suffer from excess "preparedness"; Schlegels see life as a "romance" and would avoid being too "cautious" about having their umbrella filched.[71] Wilcoxes excel at the "outer life," Schlegels value the "inner life." Not surprisingly, their domestic habits differ. Wilcoxes discuss cricket averages and stocks and shares,[72] decorate their dwellings in a manly fashion (like Carpenter's intermediate females), treat women chivalrously but not as equals, and doubt the value of female suffrage.[73] Schlegels discuss philanthropy and literature, acknowledge that their home is "feminine" and worry – perhaps to their credit as self-critical women, and to Tibby's discredit as an ambiguously gendered man – about it becoming "effeminate."[74]

These masculine and feminine raw materials, the very categories that Carpenter hoped to soften, must serve as the foundations of Henry and Margaret's partnership. Can such materials be synthesized? At an abstract, hypothetical level, perhaps. In a future utopia, maybe. But Forster's "flat" characters (such as Wilcoxes) are marked by their *in*capacity for change, which means their incapacity to synthesize values external to themselves. Margaret can bend, but Henry can only stand proudly – or be broken. Thus, although Margaret differs at first from Ruth, not being content to exercise her influence quietly, as time wears on she repeatedly succumbs to Henry's forceful manner. "Whether [he] was right or wrong . . . she must trust him absolutely," Margaret ominously thinks, when she asks for his help in tracking down Helen.[75] Henry revels in exercising absolute authority, whether in matters of detail – instructing Margaret to order mutton rather than fish pie,[76] securing a hotel – or in larger ways. He "wasn't aware" that she and Helen had "walked alone over the Apennines," and he warns that, "if [he] can manage it, [she] will never do such a thing again."[77] Rather than insisting that she can walk alone to her hotel, Margaret changes the subject when Henry asserts his spousal prerogative. Who "converts" whom at such moments? Margaret's hope that Henry's soul will be "set in order" seems delusional. With a wife formed in Ruth's mold, such a conflict would never arise, since such a hope would never arise. Ruth might soften her son's aggression by discouraging "plain questions,"[78] but Forster's narrator employs no rhetoric of her "deeper being" or her "conversion" plans for any male in her family. She takes the men as they are, whereas Margaret's hopes (inflected with New Womanly and post-Victorian values) that Henry might change, and Henry's intransigence, produce an impasse. Margaret's marriage grows harmonious only when she is so accommodating that she doesn't merely accept but actually "sides with men as they are."[79]

At some moments of impasse, it must be admitted, Margaret does defy her spouse and "lord."[80] When she stands at the door of Howards End, barring him access to her pregnant sister, she demonstrates the ferocity with which gentle Forster characters must sometimes defend their loyalties.[81] Such physical courage hints not merely at intermediacy, but at a dialectical reversal, with Margaret being transformed by circumstances into a warrior, albeit a defensive one.

But no such transformation is completed. Before Henry's forceful personality, Margaret's aggressive inclinations give way to conciliatory ones. She remains a gentle, decent, and – until fate intervenes – powerless female. Her flash of courage, however bright, wins Helen only one night of respite from a threatened fate of exile and indigence. Fortunately for Margaret, two events effect changes that she cannot. First, Jacky appears at Evie's wedding, exposing Henry as a philanderer and embarrassing him into releasing Margaret from her engagement. But Margaret has become invested in the idea of marrying Henry, and in the conviction that he is due respect from others. She rebuffs Helen and the Basts, and in ensuing conversations plays the "girl," helping him to reconstitute his "fortress" of smug self-possession.[82] Not to be foiled, though, by Margaret's collusion in Henry's hypocrisy, the "logical yet senseless train" of events intervenes again.[83] Charles kills Leonard, and his imprisonment deals the patriarch a humiliation from which he cannot recover. Henry ends the novel "bending down," asking Margaret if he did wrong in destroying Ruth's informal bequest, his body language proof of his defeat[84] and reminiscent of Rochester, another proud man humbled before his wife, at the conclusion of *Jane Eyre*.

MARGARET'S PYRRHIC VICTORY

In other words, Margaret has won! Howards End is a matriarchy, Helen's illegitimate son its heir. Two brutish Wilcox men have gotten their just deserts: prison and decrepitude. The victory denied to Isabel Archer is granted to Margaret. But this external success, as mentioned, comes at an intellectual price. The novel's rejection of patriarchal marriage is compromised by its reversion to an essentialist Victorian picture of *what women can or should be like*. That Henry dominates Margaret, before Charles's crime, more than she "converts" him, illustrates why such marriages deserve critique. But when Margaret refuses, in the aftermath of the crime, to come to terms with the connections between Leonard's grisly fate and her own comfortable one, the female psychology of the first Wilcox marriage is preserved in the second, even as the power dynamic is reversed. Margaret presides like an angel over a country estate, in defense against the encroaching city. And her outlook resembles that of the deceased wife whose attitude toward the world beyond her property was summed up by such statements as, "I had nothing so coherent in my head,"[85] "I have no side. But my husband – "[86] and "I never follow any arguments."[87] Ruth's claims that "it is wiser to leave action and discussion to men" and that she is "too thankful not to have a vote myself"[88] demonstrate that such an attitude has political ramifications. Margaret's description of how she came to her position of authority aligns her with these anti-feminist strains in Ruth's thinking. Margaret indicates that, following Ruth's incuriosity and aversion to conflict, she would rather not ask difficult questions about the reasons for her ascendancy.

Why did this ascendancy occur? In the final chapters, Margaret offers her own limited reasons; Helen offers slightly different ones; and the narrator offers a third, more extensive, analysis – an invitation for readers to adjudicate between the three. Various questions emerge, some ontological and others epistemological. Ontologically speaking, did Margaret play a large or a small role in the events that led to her good fortune? What roles were played by supernatural and natural forces, by benevolent and violent ones? Epistemologically speaking, are these forces accessible to reason? Will a paradox-based mode of analysis effectively bring them to light? It turns out that each answer is either emotionally painful or requires intellectual subtlety and persistence, traits that are valued only as long as the novel elaborates its modern – not its Victorian – vision of female virtue. Margaret played a larger role in the events than she cares to acknowledge. So too did natural and violent forces: the heroine is oblivious to these, though sensitive to the benevolent, supernatural ones. Yes, these disturbing forces are accessible to reason – but only that of a determined analyst. Finally, reason alone will not suffice, but an ability to embrace paradox is necessary to fathoming these complex conditions. The narrator's explanation, though not infallible, functions as a standard against which the sisters' more limited insights can be measured. What Margaret wins in power and comfort, she loses in analytic rigor.

The narrator offers an unvarnished account of Margaret's role in her ascendancy: "There was something uncanny in her triumph. She, who had never expected to conquer anyone, had charged straight through these Wilcoxes and broken up their lives."[89] While this grammar ("She . . . had charged [and] broken") suggests a consciously aggressive intention that Margaret never had, it is nonetheless not hyperbolic where consequences are concerned. Henry and Charles's lives could not be more profoundly transformed by the time Henry has "shambled up to [Margaret] and asked her to do what she could with him."[90] While Margaret's actions were not sufficient for this outcome (Helen and Charles also played key roles), they were certainly necessary.

Helen agrees with the narrator in one sense: she credits her sister with playing a large role. "You did it all, sweetest," she says. Whereas Helen makes no mention of conquering or breaking – and even counters this violent language with the epithet "sweetest" – she does venture a decisive interpretation ("all"). But Margaret demurs. "No doubt I have done a little toward straightening the tangle," she says, "but things that I can't phrase have helped me."[91] In all likelihood, the truth lies somewhere between Helen's "all" and Margaret's "a little." But the manner of Margaret's demurral reveals the limits of her new – or mostly new – way of thinking.

The domestic metaphor ("straightening" a tangle) contrasts strikingly with the narrator's military figure, but fits with Margaret's labor at this point in the novel. When the hostile Paul summons her to the family conclave, because Margaret is "averse to wasting her time, she went on sewing."[92] Knitting a family together is, arguably, just what Margaret is currently doing. The metaphor could have positive connotations, if Margaret has "broken" a bad thing (Wilcoxian primogeniture) and if she is untangling or sewing together a different, better thing (a family that combines, even if it does not synthesize, a diminished Wilcox man, two Schlegel women, and an illegitimate child). Margaret's metaphor suggests that she intuits much about the text into which she is woven: much about human interconnectedness that the narrator's martial diction fails to capture. But at the same time, Margaret's trope obscures the suffering involved in Helen's exile, Henry's embarrassment by Jacky at the wedding, Leonard and Jacky's rebuff thereafter, Leonard's death (which leaves Jacky alone and unprotected), Charles's imprisonment, and the grave humiliation this occasions for every Wilcox, Henry most of all.

What does *Howards End* indicate by these strengths and limits of Margaret's feminized epistemology? Is the heroine celebrated or criticized for her increasingly angelic sensibility? She does appear to relish the role of the soothing matron. Helen, in a moment of guilt (or disorientation), says that love (e.g., of a woman for a man) is not real but a "dream." Margaret, though her relationship with Henry offers scant support for her counterclaim, says "I do not agree." Is she a terminal dreamer? Helen acknowledges that she is "forgetting" Leonard, and, mincing no words, adds "I tempted him and killed him." Margaret says "don't fret yourself"; what little Leonard got from life might not have sufficed "for us," but it was enough "for him," a claim that might soothe Helen more than it convinces readers of Leonard's disposability. The narrator, in a moment of alliance with Margaret's perspective, says that at Howards End the sisters "were building up a new life, obscure, yet gilded with tranquility."[93] Does its gilded quality suggest that the tranquility is superficial, given the suffering from which it emerged – but that as long as "charging," "breaking," "tempting," and "killing" remain "obscure" (unmentioned), such tranquility can be maintained? Even if Forster does not put his thumb in the scale, something is surely missing from a heroine who was once so straight-talking that she surprised Henry by broaching financial questions, and who now describes a fatal set of circumstances as a "tangle" that time helps to "straighten."

On the other hand, Margaret's proclivity for poetry and mysticism (perhaps also evasiveness) predates her "breaking" of the Wilcoxes. When Henry prepares to ask her an uncomfortable question about Helen's pregnancy, "all Margaret's senses [forsake] her. She blushed, and looked past him at the Six Hills, covered with spring herbage."[94] Her receptivity to natural beauty is admirable, but is this the right moment to indulge it? Shortly later, when Helen confides in Margaret near the wych elm, the elder sister again takes refuge in nature: "Margaret did not speak for a moment. So tired was she that her attention had actually wandered to the teeth . . . thrust into the tree's bark to medicate it. From where she sat she could see them gleam. She had been trying to count them."[95] Margaret can hardly be blamed for needing respites under such grave circumstances. And her eye for natural beauty is impressive: she perceives a "gleam" when another's senses might be dulled by grief or fatigue. But this same aesthetic sensitivity may serve evasive purposes, or even morph into a useless obsession: she tries to count the teeth at a time when such a detail – notwithstanding the charming legend of the teeth's magical properties – could not be less relevant.

Or perhaps Margaret is not uselessly obsessed, but mystically attuned. Forster lamented England's lack of a national mythology;[96] in figures such as the sibyllic Miss Avery, the ghost of Ruth Wilcox, and the Howards-End land, this novel – sometimes artfully, sometimes awkwardly – makes mythological offerings. Margaret's attention to the gleam could signify her mystical awareness and enact the novel's "obscure" optimism, its "gilded" tranquility. Helen fears the "melting pot" that will overtake Howards End, which "logically [has] no right to be alive"; Margaret's hope lies in the weakness of logic,"[97] and the novel's hope may lie with her. That *Howards End* takes a bleak view of encroaching cosmopolitanism is provocative, and a potential source of fructifying ambivalence, given Forster's internationalist values. However, that the novel invests its heroine with mystical – but not logical – prowess suggests that, in resisting all the changes that modernity threatens to inflict upon rural England, it paints itself into an ideological corner.

The metaphor of the "tangle" raises the same ideological questions about Forster's construction of Margaret's femininity as do her retreats into natural beauty. Never is her evasiveness more pronounced than when the police question her "closely" about Charles's role in Leonard's death. "She never suspected why," the narrator comments, meaning that even with the help of hindsight, she never grasped her own role in Charles's legal fate.

> They asked to see her father's sword. She explained that Charles's anger was natural, but mistaken. Miserable questions about Leonard followed, all of which she answered unfalteringly. Then back to Charles again. "No doubt Mr Wilcox may have induced death," she said;" but if it wasn't one thing, it would have been another, as you yourselves know." At last they thanked her, and took the sword and the body.[98]

To the law, her assertion that Charles "may have induced [Leonard's] death" is more damning than she imagines it to be. But Margaret, like Ruth before her, occupies a world too delicate for "plain questions" such as *Did I tell the police anything that could be used against Charles*? In Margaret's new position, she grows evasive both ontologically (choosing not to think about unsettling things), and epistemologically (choosing not to think in ways necessary to understanding her good fortune). She is a Victorian matron for the new century, whose ignorance of the harsh male world, and whose connectedness to the sustaining energies of nature, provide the dimensions of her moral beauty, such as it is. New-Woman heroines may boomerang from modern to Victorian *roles*, but Margaret boomerangs into a Victorian *mindset*.

Through many chapters, *Howards End* answers the question *What can women be like*? by illustrating that they can be like Margaret, Helen, or Ruth; and by leaving open the question of what they *should* be like. By its conclusion, the novel largely collapses the figure of Margaret into that of Ruth. Essentialism gains considerable ground, philosophically and psychologically speaking, notwithstanding the rejection of Wilcoxian marriage. Miss Avery's comment to Margaret "I took you for Ruth Wilcox" suggests that the two women are linked symbolically.[99] That Margaret senses Ruth's spirit (the "thing" she "can't phrase," the *genius locus* of the property) speaks well of her extra-sensory intuitions, but her manner of describing it is ominous where her logical acumen is concerned. This heroine has struggled, through the greater part of the novel, to "phrase" many things, to herself and to others, as precisely as possible: her commitment to society's less fortunate, her feelings for Henry, the differences between music and literature,[100] the importance of personal relations. But after Leonard's death, as she has grown "less talkative,"[101] she has also lost her penchant for analysis.

The narrator's explanations of events, on the other hand, combine empirical and mystical epistemologies, faith in reason's powers and skepticism concerning its limits.[102] The description of the train of events as "logical yet senseless" suggests that reason (logic) can trace cause–effect relations, even if moral "sense" is more difficult to extract. Or perhaps these two opposed adjectives suggest nothing so coherent, as much as they illustrate the importance of paradox to Forster's epistemology of human relations. The narrator of *The Longest Journey* distinguishes "the knowledge of good and evil [from] the knowledge of good-and-evil,"[103] indicating with the hyphenated noun that these opposed principles cannot be separated in real life. The concept of "good-and-evil" applies directly to Margaret's case, for the "good" of Henry's humiliation depends upon the "evil" of Leonard's death and Charles's punishment. But Margaret has lost her desire to wrestle with paradoxes, to fathom such things as "good-and-evil."

What happened to the New Woman that Margaret once was? She was revoked as a figure for moral contemplation. This authorial maneuver shifts burden to Leonard and Tibby, for any readers hopeful that the rejection of Wilcoxian marriage will be complemented by a sanguine, anti-essentialist picture of twentieth-century gender.

NO HOPE FOR MEN?

Why does *Howards End* treat intermediacy obliquely and disapprovingly? Armstrong sees the ambiguously gendered narrator as at once queer, admirable (intellectually and emotionally sensitive), and efficacious (possessed of a varied arsenal of narrative tools). I find the claim of the novel's queer values to be dubious, since the narrator turns so much of this arsenal against Tibby and Leonard, leaving little hope that psychosexually atypical men point the way toward a renaissance of gender.

Margaret, whose consciousness often blends with the narrator's, uses the household as a synecdoche for the individual, as she defends healthful (though not exactly "intermediate") gender traits negatively, by criticizing unhealthful extremes. She shares not only Carpenter's conviction that extremes are undesirable, but also his sense that gender does not necessarily correspond to sex. She explains to Juley that the Schlegel household "was irrevocably feminine, even in father's time." This trait testifies to the household's love of art and its transcendence of vulgar nationalism, commercialism, and power worship. Margaret develops the association, familiar to readers of Carpenter, of femininity with cultivation. To underscore her point, she denies that a dinner party given by Queen Victoria, even if attended by literati, could be "artistic," a quality metonymically linked with femininity. Victoria, though a matriarch, is insufficiently cultivated to bring off an artistic "atmosphere." Because gender doesn't result inevitably from sex, a family household run by a male can be feminine, and a royal household presided over by a female can lack artistry. The danger in either case is that the household will tip into an extreme. Thus "all we can do," says Margaret, "is to see that [our house] isn't effeminate." "Effeminacy" is the extreme of "femininity" to be avoided, perhaps most of all when it contaminates a male such as Tibby. Conversely, the Wilcox household seems "irrevocably masculine," says Margaret, "and all its inmates can do is to see that it isn't brutal."[104] "Brutality" is the extreme of masculinity to be avoided, as it can transform a house into a jail, complete with "inmates."

Forster's preoccupations are visible in the extremes he does *not* figure (in women) as much as in those that he does figure (in men). While brutal and effeminate men both populate *Howards End*, and while Margaret describes effeminacy as something for women and families to avoid, nonetheless no woman in the novel – not even Ruth – is repudiated for this flaw. Carpenter worries that extreme homogenic women assume men's worst qualities, with their "fragrant weed" filling their dwellings, but for Forster and the Schlegels, Helen's smoking is only a joke. Margaret tells her sister "You do what you can for the house . . . the dining room reeks of smoke," and Helen retorts "if you smoked too, the house might suddenly turn masculine."[105] But there is no genuine danger that these women, or the household they dominate, will fall prey to extremes of masculine brutality. In Carpenter's formulations, gender can come dangerously unmoored from sex, assuming extreme expressions, in both men and women. In *Howards End*, notwithstanding Evie's love of sports (which maddens Helen), men are the sex more prone to brutality, as well as to pusillanimous effeminacy.

Paradoxically, by displaying brutality – the most prominent malady of extreme masculinity – men are likely to reveal a cowardice damning to their character. The bluster of the prototypically brave man, the maelstrom of "telegrams and anger" in which Wilcoxes live, may disguise but cannot cure a metaphysical anxiety, a "panic and emptiness"[106] that such men lack the imagination and moral integrity to confront. Helen makes this point for her author at a performance of Beethoven's Fifth Symphony. Beethoven's "goblins," Helen believes, observe that there is "no such thing as splendor or heroism in the world." Forster and *Howards End* are too skeptical wholly to believe or disbelieve in these romantic qualities; between Margaret's disdain for heroism[107] and Helen's yearning for it, the novel questions – without deciding upon – its value and reality. Helen, listening earnestly to Beethoven, wrestles with the question. By contrast, she thinks, men such as the Wilcoxes and President Roosevelt would consider the goblins "only the phantoms of cowardice and unbelief."[108] She attributes to such men a shallow rhetoric, by which they accuse *others* of cowardice (disguising their own fears) and blame others for unbelief (though Forster, who did not "believe in Belief,"[109] valued this trait).

Even more than his father, Charles personifies this superficial courage that Helen diagnoses as the antithesis of Beethoven's authentic intellectual bravery. Charles resolves to thrash Helen's seducer "within an inch of his life"[110] with what, according to his value code, might be a just "Belief" in his own rightness and the courage to act on it. His father counsels him to "use no violence,"[111] but Charles, little more than a schoolyard bully, speaks no other language. His father may intuit as much when, in a rare moment of tenderness, he sees Charles as a "little boy and strong man in one,"[112] a phrase that nicely sums up Forster's moral evaluation of the "strong man," whether at the head of a family or a nation.

Helen explains for her author why individuals like Charles are never more than little boys when she tells Leonard that Nietzschean supermen were never taught in their youth to say "I," the pronoun that brings pity and thus justice with it.[113] Erasing any possibility that Helen was speaking merely for herself, the narrator explains near the novel's conclusion that Charles "had a vague regret – a wish that something had been different somewhere – a wish (though he did not express it thus) that he had been taught to say 'I' in his youth."[114]

Howards End makes it clear that, if the world contains any splendor or heroism, it is not to be found in the little boy/strong man, the Wilcox/Roosevelt model of manliness. The social arena illustrates this point as decisively as does the household. The social arena also illustrates how deleterious the opposite extreme version of maleness can be: that of male effeminacy, even if it coexists, as in Leonard's case, with positive qualities. To Leonard's credit, he is gentle-hearted and sensitive to beauty in people, nature, music, and literature, as Wilcox men are not. But this same sensitive specimen is a victim of fate in the employment market and at his moment of death. That he does not inflict violence on others redounds to his credit, according to a Carpenterian and Forsterian value scheme, but that he so easily suffers it may be a symptom of his "effeminate" character – in one large, metaphorical (and unflattering) sense that Carpenter employs the term, and that the Schlegel sisters use it, in worrying about their home.

In fact, *Howards End* goes further than Carpenter in doubting the social value of effeminate men. As David Bradshaw notes,[115] the novel engages with many eugenic concerns. Is the British race deteriorating? Does the declining birth rate bode ill for the nation's future, and will this future require physically robust men like the Wilcoxes? (Bradshaw sees the novel place more value in their healthful manliness than I do.) Amid worries about national degeneracy, effeminate Leonard may be an ill omen (as may Tibby). A generation ago, Leonard might have been a yeoman farmer. In a future socioeconomic order, or after another generation of education in the Bast family, his offspring or men like him *might* find a niche in the business class, but at present he hovers on the abyss of extreme poverty. Far from having gifts to offer society, Leonard has no place in it. Henry's advice, casually dispensed, can lead him out of a relatively secure job – the one groove he fits as a worker – but no effort of his own can reintegrate him into an equally lucrative position. His head can be set to swimming by a conversation with the cultured Schlegel sisters, but his social instincts incline him to avoid a subsequent interview with them, to limit his contact with his betters. He can violate this resolution so severely as to impregnate Helen, but this does not mean he's in a position to provide for the child, nor even to know of its existence. He can admire Ruskin's prose style, but cannot bend it to suit his dingy flat; and when a bookcase falls on him, the Culture for which he has awkwardly striven becomes his symbolic killer. His sensitivity can shade into the "sentimentality" that Carpenter disliked in homogenic men, as when Leonard pains the Schlegel sisters with his callow effusions on his reading material. Worse yet, the clerk's sensitivity is, in general, bound metaphorically with weakness and vulnerability – physiological, economic, cultural. In eugenic terms, such male sensitivity would seem to have little future – a sad prospect, since Henry and Charles's version of courage holds no promise for a humane future.

Given that effeminacy reeks of degeneracy, and that brutality is worthy of a caveman, can the men of *Howards End* find other models for deportment? With his plans for self-betterment, Leonard hopes that gentlemanliness is such a model, but he could not be more wrong. When the concert ends, Margaret is "vexed" by his eagerness to "hand a lady downstairs, or to carry [her] programme."[116] The category of "lady," of course, complements that of "gentleman," and names the type of female that Carpenter believed had man's "contempt." Yet when the sisters invite Leonard to Wickham to advise him to leave the Porphyrion, he reveals his incompetence at "persiflage" with such witless comments as "the more a lady has to say, the better," and "ladies brighten – " before Helen cuts off the latter cliché with the ironic "Yes, I know. The darlings are regular sunbeams."[117] Helen is even more vexed than her sister by "gentlemanly" deportment that patronizes women and simultaneously diminishes men.

Leonard's awkward stabs at gentlemanliness are comical, but the novel condemns this value code in the persons of Henry and Charles. While the father and son plan to avenge what they term Helen's "seduction" by Leonard (whose identity they do not yet know), Henry asks his wife "you don't think that my son and I are less than gentlemen?"[118] He reveals the hollowness, even perfidy, of this supposedly honorific, self-bestowed title when he tells Margaret that it would be "false to my position in society" to allow Helen to sleep at Howards End. (Margaret reaches her breaking point at this outrageous display of hypocrisy, as mentioned earlier.) Charles reveals a chivalric code of values to be both anachronistic and dangerous when he uses a sword to kill Leonard – a sorry parody of a gentlemanly duel in defense of a lady's honor. D. H. Lawrence entertains the value of some medieval concepts for the twentieth century (as I discuss in Chapter 4), but not Forster.

Does *Howards End* employ a negative methodology only – a process of elimination – in wondering *What should a man be like, in a post-Victorian world?* Emphatically he should not be a brute, nor effeminate, nor a "gentleman." If he should be intermediate, there is no full picture of such a man in these pages. Carpenter sees intermediates as an emergent type, harbingers of better years. *Howards End* sees Henry as the harbinger of a grim future. The "Imperialist" is "healthy, ever in motion" (unlike the degenerate), and "it breeds ... quickly" (the appellative "it" animalizes the type), but unfortunately for the world, it is a "destroyer." The Imperialist "prepares the way for cosmopolitanism," a "gray" fate.[119] Whereas Carpenter scavenges through history for evidence of intermediates of both sexes as prophets, witches, etc.,[120] *Howards End* endows some women with mystical properties (Ruth, Miss Avery), but no men.

If any men might compete with Wilcoxes as emergent types, Leonard (just shy of twenty-one when the novel begins) and Tibby (an undergraduate through much of the novel) are the right ages to do so. But emergent male types would need to integrate themselves into society in order to disseminate their influence, and to couple with females in order both to reproduce genetically and to exemplify *how to build (heterosexual) intimacies for the new century*. But Leonard is poorly paired with Jackie and paired only in a reckless way with Helen, while Tibby (perhaps a terminal bachelor like Forster) is never paired at all. Instead of connecting him to larger, sustaining processes, Tibby's education "had severed him from other boys and men. He made no friends" at Oxford.[121] Much the same can be said for Leonard's truncated rise from agricultural to urban labor: it severs him from both past and future (the existence of his son is unknown to him).

Notwithstanding these men's lack of worldly potency, the novel – particularly its heroine – remains invested in a discourse of *virility*, in the etymological sense of the term, connecting moral worthiness with masculinity. "Men like the Wilcoxes," says Helen in her initial letter, "would do Tibby a power of good," though she fears that Margaret "won't agree."[122] Admittedly, Helen writes this when she still welcomes the Wilcoxes' opposition to female suffrage as a refreshing antidote to her own "cant." Even after her disillusionment with the Wilcoxes, though, Helen still casts sly aspersions on Tibby's masculinity with diminutive nicknames such as "Auntie Tibby" and "Tibbikins," indirect expressions of her ambivalent feelings toward her unmanly sibling.[123] Margaret continues such rhetorical handling of Tibby when she regrets the absence of a "real boy" in the house, who admires men as much as women, and whose presence "would make entertaining so much easier."[124]

Margaret does not restrict her discourse of virility to her brother. When Henry's past infidelity to Ruth has been exposed, and he is at his weakest, she writes him a letter that begins "My dearest boy." When they meet in person, and he embarks on a bogus repentance, she cuts him off by saying "Leave it where you will, boy."[125] (At this time she is reduced to the stratagem of playing the "girl," so that he may regain his composure. Apparently boys and girls are meant for each other, which raises the question of where the twentieth century's men and women will come from.)

At times it seems as though Leonard may exemplify the manliness that Tibby falls short of and that the Wilcoxes pursue to excess. Margaret describes him to Henry and Evie as a "real man," language that rings with virtue. But this rhetoric arouses what the narrator sneeringly calls the "real man" in Henry. The Wilcox patriarch is "thrilled to jealousy," and the narrator explains that jealousy "connects [people] to the farmyard intolerables, and calls up visions of two angry cocks and a complacent hen."[126] Forster dramatizes Carpenter's convictions about sexual jealousy and possessive love: that they belong to a primitive stage of human evolution. Henry could never appreciate this criticism of his own emotion, as his mind is at once so primitive and so conventional. He insists that no "gentleman" would have expressed suspicion, as Leonard did, that the Schlegel sisters had designs on his money; and he even calls Leonard a "brute." He employs some of the very vocabulary that Margaret and Forster's narrator use – but Henry does so inaccurately. Margaret appears to agree with him when she responds "just the senseless fear that does make men intolerable brutes,"[127] but in reality this psychoanalysis and moral condemnation apply to Henry (who is senselessly fearful in various ways) far more than to Leonard (who treats life as a romance).

Margaret's estimation of Leonard's manly virtue is corroborated by the narrator, who is not reluctant to praise strength and criticize weakness, as long as these qualities are not defined by Wilcoxes. Even as the unemployed Leonard exploits his family for money (flirting with blackmail), he "remained alive . . . to a sense of sinfulness" and in so doing avoided "the anodyne of muddledom." The narrator quotes George Meredith's lines:

And if I drink oblivion of a day
So shorten I the stature of my soul

and calls them a "hard" saying, written by a "hard"[128] man, hardness being a quality that, in a different context, could be associated with brutality. But not here. Here it reveals Leonard's commitment to truth. When Leonard sees Margaret and Tibby in St Paul's Cathedral, he develops a "desire to confess," one form of truthfulness which the narrator sees as "proof of a weakened nature." By way of explaining such "weakness," the narrator compares the confessor to the suicide: each yearns "to get clear of the tangle."[129] That Margaret shortly later invokes the same metaphor of a "tangle" suggests that her "nature" has likewise been weakened, that she has drunk "oblivion." Given Leonard's extraordinary circumstances, though, the narrator forgives his confessional impulse, explaining that "confession need harm no one – it can satisfy that test – and . . . Leonard had a right to decide upon it."[130] Leonard is consumed with remorse for having coupled with Helen; but the narrator comments that "remorse is not among the eternal verities," adds that "Helen was [also] to blame" (though Leonard forgets this fact), and reiterates that Leonard was "a real man, who cared for adventure and beauty, who desired to live decently and pay his way."[131] It turns out that there is room in *Howards End* for manly virtue, even if it is not coded as "intermediate."

But Leonard's manly virtue doesn't do much for him. It endows him with some integrity and dignity as he staggers toward his death at the hand of Charles, of the sham manliness and outward show of courage. *Howards End* begins to elaborate its own scale of toughness, in opposition to the Wilcox scale, but evinces no hope that it will gain ascendancy in the future. Physical toughness of the coarsest Wilcoxian kinds has apparent eugenic value – Wilcoxes propagate effectively two generations past Henry – but perhaps moral toughness does not.

With Leonard dispatched, and his son, under Helen's care, headed toward an uncertain future, Tibby remains the only live, fleshed-out model of *what a man might be like, if not like Wilcoxes.* Tibby is Forster's vaguely effeminate version of privileged young male adulthood: he thrives on the life of the mind (as Henry does not and Leonard cannot due to circumstances) and "disdains the heroic equipment"[132] (like Margaret and again unlike Henry). In contrast both to Carpenter's writings and to Forster's other novels, these direct and indirect evocations of Tibby's ambiguously gendered Soul-material convey little to nothing that is admirable, and much that is despicable, especially his cowardice.

Admittedly, to his credit the scholar does mature – somewhat – during his young adulthood. Though it took them many visits, men at Oxford did discover him "to possess a character and a brain," says the narrator.[133] The term "character" expresses a commendation that approaches – but does not equal – what Margaret evokes with the label "real man." Tibby has matured enough that Helen, with whom as a rule he does not get on, tells Margaret that he is "moderately a dear now,"[134] but her qualifying adverb is telling. The narrator says that, by the age of 22, Tibby has "lost his peevishness, and [can] hide his indifference to people and his interest in food,"[135] but the mere attainment of acceptable manners leaves him a long way from being a paradigm of masculine virtue. It is little wonder, given this minimal growth of "character," that Tibby judges himself to have failed his own rite of passage when he breaks his word to Helen and, crumbling before Charles's physical intimidation, spills the name "Bast." Tibby is vexed by this failure both for Helen's sake and because of "the flaw he [discovers] in his own equipment."[136] The bully and the coward are two sides of one debased male coin. Perhaps a greater degree of "heroic equipment" – even if this phrase denotes something as basic as physical fortitude – would have helped Tibby (not to mention Leonard) when he was faced with Charles's violent anger.

But to discuss Tibby's failure of heroism is to anticipate. Before depicting this anti-climax in the scholar's aborted rise to manhood, Forster develops Tibby as a semiotically complex example of non-Wilcoxian masculinity who bears vague traces of intermediacy, but who is notable, even as an adolescent, for lacking the inventiveness and courage to be what Carpenter would call a "guide toward the future." He is passive, indolent, and self-absorbed to an arguably morbid degree (recall Carpenter's critique of the association of morbidity with intermediacy). Tibby's intellectual and, especially, his aesthetic organs are finely developed: he enjoys music, cake, and studying Chinese. But despite these refinements he has few social skills and no visible sex drive. As becomes clear later, it is not surprising that such a man should lack courage when the hour calls for it.

The first glimpse into his lamentable (if less-than-morbid) passivity comes when Margaret frets about whether Juley should accompany her to Howards End, to prevent Helen and Paul's union. Tibby suffers from hay fever at this point, and the only thing that makes his life worth living is having Margaret read to him from Walter Savage Landor's *Imaginary Conversations*, which signals his sophistication, but also his desire to escape when attention to a crisis is needed (as the word "imaginary" in Landor's title suggests). Tibby's need for literary consolation is a counterpoint to Margaret's engagement in her sister's affairs, and it may hinder Margaret from acting. The narrator explains that "there was a train from King's Cross at eleven. At half past ten Tibby, with rare self-effacement, fell asleep," enabling Margaret to drive Juley to the station.[137] He is perhaps a malingerer, at least useless to the family, and at worst an impediment. Wilcoxes are to be blamed for their brutal solutions to delicate situations. Tibby is without brutality, but even less competent than Henry at engaging with matters of the heart. The introduction to his "self-effacement" is managed with gentle irony, but with their repeated exposure, his moral limitations become less humorous and more bathetic.

For example, he effaces himself once more, again in counterpoint to Margaret's practical interest in her relationships, when she and Helen find that Ruth has called on them in London, and dispute returning the call, with Margaret worrying about Helen encountering Paul, and Helen parrying the concern with jokes. When Tibby enters the room, their joking stops, since he is a male, and "the barrier of sex . . . is still high." Women may deserve extra blame for the barrier, since it is "higher" on their side, which could explain why Helen tells Margaret "all," her cousin "much," and her brother "nothing" about her personal affairs. Notwithstanding women's mistrust of men, though – even one as un-virile as her brother – Helen would risk nothing by confiding in him, since he is so narcissistic that he "seldom reported any news that did not concern himself." Though involved in a speculation about female shortcomings, the narrator cannot refuse an opportunity to criticize Tibby. And Tibby dramatizes the narrator's point when he asks a single vague question ("What's that?") about the conversation his presence has ended, before proceeding to the dining room "to eat Elvas plums." Even more than Landor's writings, the succulent food suggests decadence on Tibby's part, an ethos that was anathema to Forster.

The parallels between this scene and the one involving Landor are extended when Helen leaves the apartment and Margaret takes "decisive action," writing Mrs Wilcox that they should not meet. At this point, "Tibby, who was not feeling well, lay stretched on a sofa by the fire."[138] However misguided some of Margaret's decisions may be, she strives to correct her mistakes, and even her attempt to forestall future encounters with Ruth demonstrates her conscientious attention to personal relations. Tibby, in contrast, indulges himself in multiple ways: warmed while "stretched" on a comfortable surface. Does the motif of his ill health suggest degeneracy? Not necessarily, especially when Leonard's more extreme frailty is considered. But this young male is so immersed in reading fine literature, eating sweet fruit, and nursing his own body that his elder sister's concern over an "effeminate" household is well-founded.

His capacity for sympathy is so meager that his self-absorption can be a blessing. His sterile irony "influenced the sisters more than they knew."[139] When Leonard's discussion of his all-night walk stirs Helen and Margaret's admiration, Tibby, "who preferred his comedy undiluted, slipped from the room."[140] He sees only "comedy" where his sisters are roused to fellow feeling. His inability to admire the clerk's dignity reveals his own, not Leonard's, shortcoming. With Tibby gone from the room, Helen and Margaret are "stirred to enthusiasm more easily."[141] The sisters' enthusiasm, empathy, and curiosity – all that makes them morally admirable – is dampened by the presence of their smug and unempathic sibling.

When Tibby's infirmity or incuriosity motivates his self-effacement from a family scene, the collateral effects can be positive (Margaret driving Juley, the sisters communing with Leonard). But when cowardice motivates his inaction, the consequences are fatal for Leonard. Tibby's failure of courage before Charles highlights the missing kind of man – sensitive and concerned with personal relations, yet efficacious in the world – that Leonard never quite becomes. While the Wilcox men repeatedly behave brutishly – Charles assaulting Leonard, Henry refusing Helen respite at Howards End – these acts betoken concern for family honor. However un-Forsterian their sense of honor may be, it leads them to participate in personal dramas far more than the effeminate and hypochondriac Schlegel male.

Do Tibby's self-absorption, sterile irony, infirmity, and cowardice mark him clearly as part of a gay novelist's answer to the question *Where will sexually atypical men fit into twentieth-century life?* No more so than Aziz's various eccentricities – minus the back collar stud – thus mark him. But the collar stud adds an extra, specifically sexual, dimension to Aziz's "queerness," and the equivalent suggestions in Tibby's case are spread out over a range of details. When Helen teases her brother that "Frieda is saving up a little girl for" him,[142] the importance of his sexuality to his moral character cannot be ignored. Of course, the possibility of his coupling with a woman is never the subject of more than a tease. Joking with Margaret – within Tibby's hearing – about Jacky's intrusion in search of her husband, Helen exclaims, "I offered Bracknell, and he was rejected. So was Tibby."[143] In another Forster novel, this specter of compulsory heterosexuality, even if suggested jokingly, might be a source of pathos. But Tibby is too passive to be a protagonist in any drama, or even to indicate whether a "girl" would meet his desires, though the novel suggests that one would not. Encouraged by Margaret to model his life after the men he likes most, Tibby claims, "I like Guy and Mr Vyse most," then leans "so far back in his chair that he extended in a horizontal line from knees to throat."[144] Like falling asleep and stretching on the sofa, leaning back enacts his aloofness.

Who are these men he claims to admire, and what might they signal about Tibby's sexual preferences? Cecil Vyse appears in *A Room with a View* as Lucy's temporary fiancé, an ironist more interested in her as "a work of art" than as a woman.[145] (Perhaps it is a blessing in disguise for Cecil that Lucy breaks off their engagement, freeing him to pursue intimacies – if he is thus inclined – with men.) Tibby's preference for Cecil intensifies the insinuation that he is sexually "queer" and therefore morally culpable. Cecil's last name – Vyse – can be read as a homophone for "vice." Margaret's criticism suggests that his lack of human warmth and his unsavory sexual inclinations stem from one source. She passes a utilitarian judgment on his lifestyle in saying he seems not "particularly happy" – the wages of vice, perhaps. Alternatively, his surname might be a homophone of "vise," in which case it suggests a tendency to keep a tight grip on his feelings – an anal-retentive personality, just the opposite of Helen. According to either reading of his last name, his alleged unhappiness may be largely self-inflicted, the wages of some form of queerness. Further, says Margaret, he is "rather a wretched, weedy man," linking his moral and physical unattractiveness, and suggesting degeneracy. Whatever his surname suggests, his alleged "weediness" indicates a crucial failing: his never having come to masculine fruition. Leonard, Tibby, and the objects of Tibby's admiration all seem to be poor eugenic material. Their physical traits, sexual proclivities, and moral shortcomings stigmatize them in the very ways that Carpenter sought to rebut.

Vyse's degeneracy, Margaret suggests, may be reflected in his lifestyle. She touches on this topic obliquely, extending the chain of guilt by association. "Then there's Guy. That was a pitiful business," she says, before changing the subject.[146] Was the "pitiful business" an affair between Guy and Mr Vyse? Margaret offers no specifics. But Guy's first name – his family name is not mentioned – foregrounds the question of his sexuality,[147] as "Vyse" foregrounds the question of Cecil's (im)morality. Guy's name may be Forster's ironic hint that this bit character is no ladies' man. Does Tibby have such an idea in mind – perhaps even the "pitiful business" of a homoerotic affair – when he claims to "like" these two men "most"? *Howards End*, in collusion with its heroine, does not stipulate as much as insinuate. The narrator is willing to suggest where Margaret is fallible, when the subject under consideration is her triumph over Henry. Thus, the narrator's silence concerning her opinions about Guy and Cecil amounts to a tacit endorsement of those opinions, with their whiff of homophobia.

Even if Tibby likes these men "most," though, he is still bereft of passion for them, or for anything. Recognizing his apathy and seeking an outlet for any virile motivation he might have, Margaret stresses his need for work. But Tibby quips that her "profound desire" for effort is something with which he has "no experience."[148] Even university, where many man-loving men of Forster's time trained their previously "undeveloped hearts," cannot awaken Tibby's passion. His sisters send him to Oxford "that he might make friends," but the place remains for him a mere "memory" of a "color scheme," without the "radiance" of human intercourse.[149] His libido has been drained: a poignant predicament, but one for which Tibby deserves as much blame as do his circumstances.

Few forms of apathy could be more damning in Forster's humanist world than Tibby's lack of interest in human beings. If unrealized homogenic longings lay at the root of this apathy (admittedly a liberal inference), then Tibby's frustrated sexuality may also help to explain his lack of empathy for female suffering. His disengagement from Margaret's concern for Helen has been remarked upon. When he has an opportunity to demonstrate direct concern for Helen, who cries in frantic desperation, her tears "touched [Tibby] as something unusual. They were nearer the things that did concern him, such as music."[150] Tibby's virtual incomprehension of his sister's emotion, at a time when she needs comfort, helps to explain the negative judgment that *Howards End* and *A Room with a View* pass on Cecil, Guy, and him as a set. Tibby and Cecil can appreciate art but cannot "connect" with females, which is a bad sign if they stand for a substantial portion of the new era's male sophisticates, even if these sophisticates are not meant to couple with women sexually. In light of Tibby's unfeeling nature, the narrator's apparent compliments of his character – such as the claim that "there are worse lives"[151] than his – seem backhanded. The allusion to "worse lives," for example, anticipates the dubious assertion that Tibby "was frigid, through no fault of his own."[152] (Who else's "fault" would his frigidity be?) If frigidity indicates an inability to produce offspring, this is a significant limitation in a novel preoccupied with "inheritance."[153]

Whatever his potential for fatherhood, his lack of virility informs each of his flaws. Just as Cecil is "weedy," Tibby "had never known young-manliness," even at Oxford. This is a great misfortune, since "that quality," resonant of normal sexuality, "warms the heart till death, and gives Mr Wilcox an imperishable charm."[154] Any praise of Henry is sure to be challenged elsewhere in the text, but a man who makes Henry's limited "charm" shine by contrast must be sorely wanting. Because Tibby had not grown more virile during his years at Oxford, he "had not grown more human."[155] His effeminacy gains him no access to the narrator's limited circle of fully rounded human beings; little wonder that the sisters worry about the effect of his character on the family household.

Given Leonard's materially restricted and Tibby's spiritually pinched lives, *Howards End* envisions for neither variety of feminized maleness a fruitful expression in contemporary society. The novel's hope for a "rainbow bridge"[156] between – among other things – male and female psyches underscores its lack of a successful intermediate. This missing figure motivates Margaret's worry that the sexes are "really [separate] races."[157] Leonard and Tibby are punished in the harshest ways, whether by plot or narrative tone, for their variously un-"masculine" characters. Margaret, on the other hand, does not need to be punished for deviating from the model of angelic domesticity because she eventually conforms to it. With this old model of femininity shored up, at least temporarily, against ruin by creeping cosmopolitanism, the novel's subversive example of a marriage – a matriarchy in the English countryside – promises to be an extreme rarity.

Admittedly, both Margaret and the narrator enjoy more sanguine moods about the sexes, even when they are not indulging political hopes that women may "move forward" or anti-essentialist hopes that they may undergo "biological change"[158] in their march toward equality. Margaret makes peace with the sexes as presently, and distinctly, constituted. "People are far more different than is pretended," she tells Helen, seeing differences as a cause for appreciation, despite the fact that "men and women are worrying because they cannot develop as they are supposed to develop."[159] What lines this development is meant to follow, she never specifies, perhaps because she does not know. But uncertainty can be intoxicating. "We are evolving in ways that Science cannot measure, to ends that Theology dares not contemplate," intones the narrator, who adds that, because we have produced the "jewel" of a man's and woman's mutual love, the gods will grant us "immortality."[160] What about a man's and a man's, or a woman's and a woman's, mutual love, readers are led to wonder by Forster's life and other novels. Can this, too, be a jewel worthy of eternity? But *Howards End* eschews homogenic territory.

In the context of a paean to the "jewel" of heterosexual love, the novel's thematic tensions concerning gender differences loom large. Margaret and the narrator's faith that the sexes are "evolving" challenges the essentialist Wilcox–Schlegel binary. But nowhere does the narrative *dramatize* this gender evolution that it *asserts* to be occurring.[161] It shows, on the contrary, Wilcox men trapped in a stunted form of maleness, Margaret retreating into an angelic lifestyle, and the Schlegel sisters too lacking in affection for men or children to love more than one another and their threatened landscape. Their narrow sphere of acquaintanceship in the concluding scenes belies their humanistic slogans.

Given the way "brotherhood," like "friendship," can carry erotic – at times utopian – connotations in Forster's texts and in Apostolic culture, Helen and Margaret's intimacy suggests a possible queer utopian sisterhood. But this suggestion has no meaningful issue. Rather as the novel associates queer maleness with "vice," Margaret calls Monica a "crude feminist of the South,"[162] a cruel epithet to hurl at a woman who was Helen's best friend in her hour of greatest need. Margaret's anti-feminism and national chauvinism go unchallenged by the narrator, whereas queerness in both sexes gets severely criticized by the narrator and heroine. Any sense that *Howards End* advances a queer agenda must be supplied by a hopeful reader. The narrator's brief flights of optimism about love and the human capacity to evolve ultimately run aground, with no man womanly sexuality able to bridge the Schlegel–Wilcox gap, nor to counterbalance the novel's indictment of contemporary marriage with hope for future marriages. It remained for Forster's subsequent novels, and for Bloomsburian texts including *Women in Love* and *Mrs Dalloway*, to imagine – sensuously, conceptually, formally – future reinventions of intimacy, with the help of new masculine and feminine Soul-materials fit for a new century.

CHAPTER 4

The love that cannot be escaped

We are now in a period of crisis.[1]

A woman craves the words "I love you" from her man, and the man stubbornly withholds them, for the sake of what he considers his freedom and individuality. What could be more of a cliché, less of an occasion for original philosophical reflection? Yet *Women in Love* uses this scaffolding to construct its own reinvention of intimacy, its anti-foundational and accommodationist answers to the respective questions *What are men and women like?* and *What should we do about this*? Whereas *Howards End* uses Ruth, Margaret, Leonard, and Tibby as models to examine *what types of male and female Soul-material will be viable in the new century*, Lawrence's 1920 novel uses its two richly imagined protagonists, Birkin and Ursula, each of whose temperaments is interwoven with his or her philosophy, as vehicles for thinking through the challenges of modern couplehood.

More specifically, *Women in Love* subjects the middle-class ideal of "companionate marriage" to as broad and deep a critique as it receives in any modernist work. This ideal, defined below, was so widespread in Lawrence's time (as it remains today) that it won the support of thinkers with radically different political and cultural attitudes. And it was (and remains) woven so thoroughly into the fabric of daily life that many couples, suggests the novel, endorse it unconsciously, without realizing the choice they make in doing so. Part of the novel's project, as of Lawrence's essays, is to make explicit this choice, this (sometimes silently) ubiquitous institution of "companionship," and thereby to critique it. But critique does not entail escape, nor necessarily the desire to escape. Perhaps the novel's greatest piquancy lies in Birkin's anguished ambivalence: his partly authentic, partly factitious repulsion at the thought of companionship, and his partly generous, perhaps partly frightened concessions to it.

Because the act of saying or not saying "I love you" is so philosophically significant to Lawrence, *Women in Love*, like his essays, engages polemically with numerous overlapping discourses, from sexology and psychoanalysis to feminism to rationalism. Birkin espouses an antifeminist and anti-rational position often echoed in Lawrence's essays, so it is tempting to read him as the author's mouthpiece. But the novel uses Ursula to perform an authorial self-critique; it constantly weighs and balances the virtues of her point of view against his.

With regard to the question *What are men and women like?* while Lawrence keeps the full weight of his thumb from the scale, the needle nonetheless tilts toward Birkin's radicalism, given the novel's modernist answer *Nothing like Victorians imagined, with their beliefs in the integrity of male and female selves.* Whereas Freud un-selves his adolescent female, representing Dora as bisexual and polyamorous, Lawrence un-selves numerous men and women, probing their bisexuality, aggression, misanthropy, and death drives.

But with regard to the question *How shall we seek intimacy?* the needle inches in Ursula's direction. This should be no surprise, given Hermione's sadism, Birkin's misery during his relationship with her, Ursula's healthfulness, and Birkin's vitality in his intimacy with her. Given the additional negative examples of Gerald's sadomasochism (sadistic toward his workers, his mare, and Minette; masochistic with regard to Gudrun), and Gudrun's sadism (her cruelty to Gerald, her thrill at Gerald's cruelty to the mare and at Loerke's cruelty to his model), Ursula's normative example of how to give and receive love, without inflicting or desiring cruelty, shines more brightly. At the novel's conclusion, however, when Birkin aches for "another [same-sex] kind of love"[2] that he had with Gerald, Ursula scoffs at this "perversity,"[3] revealing the intolerant side of her more conservative attitudes toward sexual selfhood. For this reason, the needle merely inches, rather than jumps, toward her perspective concerning *models of couplehood.*

Lawrence's critics have attended separately to each of these contending features in his thought, embodied in Birkin and Ursula – both his rage against established ideas and the conventional impulses lurking beneath his radical rhetoric.[4] Lionel Trilling's "On the teaching of modern literature" identifies an adversarial attitude toward "culture itself" as characteristic of modern literature, and cites Lawrence as a spokesman for these values.[5] Conversely, Davida Pines argues that *Women in Love* remains conceptually imprisoned by the same "love-and-marriage ideal" that earns Birkin's sneers.[6] Pines is right that *Women in Love* makes concessions to this problematic "ideal" – therein lies its accommodationism – but a full account of the novel should not overlook the qualities that Trilling sees as paradigmatically modern. Like *Dora* and *Mrs Dalloway*, *Women in Love* makes an aesthetic virtue of ambivalence. Not unlike a cubist painting, the novel uses Birkin and Ursula's protracted lovers' quarrel to examine the idea and practice of intimacy from multiple angles simultaneously, and to depict it as an ongoing process – dynamic, sometimes violent, and never fully resolved.

As an attack on foundational thinking, the novel has a range of targets. Birkin describes heterosexual couplehood as stifling and conformist, blames the ideal of "love" for contemporary passionlessness, and impugns Christianity for the esteem it accords to this and other stale concepts. But couplehood, love, and religion do not exhaust his scapegoats. He considers several political ideologies as well – "democratic–equality" politics,[7] feminism, and authoritarianism – and rejects them with equal vigor. In lieu of any political mechanisms, he argues, only a new model for intimate relations – one that transvalues personal and heterosexual love with impersonal and bisexual eroticism, and in so doing contests feminists, among others – can revive a dying culture.[8]

But for their own foundational reasons, Gerald and Ursula mistrust the bisexual model he advocates. Reproducing the logic of some Victorian (and modern) conservatives, Gerald says that there can "never be anything as strong" between two men as "sex love" between a man and woman, because "nature doesn't provide the basis,"[9] and Ursula echoes him with her talk of "perversity." In her view, by contrast, Birkin's same-sex longing reveals his "obstinacy;" it is merely his "theory" about his own affection and desire, as though, she implies, the true nature of this desire is otherwise.[10] She defends a heterosexual foundationalism, to which Birkin refuses to assent: "I don't believe that," he says.[11] The novel's complex representations of Birkin's loves and hatreds suggest that Ursula's conventional-mindedness is narrow-minded.

But in other regards she is more broad-minded than he. She has much to teach him, first of all, about himself – by exposing hypocrisies in his thinking. Birkin professes disgust with sadomasochism, such as he sees in Hermione and Gerald. He affects misanthropy, as though humankind is scarcely worth his consideration – the modernist disenchantment to which Trilling refers. As part of this pose, he affects anti-patriotism, as though he is no more attached to England than to any other corrupt human collective. But Ursula helps him to recognize his own masochistic tendencies, his pathological attachment to humankind, and his sentimental feelings toward an imagined England of the past. By revealing how his protestations conflict with his disposition, she helps him to temper his anger, where it is inauthentic, and to act more authentically on his radical impulses.

Notwithstanding the hollowness of Birkin's misanthropy and anti-patriotism, however, the unmasking of these affectations is not the most important element in his moral development. Instead, the crucial refining fire for his integrity as a man and thinker is his and Ursula's contest over the nature of their intimacy. On a theoretical level, this contest yields neither victory nor defeat: they are doomed to repeat their argument, as Birkin maintains that, instead of love, he wants something "impersonal and harder, – and rarer."[12] But despite his obstinacy, she elicits from him several professions of "love" – that very word – and a willingness to "let love be enough,"[13] in other words an acknowledgment that the shape of their intimacy is not wholly his to choose.

While no clear victory is possible for either lover in theoretical terms, in practical terms certain facts are established by the novel's end. Birkin and Ursula are married. Their form of intimacy – gentler and more egalitarian – has endured, whereas Gerald and Gudrun's has not. Moreover, the protagonists' bond is exclusive: Gerald is dead, whatever love Birkin would have liked to cultivate with him, and Gudrun has departed from their geographical and emotional orbit. The protagonists find themselves, as Pines stresses, in an all-too familiar kind of intimacy: monogamous, heterosexual, legally sanctified, and self-contained. Birkin disdains a society "all in couples, each couple in its own little house, watching its own little interests,"[14] but he and Ursula end up reproducing this norm.

Maintaining a vital intimacy, this novel indicates in its less idealistic moments, entails some capitulation to inherited institutions. But how far need Birkin capitulate to inherited sentiments, such as Ursula's idea that "love is the greatest"?[15] In fact, his concessions to "love," and to the model of marital companionship implied by this term, partially vindicate the establishment precepts, espoused by a diverse array of thinkers, which Lawrence's essays associate with bourgeois sterility. It remains to explore, then, what the ideal of marital "companionship" looked like to Lawrence, why it elicits his mistrust; and how *Women in Love*, over the course of its genesis, arrived at its tense peace with the ideal.

COMPANIONSHIP, SEXUAL DEVIANCE, AND THE MANUSCRIPT HISTORY OF *WOMEN IN LOVE*

"Companionate marriage" as a modern Western ideal has been traced to writings including John Milton's 1643 "Doctrine and discipline of divorce" and his depiction of Adam and Eve in *Paradise Lost*; as a middle-class habit, it has been celebrated as an eighteenth-century achievement.[16] During the mid-Victorian years, the sexes' separate spheres, and the intellectual limitations of domestic "angels," vitiated the ideal. But in the twentieth century, with an expanding middle class, large and stable marriage rates, shrinking family sizes, and a broad social reaction against Victorian gender roles, the companionship ideal was reinvigorated. Its theoretical components are various, sometimes in tension with one another and with the practice of married life, but can be summarized as follows. (1) Marriage will comprise one man and one woman. (2) Marriage will be monogamous and lifelong. (3) Marriage confers economic and social benefits: a stable and comfortable domicile with fewer children and servants than Victorian households contained, hence privacy for as many family members as possible; a dependable income – perhaps generated only by the husband – sufficient to sustain middle-class respectability. (4) Spouses should be equals: neither moral nor intellectual superiority belongs to the man. (5) In spite of the supra-individual quality of permanent commitment, the individuality of neither spouse should be subsumed. Equality – and space of one's own, especially for the wife – are helpful guards against this danger. (6) Marriage, being "companionate," entails more than economic convenience; spouses cultivate emotional and intellectual bonds unique to their personalities. (7) Tenderness, mutual respect, and longevity may mitigate against passion, but the sacrifice is more than compensated for.

The reach and power of this ideal derive from its wide scope of advocates. It is not surprising that a secular liberal such as Bertrand Russell should champion its more progressive tenets (numbers 4, 5, and 6). It is to be expected that thinkers clearly identified with the establishment, such as Edward Lyttleton or the Rev. James Marchant, would endorse its more conservative elements (numbers 1, 2, 3, and 7).[17] Nor is it surprising that a more idiosyncratic conservative and religious thinker such as Denis de Rougemont should value the same tenets. But the rhetoric of *Women in Love* highlights the collusion, as Lawrence sees it, between seeming rivals such as Russell and Rougemont in solidifying this oppressive ideal. Different as their emphases may be – with Russell seeing companionship as a force to liberate couples from the coercion of traditional morals, and Rougemont seeing agape (akin to companionship) as a bulwark against the destructive powers of erotic passion and modern atomization – for Lawrence the worldviews of such thinkers are two sides of one coin, where intimacy is concerned. That companionship has, from Lawrence's point of view, such an extensive array of advocates, helps to explain why Pines sees *Women in Love* as an establishment text. What room does Lawrence (or Birkin) have to maneuver outside the discourse of companionship when it casts such a wide net, and when Ursula is such an effective spokesperson on its behalf?

Russell, as discussed in the Introduction, added his voice to those of feminists, secularists, and others determined to define twentieth-century intimacy against what they felt to be oppressive Victorian models. His anti-Victorianism led him to support the fight by Colorado judge Ben Lindsey on behalf of "trial marriage" – or "companionate marriage"[18] – divorce by mutual consent, and sexual freedom for young couples. Trial marriage was meant to allow couples to cohabit without the social and psychological burdens of legal matrimony. Lindsey, Russell, and their allies felt that a marriage should not be legally binding until a wife's first pregnancy, at which point the parents' rights are subordinated to the child's.

The sociologist Anthony Giddens uses the term "companionate marriage" in an historically broader sense than Lindsey, dating it to the period when Mary Wollstonecraft espoused sexual equality consistent with republican principles, and lamented the social construction of women as men's helpmates. Giddens describes "romance" as a form of storytelling, and matrimonial companionship as a venue in which ordinary citizens can narrate their own love lives.[19] For Giddens, the "democratization of intimacy" means that love is pursued by women in conjunction with – not under the coercion of – men, and by couples free from the coercion of families, churches, and communities. Russell and Lindsey articulated for their time these principles that Giddens says had long been emerging.

Russell views this emergence with a sense of long-term optimism, impatient though he is for "conventional moralists" (whom he sees as cruel) to disappear. He claims, for example, that post-World-War-One feminists are preferable to those of Wollstonecraft's generation, since they make no attempt to fetter male sexuality. As a compliment to this observation, he says not only that free, spontaneous love is good, in general, for both sexes, but specifically that premarital sex is healthy for women.[20] Such polemically anti-Victorian ideas about sex made Russell a lightning rod for conservative outrage.

How could such a thinker, from Lawrence's point of view, contribute to the same hegemonic ideal as Rougemont? Russell, after all, repeatedly attacks Christianity. He specifies Saint Paul (one of Rougemont's touchstones) as the source of many pathological ideas about sexuality. He deplores any language that mystifies companionship: talk of the "mystery" of love or the "tragic tension" between a man and woman who share a household. Russell also echoes sexual radicals such as Edward Carpenter in his refusal to valorize jealousy (what he calls the spouse in the role of "policeman"): he speculates that monogamy is a passing phase in the history of human sexuality, sees infidelity as a fact of life, and hopes that patterns of jealousy are correctible cultural pathologies.[21]

These attitudes might seem to make Russell the polar opposite of Rougemont, whose critique of eroticism aimed to contain many of the instincts that Russell hoped to grant wider freedom. *L'Amour et L'Occident* (1939, tr. *Love in the Western World* 1940) is a frankly Christian apologetic that appeared in English a decade after Lawrence's death. It articulates a mistrust of past and present eros shared by British, American, and European thinkers throughout the Victorian and post-Victorian decades, and grounded in the belief that, because Christianity provides believers with a god in human form, it teaches them how to love in *this* world. Rougemont champions *agape* (which, from the point of view developed in *Women in Love*, is the Christianized version of Russell and Lindsey's "companionate" marriage) as the model of intimacy most conducive to human happiness. Rougemont says that novels threaten this model by disseminating erotic values. Indeed the vocabulary of *Love in the Western World* provides opportunities for incisive critiques of Birkin's longings and pathologies, just as Lawrence's novel anticipates Rougemont's apologetics. The history of love in the West, as Rougemont tells it, is the history of eros leading men and women toward self-deception, suffering, and death, versus the divine Christian love which can be a gateway to rational companionship.

Eros means passion and passion means suffering, says Rougemont, so how did this state of being come to haunt the West, given that the Greeks and Romans saw love as a sickness?[22] The cult of love has multiple sources, primarily the chivalric codes of twelfth- and thirteenth-century society. Courtly love, with its exaltation of the lady as an unattainable object of the knight's longing, arose as a reaction to the brutalities of feudal society. It is not, of course, reflected in our laws today, and even in medieval times it may not have been more than an ideal, says Rougemont, but nonetheless its imperatives remain ours – in our dreams.[23] Rougemont sees these "dreams" at work in myths, including the Romance of Tristan and Isolde, in which the protagonists' erotic longing for one another betrays a necessity "stronger than the need of their happiness"[24] or their lives; it is not a feeling they can control, nor one they choose to have; it results from a magic potion they drink. This longing is not primarily sexual – though unbridled carnal desire is anathema to Rougemont – but a desire to escape from ordinary life into a more intense, more adventurous, and seemingly more *real* existence. But the desired life is not real, it is a false and dangerous ideal. The logical extension of eros is suffering, because in suffering the lover feels himself more alive – hence he *craves* suffering – and the logical culmination of eros is death, as only death can fulfill a passionate desire to exceed all boundaries. The Tristan myth depicts rules of conduct by virtue of which the lovers, for a time, can contain their passions;[25] but eventually they meet their mortal erotic fate, and the myth testifies indirectly to the truth too dark to speak openly: that passion is an antisocial force linked with death.[26]

In addition to chivalric codes, myths and Romances, and lyric poetry which celebrates unhappy yearning lovers, eros finds another historical source in Manicheanism, "essentially a lyric faith," which sees the soul as divine, as imprisoned in created forms, and as something that reaches the Light through the "death" of askesis.[27] Through each of these sources, eros beckons to the West with its exhilarating dangers. But Rougemont diagnoses multiple layers of sickness in the desires to escape ordinary life, to thwart one's own happiness, to suffer, and to die. He underscores that erotic love is egocentric: Tristan and Isolde don't really love one another, they love being in love, and need one another to be aflame; each beloved is merely a vehicle, a fuel, for the lover's feelings. Birkin suffers from these layers of sickness, and Ursula (who, given her anti-religiosity, shares surprising affinities with Rougemont) would have Birkin healed by loving her in ways similar to how Rougemont would have Christians love one another.

While Manichean mystics and Romance heroes experience eros in "heroic" ways, says Rougemont, for 90 percent of twentieth-century citizens the feeling has been democratized into the dull routine of adultery. Statistics testifying to the frequency of adultery belie any self-deceptive poetic ideas that American or European masses might entertain about their own flights of "passion." Adultery remains a source of suffering, however, even if it drains the cult of passionate love of its aesthetic, spiritual, and tragic dimensions.[28] *Love in the Western World* has the therapeutic aim of weaning middle-class dreamers from their dreams.

Like Rougemont, Lawrence was anything but an advocate of casual infidelities. The Foreword of *Women in Love* responds to the American accusation of "Eroticism" with the questions "Which Eros? Eros of the jaunty 'amours,' or Eros of the sacred mysteries? And if the latter, why accuse, why not respect, even venerate?" Ursula Brangwen is not Emma Bovary; *Women in Love* does not depict a woman's "jaunty amours." But while Lawrence shared Rougemont's contempt for democratized and trivialized eros, the two had different attitudes toward what Rougemont calls Tristan's "falsely sacred" eros, but what Lawrence calls "sacred mysteries" and Birkin refers to in similarly reverent (and potentially morbid) ways. Ursula, Rougemont's secular proxy, leads Birkin toward a more conventional form of companionship that she believes is more likely to yield happiness than "sacred mysteries."

For Rougemont, the Christian incarnation negates other religions that lack human gods, and that thus condemn man's finite life.[29] These religions are erotic. But in Christianity, says Rougemont, Christ's death becomes the first condition of a new spiritual life whose essence, agapic love, "brings forth our neighbor" as more than a vehicle for our egocentric passion.[30] For Rougemont, eros is a poisonous idealization, and his religion provides a life-restoring de-idealization: a Christian spouse will seek no "illusory flight out of the concreteness of life." "It is better to marry than to burn," says Saint Paul, which Rougemont approves as an admonishment against burning with passion.[31] Marriage rationalizes the lover's eros, enabling the beloved to emerge on his or her own terms. This agapic project has Ursula's support. To what degree *Women in Love* sides with her, or shares Birkin's erotic longings, which it refuses to see as "illusory flights," remains an aesthetically productive enigma.

Like Ursula, Russell (also from a secular perspective) shares Rougemont's pro-agapic, anti-erotic values. For this reason, thinkers with radically different attitudes toward religious traditions and progress could, from Lawrence's point of view, reinforce the same dull modern principles concerning intimacy, sexuality, and selfhood. Russell inveighs against Romantic love in much the same vein that Rougemont inveighs against eros. Americans divorce frequently, says Russell, because they are Romantics, which means they cope poorly when their ideals meet the realities of matrimonial life. In a tone of humorous disenchantment, he says that marriage is more likely to be "what is called 'happy'" if neither party expects too much from it.[32] Imagining love to be a "sacred mystery" is a perfect recipe for excessive expectations. But Russell's anti-idealism does not prevent him from singing the praises of love. He says that love "breaks down the hard walls of the ego," which are among the greatest impediments to happiness; that it is in itself "a source of delight," that its absence is "a source of pain," and that it enhances other pleasures, from music to nature.[33] These are, of course, self-consciously mundane observations about ordinary love, the feeling for which Birkin expresses boredom and disgust. When Russell defends Lindsey's model of marital companionship, he illustrates the breadth of the status quo which Birkin questions: it stretches from one side of the Atlantic to another, enlisting the support of judges and philosophers, secularists, and Christians. Birkin could hardly avoid succumbing to such an ideology.

But Lawrence and his protagonist are determined rebels, eager to exploit any fissure or decry any blind spot in the ideology. *Love in the Western World*, for example, neglects to examine homosexuality and thus to make explicit that heteronormativity[34] is a pillar of the establishment love that it defends. But *Women in Love*, in opposing Birkin's erotic yearnings to Ursula's agapic values, makes the question of what Freud called the "sexual object" central to its critique of modern love.

One reason, the novel implies, that love and companionate marriage are oppressive is the heterosexist assumptions on which they are based. Birkin's attraction to Gerald dispels the notion that "nature" provides the "basis" only for opposite-sex "sex love." When the two men wrestle naked by the fire, the encounter is so charged with erotic askesis that Birkin feels "as if [his] whole physical intelligence interpenetrated into Gerald's body." It is also violent: the men "had a real struggle. They seemed to drive their white flesh deeper and deeper against each other, as if they would break into a oneness."[35] The significance of the wrestling is multifaceted: both somatic and spiritual (involving Birkin's "physical intelligence"), both sexual and violent, both polarizing (they drive their flesh "against" each other) and unifying (they drive "deeper" against one another – the preposition *into* would seem more apt than *against* – and they approach "oneness"). Birkin's sexual nature is complex and self-contradictory, bound up with other, non-sexual psychic drives, unlikely to be satisfied by an exclusively heterosexual life, and unlikely to be satisfied if his ego remains ensconced within the cozy confines of agapic love.

Despite Lawrence's theoretical commitment to his own version of polymorphous erotic perversity, with Birkin's decision to marry Ursula – to form one more "couple . . . watching its own little interests" – *Women in Love* largely renounces erotic idealism and accommodates the agapic norm. Whether Gerald's sadomasochistic tendencies or his maleness establishes Ursula as a more fitting partner for Birkin, one way or another Birkin's marriage normalizes him sexually: his desires focus on a single opposite-sex object. Likewise, Freud's *Three Essays* balance their theoretical commitment to polymorphousness with a practical commitment to psychic health and normalcy – which generally imply a curtailing of "perversions" – although Freud never adopts a tone as angry as Ursula's, toward same-sex desires.

It should be stressed that these two thinkers' anti-essentialism does not lead them to substitute one putative sexual essence for another. For Freud, polymorphousness does not entail a set of desires that individuals must fulfill in order to achieve self-realization. Rather, it describes a set of potentialities, some of which are bound to be explored less than others. Thus, Freud's theory does not box him into a political position, in which he is logically obliged to advocate homosexual liberation, for example. Instead, it leaves him free to measure the moral attractiveness of an individual's same-sex and opposite-sex love objects by a combination of shifting factors, from the pleasures they promise to the dangers they entail. The anti-essentialism in (the published version of) *Women in Love* is similar: the wrestling scene does not imply that Birkin requires a permanent male sexual partner in order to be "fulfilled."[36] When Birkin tells Gerald that "life has all kinds of things . . . there isn't only one road,"[37] he means to reassure Gerald, who doubts whether he will ever "love" a woman. But Birkin describes his own predicament as well, in claiming that the future contains multiple possibilities.

This anti-essentialism, however, had not always been part of the novel's theoretical design. Its composition history shows that Lawrence experimented with a more essentialist conception of (at least male) sexual desire, before arriving at a depiction of Birkin that leaves the author – as Freud's theory leaves Freud – politically non-committal. One outline unfolded into what eventually became both *The Rainbow* (1915) and *Women in Love* (completed in 1916, published in 1920).[38] Ursula appears in the earlier novel, wherein her affair with Winifred Inger establishes her polymorphous sexual curiosity. In combination with this lesbianism in *The Rainbow*, the wrestling scene in *Women in Love* suggests that monogamous heterosexual partnerships fail to answer to the emotional needs of either sex. The cancelled Prologue of *Women in Love* strikes a note of more radical disaffection, and says that in denying his same-sex longings, Birkin betrays himself.[39] Birkin carried on sexual relations with women, and "wanted all the time to love" them in the passionate way he loved men, explains this excised text, "but he could not." Commenting omnisciently, the narrator asks "how can a man *create* his own feelings," and answers "he cannot."[40] The canceled Prologue flatly contradicts Ursula, passing a similar judgment against his heterosexual experiments that she passes against his desire for Gerald, when she calls it a mere "theory."

But despite the clarity of these opposed theories about Birkin's sexuality, the final draft of *Women in Love* embraces neither form of essentialism. The crucial fact about the Prologue, as Frank Kermode argues, is that Lawrence abandoned it, evidence that he considered and rejected any "theory" or "metaphysic" that implicitly equates bisexuality with sexual authenticity.[41] The nausea with which Ursula reacts against her affair with Winifred helps explain her hostility, in the later novel, to the idea that Gerald could be an "eternal" object of Birkin's love.[42] Ursula's psychosexual trajectory, in other words, contrasts sharply with that of the heroine in *Mrs Dalloway*. Ursula forgoes Winifred for Birkin, rather like Clarissa forgoes Sally for Richard (admittedly, Clarissa's physical intimacy with Sally never proceeds beyond a kiss). But whereas Ursula repudiates her lesbian experiences, Clarissa treasures her kiss as a "present . . . infinitely precious."[43] Were *Women in Love* as sympathetic to lesbianism as Woolf's novel, Ursula might view her past differently. But Lawrence's novel neither avows nor disavows Ursula's heterosexist bias. The moral integrity and psychic health she brings to her intimacy with the sickly Birkin endow her with considerable authority. But with its concluding note of irresolution, *Women in Love* refuses to construct either protagonist as infallible, either as a theorist of selfhood and desire or as a practitioner of intimacy.

Ursula's authority as a proponent of "love" – thus as a representative of the civilization Birkin mistrusts – stems not from her reactionary ideas about same-sex desire, but because she answers his need for lambency and finality, dynamism and permanence, as no one else can, especially once Gerald dies. Birkin's two most intimate relationships, prior to that with Ursula, explain why he half desires, all along, to submit to this feeling and to the institution of companionship, even as he continues to attack "culture itself." The degradations of his affair with Hermione and the incompleteness of his friendship with Gerald leave him longing to be sexually and emotionally enlivened by a woman. While the life open to him with Ursula is hardly conventional in all ways, it does ground him in a tried-and-tested bourgeois arrangement: marriage.

FEMINISM AND THE PRACTICAL APPEAL OF CIVILIZATION

Birkin attacks the companionship model from many angles, and his language is echoed in Lawrence's essays. Nonetheless, Ursula successfully repels his attacks, in part because she exposes ignoble motives – both chauvinism and cowardice – that lie behind them. Birkin worries that love is a "dance of opposites," a "tick-tack" of pride and subservience[44] – a far cry from the equality that supposedly undergirds companionate marriage. Even when subservience is not an issue, Birkin denigrates the "emotional plane" as a place where lovers can "meet and mingle." This place, he says, pertains only to the "branch," not the "root," of the "impersonal me."[45] Nonetheless, "mingling" there ignobly compromises the two partners' separate selves, and thus violates the fifth component of companionate marriage: that neither spouse's individuality should be subsumed. Of course, neither "companionship" nor "individuality" (in the rationalist's sense of these concepts) appeals to Birkin, which is why the "interpenetration" of his and Gerald's "physical intelligences" is invigorating. On the one hand, "interpenetration" and "mingling" are alike, as both involve a blurring of boundaries, a softening of the self's integrity. On the other hand, though, they could not be more different, as mingling entails only the most tepid stepping forth, whereas wrestling ascetically empties Birkin and Gerald of personal emotions, and brings their "impersonal" roots into adventurous, athletic interaction.

Birkin's preference (if one can be inferred) for interpenetration over mingling might suggest courage on his part, given that he – a member of the socially privileged sex – disdains the "tick-tack" of a power seesaw, and welcomes a physical contest with a more powerful man. Such courage, if it is not a sham, could bode well for his skills as an intimate partner. As a matter of fact, in his mistrust of "mingling," and in Ursula's mistrust of his motives, *Women in Love* reflects a debate within post-World-War-One British feminism concerning distinctions between the sexes. Prior to the granting of partial suffrage in 1918, British feminism was largely concerned with issues of fairness, such as equal pay for equal work. Giddens says that the same transactional struggle, the same process of "democratization," that continues to transform public life also incites subversion of male domination behind the household door. This transformation of private experience according to the dictates of a public movement is exactly what raises Birkin's – and Lawrence's – ire. But do the protagonist and author strive courageously to guard the life of the heart against public discourse, with all its "tick-tacks," for apolitical reasons – simply because they value lovers' freedom – or in service of a (masculinist) political agenda, as men's sexual privileges slip away, in a liberalizing world? (Perhaps it is less threatening to Birkin's male pride for his root to interpenetrate with Gerald's than for his branches to meet and mingle with Ursula's.) This is the self-critical question that Lawrence poses throughout *Women in Love*, with the help of Ursula, whose voice is absent from Lawrence's essays.

Although they had different reasons for doing so, some post-World-War-One feminists worried, as Lawrence did, about the influence of public discourse on intimate life. "New feminists" including Eleanor Rathbone held that women had "special concerns" necessitating such legislation as allowances for mothers. Conversely, "equality feminists" such as Ray Strachey worried that emphasizing sexual distinctions would perpetuate Victorian gender roles and harm women's private lives.[46] While Lawrence feared that feminist discourse in general would make women assertive, Strachey worried that "new feminist" discourse would make women self-abnegating. Each thinker acknowledges the large role played by social forces in character formation. Ursula strikes a Stracheyan note in wondering whether the "pure . . . duality"[47] and sexual "polarization" that Birkin desires would favor men's interests by molding men and women into partnerships of uncommitted, independent-minded individuals.

She also wonders whether his death-haunted erotic desires will serve either of their interests. Her more rational desire for an equal union, though not beyond reproach, weakens Birkin's attacks on "culture itself," and on love. Her voice in *Women in Love* makes it impossible *not* to detect inconsistency when Birkin – defender of living process over dead ideals – alludes to "the one last thing one wants," nor to detect desperation when he says that one should "throw everything away" for the sake of his mystical goal. Ursula presses him to name this goal, wanting him to say "love" – that staple of traditional discourse – but instead he calls it "freedom together,"[48] reiterating his distaste for mingling. This sounds courageous, but Ursula cannot trust his talk of "throw[ing] everything away" as long as he refuses to break from Hermione.

When Ursula exposes Birkin (to himself) as a coward, and his radical, mystical rhetoric as so much bluster, his reflex is to challenge her in turn. He demands from her a "final" and "infallible" pledge. But finality is negatively connoted in this novel that values becoming over being. Rather than exposing Ursula's fear of commitment, Birkin's demand reveals his cowardly impulse to escape a world of unpredictability and change. His pathology is evident in the "clang of mistrust and almost anger in his voice."[49] Birkin's anger has been well established by this point in the narrative. While not attractive, it has some justification in the corrupt social order against which he rails. But his clanging "mistrust" is a damning flaw. His inability to trust himself, Ursula, or his own ideas undermines the credibility of the erotic model of intimacy that he defends.

In contrast to his mistrust, and the suggestion that his mystical protestations might be symptoms of desperation, Ursula's strength is confirmed and the novel suggests a connection between her personal integrity and her conventional aspirations as a lover. Ursula, says the narrator, "could not submit" to Birkin's doctrine that love "gives out in the last issues."[50] This refusal ramifies on two levels. One might appear apolitical (a conventional preference for love and equality over the more demanding "equilibrium"),[51] but if Ursula is right to suspect that Birkin's mysticism is not politically innocent, then her refusal to "submit" affirms the democratic principle of equality in intimacy. Birkin's hope for "duality" in "polarization" echoes the separatist rhetoric of the new feminists, and Ursula's valuation of companionate love recalls the political aspirations of Wollstonecraft and Strachey.

Is "polarization" – i.e., Birkin's desire that the male and female be defined as separate centers of consciousness, even separate principles – thereby invalidated as a lovers' goal? *Women in Love* provides no such resolution.

Rather, Ursula's refusal to accept Birkin's doctrines enacts the principle of polarization. Lawrence's essays discuss a male preference for individuation and a female preference for connection. When Birkin's "polarization" contends with Ursula's "love," and neither wins, the male principle is illustrated in action. The lovers are connected because they are polarized.

CONTRA FEMINISM, CONTRA POLITICS

Women in Love, in other words, sustains an antifeminist reading – one sympathetic to Birkin's philosophical agenda and disenchantment with civilization – as surely as it sustains a reading sympathetic to Ursula's feminism and her more accepting attitude toward civilization. Many of Lawrence's other writings develop antifeminist themes as well. *The Plumed Serpent* (1926) criticizes "well-dressed, beautiful women" who keep "their souls for themselves, in a sort of purse."[52] Clothing and purses invoke the *amour propre* and economic privilege of the bourgeoisie – a favorite target of the author's – and suggest that such women never give their "souls" to male lovers in passionate abandon. Birkin develops the antifeminist component of this anti-bourgeois attitude when he calls Ursula's "female ego" a "rag doll." Her "ego," like another woman's "soul," stands for the personal part of her that Birkin sees as the enemy of her "complete self,"[53] which can apprehend cosmic, natural, and sexual forces in their full magnitude. The goal of sexual intimacy, says Birkin, is to discover the "unknown" where an "isolated me" can experience "primal desire" and "approach" the beloved. Language that reinforces the sense of social "obligation"[54] can only hinder men and women from discovering this "beyond," according to Birkin and his author.

No one is more fettered by a sense of social obligation and alienated from their own nature, Lawrence implies in the essay "Cocksure women and hensure men" (1929), than the eponymous women, whose fear of their "henny" promptings leads them to "miss life altogether" in pursuit of social justice.[55] The essay's glib philosophical assumption is belied by such fictional texts as *The Rainbow*, wherein Ursula's polymorphous traits render suspect the notion of a simple "henny" nature. But other essays reinforce the impression that "cocksure" women symptomatize a cultural anxiety in the face of sex. "If only our civilization had taught us how to let sex appeal flow properly and subtly . . . we might, all of us, have lived all our lives in love," runs Lawrence's diagnosis in "Sex versus loveliness."[56] The solution to ennui and misery, he says, lies in a perfected relationship, driven by "sex appeal," between men and women.

According to a line of reasoning shared by Lawrence's essays, Birkin, and Ursula, feminism is only one example of a political ideology that leads away from this solution. Politics and religion – institutional life in general – is the culprit; feminism is but one face this villain shows. Ursula accuses political man of transforming the sea into "a murderous alley and a soiled road of commerce," and says that he "claims," "shares up," and "parcels out" the air to "owners," "trespasses" it to "fight for it."[57] Her views find support in Lawrence's essay "Democracy." "Politics, what are they?" asks this diatribe. "Just another, extra large, commercial wrangling over buying and selling – nothing else."[58]

Because "politics" in the broadest sense is "murderous" and "soiled," none of the foundational solutions offered, for society's ills, by various ideologies, can help intimacy-seeking men and women. The Christian foundations of charity and love, according to which Gerald's father hopes to treat his workers, are no better than the authoritarian foundation – embodied by Gerald – of a personality cult. Neither foundation is better or worse, where intimacy is concerned, than that of "equality." That Gerald as a boy "longed to go with the soldiers to shoot" the workers[59] who riot after losing their jobs, for example, illustrates the sadistic elements of his authoritarian personality. The same elements may have led him to shoot his brother "accidentally."[60] They enable his sordid affair with Minette – who attracts him by stabbing another man with a fork – and his destructive relationship with Gudrun, which leads him almost to strangle her, before he acquiesces in his own death. The same personality that craves a relation of violent domination and subordination between owner and employees also craves such relations in his sex life. While the sexual relation precipitates Gerald's death, his relation with his workers also brings him suffering. Even after he bent their desires to his will, when Gerald "went to the mirror and looked long and closely at his own face, at his own eyes, seeking for something," he feared that "it was not real, it was a mask," and hence he was "afraid, in mortal dry fear, but he knew not what of."[61] His authoritarian will destroys both his official and his intimate relations, and leaves him without the sense of self that could yield "equilibrium."[62]

SADOMASOCHISM AND URSULA'S INTEGRITY

It is not only political ideologies, therefore, but also an individual's impulses, that can poison his intimate relations. Gerald's monstrous cruelty, which he eventually turns on himself, constitutes a resounding authorial judgment against sadomasochistic impulses, and speaks more loudly against a "tick-tack" of pride and subservience than anything Birkin says. Yet Birkin himself, despite his disgust at Gerald and Minette's pathological attraction to one another,[63] falls prey to his own masochism, and requires the tutelage of his practical- and normative-minded lover to overcome it.

Ursula's wisdom contrasts with Hermione's craving for domination and subordination. When Hermione, shortly after Birkin leaves her, tells Ursula of his violent reactive tendencies, Ursula says, "humbly" and empathically, "yes, you must have suffered." Hermione's response reveals her psychic illness. "One must be willing to suffer," she explains, "if you are going to help him." "I don't *want* to suffer hourly and daily," counters Ursula, "I think it is degrading not to be happy." Ursula's simple assertion causes Hermione to "stop and look at her a long time," and to recognize "Ursula's far distance from herself. For to Hermione suffering was the greatest reality." Hermione feebly agrees that one "should" be happy. But for her, happiness is "a matter of will,"[64] whereas Ursula's capacity for joy issues from a less dangerous source. In leaving Hermione for Ursula, Birkin exchanges, for a pitched battle of "wills," a relationship predicated on different terms, although Ursula recognizes the role played by "will" in his purportedly egoless "beyond."

Willfulness, sadism, masochism – characters in *Women in Love* brim with these qualities, and the novel makes their unattractiveness abundantly clear. As part of his anti-essentialist project, his post-Victorian answer to the question about *what men and women are like*, Lawrence returns relentlessly to the human capacity for cruelty and destruction. His ideas about *how intimate relations can be reimagined* in the new century depend on this dark vision of the unconscious, reminiscent of the Freudian id.[65] Ursula struggles mightily, by argument and by example, to defend her preference for a unitary, rational, heterosexual, humane, and life-embracing selfhood. Does this ideal diverge so radically from the personalities around her, including Birkin's – fragmented, irrational, bisexual, sadistic, and death-driven – that it is merely an idle fantasy?[66]

At times Birkin's personality, almost as much as Gerald or Hermione's, suggests that Ursula's idea of emotional health cannot apply to him. Ursula encounters Birkin by the fire looking "like some crouching idol, some image of a deathly religion . . . pale and unreal . . . almost phosphorescent." She asks if he feels well, and he – who scorns others for evading their inner promptings – answers, "I hadn't thought about it." Never is Birkin's peevishness, nor his penchant for irrationalism, so clearly pathological as when the narration specifies how tenuous his residence is among the living.

At such moments, the wisdom of Ursula's normative preference shines. She refuses to accept his evasion. "Don't you know [how you feel] without thinking about it?" she asks. Her talent for hectoring him rivals his ability to hector her and others, with a key difference. She has precise goals in mind, such as exposing a contradiction in his theory or a pose that is unworthy of him. When Birkin deflects her question, she repeats it – an argumentative tactic of which he, too, is fond – "Don't you know whether you are unwell or not, without thinking about it?" With the persistence of Socrates questioning a pupil, she invokes Birkin's own principle: surely he, an enemy of hypertrophied consciousness, would agree that "thinking" should not be necessary to apprehending one's wellness. The exchange concludes with Ursula enjoining him to stay in bed: "you *ought* to suffer, a man who takes as little notice of his body as that."[67] She accuses him of courting his own illness. Though he resents her accusation at the moment, upon reflection he recognizes its justice. "Ursula was right," he thinks. "He knew that his spirituality was concomitant of a process of depravity, a sort of pleasure in self-destruction." Hence "he wanted her" revivifying influence.[68] Tristan lacks such an option, since his lover is as erotic – as self-destructive – as he is. But Ursula opens the path of agape to Birkin.

She admonishes him just as Lawrence would have her do, in a manner free of bullying – free of sadistic impulses, even disguised ones. In *Fantasia of the Unconscious*, Lawrence says that the use of "coaxing and logic and tricks" to get a child to take castor oil – a question such as "You love your mother, don't you, dear?" – is "sickening cant," "the most hateful of all things." The "appeal to love based on false pity" is a sure sign of the parent's "bullying . . . spiritual will." Lawrence prefers the mother who asserts, "Child, you've got to swallow this castor oil . . . . I say so because it is true. So open your mouth."[69] When Birkin behaves like an irresponsible boy, Ursula adopts the role of a strong mother. She rebukes him without subterfuge, without the tone of an angelic minister. She speaks not on behalf of "ideals" – *Fantasia* says that to impose these on another person is "criminal" – but from feelings of empathy and revulsion. "I hate people who hurt themselves," she says, shaking her hand, when she hears that Gerald has injured his hand in machinery; "I can *feel* it."[70] Birkin rebukes others for betraying their vitality or practicing cruelty on themselves, and Ursula rebukes him for the same reason.

Ursula brings the same passionate, straightforward – and conventional – moral attitude to bear on men's sadism as on their masochism. She condemns as "unnecessary" Gerald's "torture" of his mare – tellingly, a female animal – though Gudrun finds it arousing and Gerald justifies it by saying that the mare is "there for [his] use."[71] Loerke's statue of a nude girl on a horse recalls Gerald's mare. It provides occasion for Loerke to explain his instrumental attitude toward his human and equestrian models, and for Ursula to express her author's repulsion at such an approach to art.[72] The conventional-minded heroine is morally alert in her concern for the welfare of an animal, her outrage at the exploitation of a young female model, and in the offense she takes at the anti-humanism in modernist aesthetics. Her protests against the magnate and modernist's heartlessness express anti-instrumental principles that Birkin shares, but he never finds occasions to intervene so precisely on their behalf.

But Lawrence's critique of domination and subordination should not be mistaken for an endorsement of democratic "equality" nor Christian "love." When the narrator of *Women in Love*, dripping with irony, says of Gerald's father, "Oh, he wanted love to be the directing power" of the mines,[73] he conveys contempt for this ideal.[74] Birkin's concept of the "tick-tack" or "dance of opposites" explains how the same workforce that relies on Mr Crich's loving charity can be bent to Gerald's domineering will. In either case they are subjected to a "directing power." The father's Christian love is not the opposite of the son's will to power, but the other side of one family coin. So infected is the concept of "love," insists Birkin, that "we hate the word because we have vulgarized it. It ought to be prescribed, tabooed from utterance, for many years, till we get a new, better idea."[75] The word has been vulgarized in part due to its co-option by institutions such as the Crich family mines. Love contributes, therefore – Birkin believes – to the crisis from which he seeks a way out, rather than pointing the way toward health, as Ursula intimates.

BIRKIN'S PATHOLOGICAL MESSIANISM

But just as Birkin's rhetorical attacks on sadomasochism mask his masochistic tendencies (until Ursula weans him from them), so too his attacks on love and spiritualism mask his loving and spiritualistic tendencies (until Ursula weans him from them). Ursula recognizes humankind as the object of Birkin's residual spiritualism. His desire to save it reveals his attachment to the foundational Christian principle of universal love, which hinders this would-be anti-foundationalist from freeing himself into an impersonal unison with Ursula. With consummate insight, she sees his resistance to her diagnosis, and his misanthropic acting out, as poses. "If only man was swept off the face of the earth," he declaims, "creation would go along marvelously." She responds with an ontological prediction – "man will never be gone" – that he never refutes, and she demonstrates a better understanding of him than he has of himself. "Ursula watched him as he talked," reports the narrator, the omniscient point of view blending with hers. "There seemed a certain impatient fury in him . . . and a final tolerance." She sees beneath his pose of intolerance, but she is too perspicacious to regret his pose and treasure his "final tolerance." Instead, "it was this tolerance she mistrusted, not the fury. She saw that . . . in spite of himself, he would [try] to save the world." She is intolerant because "she wanted him to herself"; she "hated" knowing that he would make the same declamations about the end of man "to anybody who came along," which amounts to "prostitution."

Impelled by her desire to have him "to herself," she exposes a contradiction in his dogma, as she simultaneously attacks his attachment to humankind and defends "love." "You believe in individual love," she asks, "even if you don't believe in loving humanity?" Predictably – they have discussed the topic before – he answers "I don't believe in love at all." Then why "bother about humanity?" she asks. "Because I can't get away from it," he answers. She recognizes this answer as an evasion. "Because you love it," she says. She is right: Birkin does "love" humanity according to his own definition of love. His attachment to it is infected with Christian pity and egotism – just the kind of sentimentalism that prevents lovers from reaching the "beyond." (Rougemont might see in this love the seeds of a spiritual renewal, but neither Lawrence nor his protagonists subscribe to such a theology.) Birkin is "irritated" by Ursula's diagnosis because it is accurate. He attempts a second evasion. "If I do love it," he says, "it is my disease." But this is another pose – he merely pretends to be disgusted with himself – by which she refuses to be taken in. "It is a disease you don't want to be cured of," she says. Not surprisingly, says the narrator, "he was beginning to feel a fool."[76] Birkin's pride is so piqued by her correct diagnoses that he "withdraws" into an "insufferable aloof superiority" – for the time being.

But Ursula has begun to lead him out of his poses and self-contradictions. She understands them because she shares Birkin's morbid feelings. In condemning political man, she thinks with (erotic?) joy of the "kingdom of death," in a reverie reminiscent of and likely inspired by Birkin. "This remained to look forward to," she muses, "the pure inhuman otherness of death."[77] She and Birkin are not alone: *Women in Love* is suffused not just with sadomasochism or individual erotic longings, but also with "end-of-the-world" and annihilation sentiments. Encountering "common people" in a colliery town, Gudrun wants "not to know that this exists" and would like for the people to be "all annihilated, cleared away, so that the world was left clear for her."[78] With Loerke she delightedly imagines various scenarios of the "destruction of the world."[79]

Ursula, Gudrun, and Birkin were not atypical in their misanthropy and morbidity.[80] Even prior to World War One, premonitions of the world ending, of race death and national death, were prominent. Intellectuals, journalists and politicians, beginning in the late-nineteenth century, "talked and wrote in terms of a vulgar Darwinistic world of struggle"; in 1898 British Prime Minister Salisbury saw the globe divided into "living" and "dying" powers;[81] in 1918 Oswald Spengler claimed the West was in "decline" and compared human cultures to organisms, with natural cycles of growth and decay.[82] Written during the war, *Women in Love* participates in this discourse.

Although Ursula has morbid feelings, she does not wallow in them, nor mistake them for insights, as Birkin and Gerald sometimes do. Gerald's suicide dramatizes their likely issue, when they are erotically channeled and not checked by influences such as Ursula exerts on Birkin. The hero's presumptuous psychoanalysis of Gerald – "You seem to have a lurking desire to have your gizzard slit"[83] – is eerily prescient, but may reveal as much about Birkin's morbid preoccupations as it does about Gerald's. Birkin's fascination with decay and corruption, though it parallels his author's fascination, often issues from Birkin's short temper and tenuous health. Birkin's "dislike of mankind, of the mass of mankind," says the narrator, "amounted almost to an illness."[84]

Ursula recognizes his savior fantasies as the reverse side of this illness, an attachment to what he wants destroyed. This paradox-based mode of analysis is central to the novel's psychology. The narrator says that because Gerald, in his worship of industrial efficiency, "did *not* act on the other [Christian] ideal, it dominated him."[85] Birkin says of Loerke, "He *hates* the ideal utterly, yet it still dominates him."[86] Birkin is quick to point out the paradox of being dominated by what one hates – as it applies to other people. But he requires Ursula's help to see how trapped he is by this dynamic. Like an effective therapist, she teaches him to recognize and thereby transcend his pathologies.

THE PATHOLOGY OF PATRIOTISM

In addition to his sadomasochism and his love of humankind (each masked by contrary protestations), he is also pathologically attached to a sentimental idea about England (which he masks beneath anti-patriotic pronouncements). With regard to this sentimentality also, Ursula tutors him. He appears to have escaped provincial patriotism, even attachment to the idea of nationhood, when Gerald asks whether the "national hat" or "racial hat" can be "an old hat," and Birkin says that it is "pretty well bound to be," that he prefers his "pleasant liberty of conduct" to any such patriotic symbol. Given that the subtext of their conversation is the possibility of war, of "race or national death,"[87] his assertion is highly provocative.

Birkin's anti-patriotism – his rejection of the nation as a foundation of one's identity – is plausible because he entertains no facile admiration of other nations. When Hermione pompously speaks of Italy "coming to national consciousness," Birkin retorts, "their nationalism is just industrialism – that and a shallow jealousy I detest."[88] When he returns from travel, Ursula tells him that she's "done" with England, and he responds "It isn't a question of nations. France is far worse." She agrees, and claims to be "done with it all."[89] Birkin's dislike of political mankind, bitter though it is, at least rests on a cosmopolitan's exposure to various national attitudes. Even the Austrian Alps, near the novel's end, seem to him and Ursula no more fertile a ground for personal and interpersonal discovery than France or England.[90] His travels appear to have freed him from undue attachment to England, or to anywhere – a frightening freedom perhaps, but an ennobling one.

But in the chapter entitled "The chair," Ursula leads Birkin – rather than him leading her – away from national attachment.[91] Birkin, as the chapter begins, reveals his irrational love of the idea of England, a politicized form of thinking that diverts his energy from Ursula and himself in the immediate present – from the man–woman relation that is "the quick and central clue to life."[92] After he and Ursula purchase a birch chair in a jumble market, he lapses into nostalgia. "My beloved country," he exclaims, "had something to express even when it made that chair." Birkin finds very little about twentieth-century England "beloved"; his outburst strikes a false note, and Ursula confronts him. Doesn't England have something to express now, she asks. "She was always angry," comments the narrator, "when he took this tone." He answers in a knee-jerk manner. "No it hasn't," he says. "When I see that clear, beautiful chair, and I think of . . . Jane Austen's England – it had living thoughts to unfold . . . There is no production in us now, only sordid and foul mechanicalness." She continues to challenge his self-righteous "tone." "Why must you always praise the past at the expense of the present?" she perceptively inquires, and adds, "*Really*, I don't think so much of Jane Austen's England."[93]

She is perceptive not because she devalues Austen's era, but because she exposes Birkin's love of a (supposed) glorious national past as symptomatic of his dependence on ideals. The "past," in her formulation – or the time of "Jane Austen," in his – like "England," is an abstraction. It is a "nowhere" to which Birkin, in a facile mysticism, can seek only an "illusory flight," away from what Rougemont calls "the concreteness of life." As Ursula reminds him, "one must live somewhere." When he says he is "sick . . . of the accursed present," she agrees "I hate the present," but has the wisdom to add "I don't want the past to take its place."[94] She is determined that they will cultivate a life in their real surroundings, not in a bygone century. Perhaps her family experience, described in *The Rainbow*, motivates her realism. She comes from a salt-of-the-earth farming community, steeped in English blood intimacy, which she left because of its narrow horizons. Disinclined to romanticize Marsh Farm, she is also disinclined to romanticize Austen's England. When she gives the birch chair to another young couple, she symbolically divests Birkin of his imaginary past that threatens to interpose itself between them.

LOVE AS A LAST RESORT

Ursula helps to cure Birkin's masochism, love of humankind, and patriotism. But none of these cures is painless. "A new relation," acknowledges Lawrence, "will always hurt," but, he adds, so will "life."[95] Emerging from his relations with his own illness, with humankind en masse, and with an idealized past, into a fuller "love" with Ursula – no matter how useful it is to make peace with this feeling – cannot but be difficult for Birkin.

Birkin seeks a revivifying intimacy largely because of his and his author's exhaustion with the social world and its grand foundations, such as "love," equality, and authoritarian leaders. But his exhaustion is an habitual pose, a pathology of which Ursula is rightly intolerant. When he says he doesn't "love" so much as "believe in" her – and qualifies even this tepid assertion by adding "if I *do* believe in you" – Ursula dislikes his "relapse into weariness and faithlessness." The language of "relapsing" associates his weariness with sickness. The religious connotation of Birkin's *faith*lessness [my emphasis] raises the stakes of his failure to believe more fully in his beloved. Christian faith may be rejected by the novel, and by its heroine, but Ursula demands a different kind of faith from her partner. When she asks if he finds her "good looking," he responds "I've seen plenty of women . . . I'm sick and weary of seeing them." His use of the word "weary" confirms Ursula's diagnosis of his "relapse," and she responds with a cutting witticism: "I'm sorry I can't oblige you by being invisible."

Such exchanges reiterate his advocacy of impersonal unison (eros), and hers of personal love (agape). By reminding Birkin of her "visibility," Ursula asserts the precedence of her *self* over his weariness with the world and his erotic desire for the "beyond." Ursula hopes for more from love than Russell does, when he discusses couples who are "what is called 'happy,'" but she shares Russell's ironic disregard for mystifications. Although Birkin speaks for his author in craving a new vocabulary for intimacy, Ursula's witticism deflates him. It leaves him taking "no notice of her . . . talking to himself" – self-absorbed, as Rougemont says that erotic lovers are. Birkin's mystical philosophy devolves at such moments into solipsism. "Your womanly feelings," he tells Ursula, "are all bagatelles to me." His own (presumably "manly") feelings should also be "bagatelles," if he is committed to the "impersonal" intimacy of which he speaks, beyond the "emotional, loving plane."[96]

But Ursula resists this conceptual paradigm. She tells Birkin that he is "very conceited," and that he can't know "what [her] womanly feelings are."[97] He had not claimed, of course, to "know" those feelings, but not to care about them. On the "plane" where Ursula prefers to dwell, however, such feelings in either partner are not "bagatelles" but of such importance that she presumes to psychoanalyze him. "I think you want to tell me you love me," she says, "and you go all this way round to do it." He calls her analysis of him "meretricious persiflage," but this only causes her face to relax into laughter, and she interprets it as "a deep confession of love to her." There is far more reason to believe her interpretation than his protestation – and not only because of the numerous occasions on which he uses the word "love." After she says that he loves her, for example, he immediately reverts to his mystic theorizing about the "equilibrium" of "stars." The narrator, speaking through her consciousness, sees his "earnestness" as "ridiculous." She wonders "why drag in the stars?" even as she feels how much she "likes" him – an encapsulation of the ambivalence that underlies their intimacy.[98]

Lawrence's ability to see his own conceptual paradigm, as elaborated by Birkin, as "ridiculous" is crucial to his artistic method. When Birkin invokes Adam as an exemplary male for keeping Eve "like a star in his orbit," Ursula has the proof she needs that "equilibrium" means inequality. "You've given yourself away!" she cries, and he admires her spirited challenge. Unable to "wriggle out" of the contradiction into which he has talked himself, Birkin instead stands "smiling in frustration and amusement and irritation and admiration and love." The narrator's use of the word "love" to sum up Birkin's attitude vindicates what Ursula has been fighting for. Though Birkin thinks the word has been "vulgarized," in this context it gives shape to a range of feelings – "frustration, amusement, irritation, admiration" – encompassing the positive and negative, passing and abiding. "She was so quick," runs the explication of his feeling for her, "and so lambent, like discernible fire, and so vindictive, and so rich in her dangerous flamy sensitiveness." Birkin loves both her positive traits (quickness, lambency, richness) and her ominous ones (vindictiveness, dangerousness). To this set of contradictions he "delivers" himself, and his own vocabulary of "the unknown"[99] is no better at naming the contradictions than Ursula's well-worn term, "love."

But it is one thing for the narrator to describe Birkin as "ridiculous" and to name his feeling "love." It is quite another thing for Birkin to do the latter. Having countered his psychoanalyses of her with hers of him, Ursula launches her decisive assault. "Say you love me, say 'my love' to me," she pleads. In his feminized position of sweet reluctant amorous delay, Birkin "grimly" admits "I love you right enough. But I want it to be something else." Stubborn to the last, he refuses to bow to the old vocabulary. Equally determined, Ursula repeats her imperative, with masculine insistence: "Say 'my love' to me, say it, say it." Birkin enfolds and kisses her, saying "Yes – my love, yes – my love. Let love be enough then. I love you then – I love you. I'm bored by the rest."

This may seem to be a successful assault by Ursula, but Birkin is a cagey tactician. He hedges his bet by claiming to be "bored by the rest" – a partial reversion to his old lethargy, even as he seems enlivened by "love." He doesn't specify what he means by "the rest"; perhaps he refers to his old poses, meaning that he is bored of being bored, weary of weariness. Such an attitude – laden with fatigue – gives scant evidence of a radically transformed man. He murmurs his confession, says the narrator, in a "subtle voice of love, and irony, and submission" – a voice that contradicts itself. Birkin has long feared the "submission" that comes with "love," and his irony protects him against it. To a significant degree, he embraces his *felix culpa* when he owns up, to himself and to Ursula, that he is in love. But he is too stubborn, or too terminally ironic, or too little able to escape from the selfhood he claims to loathe, to capitulate fully. Their quarrels will persist, it seems, as long as their intimacy persists, with Ursula insisting that she should be "enough," and Birkin mourning the loss of "another kind of love" that would have made him "complete, really happy."[100]

Nonetheless, Ursula secures a far-reaching – if less than 100 percent – victory. Birkin begins *Women in Love* embittered, in a spiteful relationship with a cruel woman, determined fundamentally to alter the terms in which sexual intimacy is conceived. When the novel concludes, he is in a revivifying relationship with a woman in whom he perceives a "golden light,"[101] who combines lambency with moral decency, independence from sordid social conventions with appreciation of the traditions of feeling worth preserving. He begins the novel determined not to love, because the emotion is not good enough for him, and ends it very much in love, however tenuous his peace is with the feeling.

Notwithstanding its author's philosophical and political radicalism, *Women in Love* approaches the quandary of modern intimacy in a spirit of ambivalence and of some compromise. Whereas *Mrs Dalloway* endorses Clarissa's choice of Richard, though they arguably love each other too little, *Women in Love* endorses Birkin's partnership with Urusla, though they arguably love each other too much – love being a threat to Birkin's erotic ambitions. Born from Lawrence's quest to forge an authentic intimacy with Frieda, and to spare no self-criticism in doing so, *Women in Love* shows Birkin and Ursula – whatever their capacities for theoretical imagining – desperately seeking one another's commitment in a world of clashing ideals and shaky foundations.

PART III

Domestic angels

CHAPTER 5

Woolf's sane woman in the attic

> Oddly enough, she [Clarissa] was one of the most thoroughgoing sceptics he [Peter] had ever met . . . she said to herself, As we are a doomed race, chained to a sinking ship . . . let us, at any rate, do our part; mitigate the sufferings of our fellow-prisoners; decorate the dungeon with flowers and air cushions . . . she evolved this atheist's religion of doing good for the sake of goodness.
>
> She could see what she lacked . . . something central which permeated; something warm . . . Then, for that moment, she had seen an illumination; a match burning in a crocus; an inner meaning almost expressed.
>
> They had to be together, share with each other, fight with each other, quarrel with each other. But . . . when Evans was killed . . . the panic was on [Septimus] – that he could not feel.[1]

In its ambivalent portrayal of its heroine's marriage, *Mrs Dalloway* provides a crowning example of Bloomsbury's anti-foundational pragmatism – a complex response to the paradoxes of modern life that numerous Bloomsburian texts share with other major modernist works. Conrad's *Heart of Darkness* and Freud's *Civilization and Its Discontents* both expose the absence of a foundation (natural or god-given) where a foundation would give comfort, but hold out civilization – a product of human artifice – as a surrogate refuge. Conrad's Marlow analyzes threats internal to a civilized society and individual. Bitterly aware of the hypocrisies on which the "whited sepulchre's" contract is founded, Marlow nonetheless holds fast to the "saving illusion" of civilization's decency, lest he become another Kurtz – or Septimus Smith.[2] Clarissa holds fast to her union with Richard, though hardly unaware of his limitations, or of Sally's and Peter's appeals. *Civilization and Its Discontents*, which postdates *Mrs Dalloway* by five years, asserts that civilization exacts neurosis as a price of membership. Freud accepts neuroses, rather like Marlow accepts disingenuousness, as a necessary and fair price.

The anti-foundationalism *Mrs Dalloway* shares with these texts shows in its treatment of marriage. Clarissa's love for Peter and memory of Sally's kiss explode any notion of female desire being monogamous and heterosexual, of marriage and its obligations being "naturally" suited to women. In part, *Mrs Dalloway* also shares the pragmatic conservatism of these two texts, evincing support not only for the Dalloway marriage, but also for Clarissa's traditionally feminine role within it – despite the marriage's lack of foundational support. But only in part. Woolf's elusive, protean tone slips, almost imperceptibly, from sympathy to judgment, even to satire. In its less sanguine passages, the novel suggests that Clarissa's marriage (and its mirror, Septimus's) has been a self-betrayal. Ultimately, neither judgment of the Dalloway marriage – and thus neither general thematic suggestion about marriage itself – wins *Mrs Dalloway*'s full support. Rather, the novel's moral energy tugs in competing directions, toward two compelling but irreconcilable judgments of Clarissa's exclusive partnership forged in the face of competing loves.

According to the pragmatic reading, the potential threats to the Dalloway union (Sally and Peter) ultimately redound to its credit. Unlike Sally's love – a passing late-adolescent enthusiasm – Richard's lasts, albeit in its feebler, clumsier way. Unlike Peter's love, Richard's is not oppressive. It provides Clarissa with space, both physically (a room and ominously narrow bed of her own) and psychically (in which to work through her problems, to live a private life). Far from a "dungeon," the privacy of its attic room notwithstanding, Clarissa's household can always be decorated with flowers; it is where her "atheist's religion" of life-love finds its fullest expression.[3]

Further, according to the pragmatic reading, the value of marriage shines in contrast to the other social praxes – psychiatry and religion – that *Mrs Dalloway* repudiates. Whatever his buffoonery, Richard is not Dr Bradshaw nor Doris Kilman; the comforts he provides are not their torments. His flaws bolster the novel's pragmatic argument: though marriage entails disappointments, it is one institution, one social refuge – in the wake of the Great War's dislocations, and in spite of (or in *light* of) the heart's polymorphous desires – deserving of loyalty. The passions that may have threatened Clarissa Parry or Clarissa Walsh's psychic equilibrium are effectively compartmentalized by Clarissa Dalloway.

Finally, according to this sanguine line of interpretation, the heroine's healthful compartmentalizing is aided by the novel's compartmentalization – its bipartite rendering of the Clarissa–Septimus struggle to remain sane. The death of the "scapegoat" Septimus,[4] on such a reading, is a ritual sacrifice, helping the heroine to cope with her various traumas, without succumbing either to rage or to melancholia.[5]

But has Clarissa's psychological compartmentalization been as effective as such optimistic readings hope? Ample evidence suggests that the heroine not only loved, but continues to love, Peter more than her husband. And the dystopic dimensions of the Dalloway marriage do not end there. *Mrs Dalloway* may be a *memento mori* not just for victims of the War, but for lost homoerotic possibilities, suggested in the latter two epigraphs to this chapter. The match in the crocus – in a different, freer society – might have ignited Clarissa into a more passionate and confident woman. Should a deep connection be inferred between the illness in her heart and the lesbian desire she has largely suppressed for three decades?

Such an inference might seem arbitrary, if Septimus's tragedy did not mirror Clarissa's in its deepest psychosexual dimensions. Read merely as war trauma, Septimus's apparent inability to feel could result from delayed shell shock, as Bradshaw speculates. But Bradshaw is hardly trustworthy, and the depth of Septimus's attachment to Evans suggests anything but an inability to feel. Clarissa and Septimus, on the dystopic reading, have both lost an object of passionate same-sex love: she to social convention, he to death. Each has retreated, in the wake of this socially proscribed sexual–emotional possibility, into a legal, heterosexual union that cannot be fulfilling. The two psychic halves of the one protagonist are left with only improper places (their stunted memories) for their most central passions. Septimus can be read as an end in himself, as more than a functional figure in Clarissa's drama, whose death sustains her life. On such a reading, his suicide is not only horrific in its own right, but a foreshadowing of one possible future for Clarissa. Septimus, after all, is blessed with a spouse even more solicitous than hers. But his suffering, psychosexual and otherwise, overcomes him: he succumbs to the disintegration that always threatens the heroine, sexually compromised like him.

Which reading – the pragmatic or dystopic – finds more support in the text? Critics disagree, both in psychological and in cultural–political terms. Lucio Ruotolo reads Richard as a good husband for Clarissa, who permits her the "unguarded moments" that promise psychic health, and that mark Clarissa's transformation from an object of satire in the sketch "Mrs Dalloway in Bond Street" to one of sympathy in the novel.[6] Conversely, Elizabeth Abel sees civilization's resounding discontents, for a bisexual woman such as Clarissa, epitomized in Peter Walsh's masculine intervention, his violent breaking of the tender moment – never to be repeated – between Clarissa and Sally. Indeed, Peter's intervention operates like a concretization of the immaterial forces of repression (social codes, the superego) delineated in *Civilization and Its Discontents*. Shirley Neuman expands Abel's reading, interpreting *Mrs Dalloway* as a revision of *Heart of Darkness*, fearful of the many "specters of domination" in a patriarchal civilization. According to Neuman, "horror" permeates Woolf's novel as thoroughly as Conrad's, condensing most painfully in Peter's intrusion.[7] I aim to synthesize the insights of both critical camps into Woolf's portrayal of the Dalloway marriage, within the context of the reinvention of intimacy.

SEXOLOGY AND ANTI-ESSENTIALISM

The reinvention of intimacy had numerous interrelated components, from increases in the frequency of marriage and divorce to redefinitions of sexuality to anxieties about women's proper marital and social roles.[8] These tumultuous developments held perils for many, but also promises – for feminists, gays, and others enjoying their liberation from Victorian mores, their increased freedom of movement by automobile and train,[9] and their freedom as consumers in a burgeoning market (with airplanes tracing advertisements in the sky and radical experimentation transforming the arts). New forms of intimacy emerged between well-to-do husbands and wives living in smaller families with fewer servants than their Victorian forebears,[10] and between same-sex couples testing the fluid boundaries of friendship and romance. Individuals such as Clarissa Dalloway struggled to see their intimate lives as narratives over which they could exert control, as self-authoring subjects. Confluent with these emerging conceptions of intimacy and the self, myriad currents of reactionary and liberatory energies swept through popular and high culture, vying to define the national sentiment. *Mrs Dalloway* plunges into contemporary debates with a combination of philosophical radicalism, social pragmatism, and intimations of nihilistic despair.

The novel's philosophical radicalism lies in two areas: its broadly Freudian conception of sexuality, and its representation of Clarissa's decentered self-authorship in love. Its political ambivalence – its vacillation between sympathetic and satiric regard of the marriage and Clarissa's role within it – can be traced in its protean tone. Throughout its vacillations, however, and suggesting that its pragmatic support of the marriage carries decisive weight, *Mrs Dalloway* maintains a core liberal and Bloomsburian value in the sanctity that it grants Clarissa's private life.

In its radical conception of (bi)sexuality, the novel resonates with sexology and psychoanalysis, as a critique of two intertwined prejudices against homosexuality, one philosophical and one moral. The philosophical prejudice, treated at length in Freud's *Three Essays* (1905), assigns a reproductive teleology to sexual desire. According to the prejudice, sexual desires that diverge from this purpose – chief among them, same-sex desires – are unnatural. Unnaturalness, abnormality, and moral despicability (even criminality) get yoked together, as the philosophical urge to classify and essentialize slides into a moral urge to normalize.[11] Homosexual desire can be no less "natural" than heterosexual desire, Freud argues, if normal, genital-based adolescent heterosexual desire is itself a conglomerate of multiple infantile desires, which are combined in the process of coming to sexual maturity, and can come apart in analysis as well as in practice. Since all sexual subjects are polymorphously perverse, the idea of "normal" desires (whose object is the opposite sex, and whose aim is genital) being "natural" seems hollow.

Even the concept of "normality" – defined as monogamous heterosexuality – gives way to the Freudian and sexological critique. Memoirs, case studies, and other research compiled by Edward Carpenter, Havelock Ellis, J. A. Symonds, Karl Ulrichs, Richard von Krafft-Ebing, Iwan Bloch, and others reveal a range of "perversions" to be far more widespread than common assumptions would allow.[12] The line between normality and abnormality blurs.

Thus Freud and his precursors assault the philosophical prejudices against same-sex and other "perverse" desires. For many of Woolf's contemporaries, the "scientific" prejudices against bisexuality and abnormal desires (with their specious invocations of "naturalness") and the moral prejudices (with their accusations of degeneracy) fell together. But such was not the case for the self-hating homosexual Otto Weininger, whose 1903 *Sex and Character* argues that all people abide in a permanent bisexual condition, with vestigial traits of the other sex (visible in men's nipples and women's facial hair), but that such traits should be engineered out of their personalities, so that the Platonic types of man and woman can be realized in society. Weininger's combination of anti-essentialism and reactionary politics exaggerates the divisions between radical psychology and conservative social thought in texts such as *Women in Love*, and illustrates the range of possible responses to the new century's increasingly visible homosexual culture. *Mrs Dalloway*'s pragmatic embrace of marriage, in the face of its explosively post-Victorian conception of sexuality, parallels Weininger's ambivalence in some ways, though of course Woolf's pragmatism lacks his vicious prejudice. To other establishment and anti-establishment thinkers, to critics on the right and the left, the reinvention of intimacy presented similar conundrums.

Woolf's novel enters these debates, first of all, by depicting sexuality, in the spirit of sexology, as a dense and dynamic phenomenon. Its heroine exemplifies Weininger's theory of permanent bisexuality: Clarissa is a tangle of paradoxes, masculine and feminine at once. Her posture is repeatedly described as upright; she "stiffens," waiting for a van to pass; she slices "like a knife through everything," recalling the phallic symbol associated with Peter; if she "could have had her life over again," she thinks, "she would have been . . . interested in politics like a man; very dignified"; she sees her face in the mirror as "pointed, dart-like, definite," and her own personality as "rigid."[13] When Peter brandishes his pocket knife, she counters with a sequence of two rival phalluses: scissors and then a needle, for mending her dress.[14] These images represent only the beginning of the masculine-Clarissa motif. Yet she derives her greatest joys from attending to the domestic sphere: shopping, organizing a party, receiving flowers from her husband. She loves, in turn – or wonders whether she loves – three people: two men and Sally; and Sally had been interested in politics like a man, with her socialistic utopianism, her interest in Plato and Shelley, her guidance of Clarissa's reading. All of these romantic relations cast Clarissa in a feminine light.

Such a feminine light, moreover, flatters female characters, considering how two women cast in a masculine light – Millicent Bruton, with her "erect," "ramrod bearing,"[15] and manly interest in politics; Doris Kilman, with her unbridled lesbian desire and domineering sanctimony – seem monstrous for it. Their very names – "brute" and "kill" – suggest the violence and horror with which the novel frequently associates such masculine womanliness. At times, *Mrs Dalloway* approaches the antipathy to such women that Ursula expresses toward homosexuality when she calls it a "perversity,"[16] that Lawrence expresses when he compares effeminate Bloomsburian men to "beetles,"[17] and that Weininger expresses generally toward men and women who diverge from his Platonic ideals. How, then, could any masculine woman in *Mrs Dalloway* not bear some taint of Kilman's monstrosity; how could androgyny, in any female character, not be frightening?

Beyond the playful contradictions of Clarissa's upright housewifeliness, for example, numerous passages suggest that her traces of androgyny reveal a frozen state of development.[18] "Fear no more the heat of the sun," Clarissa counsels herself more than once, as if, in preparing for mortality, she continues her decades-long avoidance of heat and passion, of the *élan vital*. She remembers, "through some contraction of this cold spirit, [having] failed [Richard] . . . again and again."[19] Peter calls her "cold, heartless, a prude."[20] In a private tirade, she excoriates love as scathingly as religion: "Love and religion! thought Clarissa . . . how detestable they are!"[21] This sounds suspiciously like the language of a woman in retreat.

Septimus Smith's androgyny carries similar suggestions of arrested development or maladjustment. On the one hand, his metaphorically feminine qualities speak well to his compassion and gentleness: his Christ-like suffering, his concern for the trees, his participation with Rezia in making hats. On the other hand, though, it is during his states of most severe distraction – bordering on disintegration – that these feminine qualities emerge most intensely. They are anything but signs of what *A Room of One's Own* calls a genius's "incandescent mind," possessed of male and female brilliance in healthy equilibrium.[22]

But the unsettling cases of Clarissa and Septimus do not constitute the novel's final judgment on androgyny, as Sally Seton demonstrates. Sally's sexual bravado (running naked down halls), her voracious intellectual daring as a reader of political philosophy (implicitly a rebuke to the drawing-room Victorian female), her brandishing of a cigar (a symbol no subtler than Peter's knife) can at worst be called childish, and at best intoxicating. Feminine and masculine traits circulate in and out of both male and female characters in *Mrs Dalloway*, carrying wildly divergent moral connotations, depending on circumstances: such is the essence of the novel's sexual anti-essentialism.

Nor is Sally the only woman whose psychic contradictions are admirable. Clarissa, the same woman whom Peter calls "cold" and who terms love "detestable," treasures the sensation of the match burning in the crocus as a precious gift. Merely entering a florist's shop surrounds her with metaphorical heat, as "every flower seems to burn by itself, softly, purely." The *élan vital* surges through her, in the midst of "delphiniums, sweet peas, bunches of lilac . . . masses of carnations . . . roses, irises" – a collective image of overwhelming, feminized fecundity.[23] The same heroine is not only masculine and feminine by turns, but hot and cold by turns. So fluid, moreover, are the connotations that *Mrs Dalloway* attaches to any trait, that even coldness can be associated with sexual possibility: Clarissa "could remember going cold with excitement" at the thought of Sally's proximity, "and doing her hair in a kind of ecstasy . . . with the rooks flaunting up and down in the pink evening light."[24] Paradoxes saturate descriptions of her sexuality, whether at the level of one-word motifs or extended passages.

The celebrated attic scene highlights Clarissa's irresolvable contradictions,[25] as well as the novel's commitment to paradox and fluidity, not merely as stylistic gestures, but as epistemological paths. At midday, says the narrator, "women must put off their rich apparel."[26] But no unitary essence lies beneath the "apparel," however tantalizing its "putting off" may be. Next to Clarissa's bed, perhaps the initial clue to her sexuality, lies Marbot's *Memoirs*, into which she has "read deep[ly]" – the modifier "deep" suggesting her own psychological reaches. Even this initial clue is opaque. Marbot's military account might stir Clarissa's thwarted masculine impulses. Or it might be a daydream only, a longed-for but impossible release from the femininity that imprisons Clarissa because it constitutes her. Further complicating the paradox, the narrator specifies Marbot's "retreat from Moscow."[27] "Retreat" carries negative connotations, and suggests that Clarissa's self-removal to the attic may reveal her own weakness. Yet, in a novel of consciousness such as *Mrs Dalloway*, an inheritor of Jane Austen and George Eliot's tradition of moral growth via introspection, what could be nobler than a scene of such extensive self-reckoning – complete with a moment before a mirror – than Clarissa's time with her reading and herself?[28]

Yet the central insight yielded by her introspection – the match in the crocus – refuses fixed meaning. Clarissa can tell herself, "No, the words ['She is beneath this roof!'] meant absolutely nothing to her now. She could not even get an echo of her old emotion." But immediately thereafter, Clarissa will feel "the old feeling . . . come back, as she . . . began to do her hair" – the image of doing her hair linking her present palpitations to her "ecstasy" at Bourton, where the rooks flaunted.[29] Much of the attic scene's retrospective narration suggests the authenticity of the "old feeling," and Clarissa's evasiveness in denying it. "All that evening [at Bourton] she could not take her eyes off Sally" – very like a woman in love. "They sat up till all hours of the night talking"[30] – very like two women in love. But Sally's reappearance, thirty-three years later, as a rotund mother pleased with herself and her five boys, suggests how dispensable to her, in the long run, was "the most exquisite moment of [Clarissa's] whole life."[31] Perhaps, then, the moment should be dispensable to Clarissa too; perhaps her marriage is where she belongs psychologically; perhaps only a man could satisfy her as a permanent partner. The moment in the garden, "exquisite" as it was, may reveal nothing permanent or necessary about her sexuality.

Freud argues, after all, that the sex instinct is not unitary, but that healthy equilibrium can be achieved when desires assume "normal," heterosexual objects and aims.[32] Nowhere is the multiplicity of Clarissa's mind better demonstrated than in its fluctuating choice of sexual object, "sometimes yielding to the charm of a woman ... confessing, as to her they often did, some scrape, some folly ... she did undoubtedly then feel what men felt."[33]

"Undoubtedly" is a strong word to describe a mind so fluid; perhaps Clarissa's longing for close, confessional – erotic – contact with a woman is, after all, a perdurable feature of her psyche. In this case, a lifelong monogamous commitment – morally, emotionally, and juridically speaking – to one man might make sense for her only as an adjustment to rigid bourgeois conventions. It might constitute a self-betrayal, condoned by the author – if at all – only from a sense of its necessity.

Can a heroine be right not to have pursued a woman she admires, who bestowed on her a "present ... infinitely precious"[34] of fuller self-awareness? Can she be right not to have married a man she loves more than her husband? Such questions haunt the novel, though they are impossible to phrase satisfactorily, since they beg other questions, in endless regress. Asserting whom she loves most authentically requires a definition of love, yet Clarissa worries over this term. "But this question of ... falling in love with women," Clarissa wonders in the attic, "take ... her relation in the old days with Sally Seton. Had that not, after all, been love?"[35] The narrator marshals considerable evidence that the answer is Yes, and bolsters this evidence with a rhetorical question – "what was this except being in love?"[36] – but provides no definite answer. Richard's heart fairly bursts with feeling as he hands roses to his wife, and much seems to be communicated on an unspoken level – but the words "I love you" announce themselves only by their absence.[37] Wilde's love dared not speak its name in its time; while numerous shades of love – including some that are socially acceptable – inspire *Mrs Dalloway*, its characters nonetheless have continual difficulty speaking the name of their hearts' desires. Their inarticulateness implicitly chastens readers who would formulate definite distinctions between the characters' true, and their misguided, affections.

This principle of uncertainty applies both to Septimus and to Clarissa. Whether Rezia is a fit partner for Septimus can never be fully ascertained. That she is unable to prevent his disintegration may testify only to the powerful combination of forces, including war trauma, which he cannot overcome. In this context of contingency and necessarily limited knowledge, the burden of proof, where the Dalloway marriage is concerned, lies more heavily on its detractors than on its supporters. Septimus disintegrates and Clarissa does not; the question "why" presumes at least some credit to her marriage. We know, after all, how valuable her privacy is to Clarissa, how stingy Peter would likely have been in granting it to her, and how generous (perhaps unthinkingly) Richard is. We know how dearly Woolf wanted women, especially women artists, to have rooms of their own in which to imagine, and the financial means to do so, unhampered by fear or bitterness. Admittedly, Woolf hoped women could find such means independent of matrimony;[38] and, admittedly, Clarissa is not a writer. But the hostess-heroine is an artist figure, and her marriage provides her not only the means to host, but also the space in which to imagine herself into being, the opportunity continually to renarrate her own life story.

Even beyond her self-invention, we sense – in the care she dedicates to giving a party for important people, in the delight she takes in masses of flowers, the concern she demonstrates for the food she'll serve, for her table settings, her dress – how important material comforts are to her well-being. (The same seems true for the older Sally, despite her dashing youthful brush with penury.) We recognize – from the repeated mentions of her heart, her illness – how vulnerable Clarissa is, how in need of protection and stability (financial, social, etc.). We sense that her capacity for passionate attachment carries seeds of danger as well as seeds of ecstasy and self-discovery. We recognize how many of her basic needs only Richard can meet. Finally, the historical conditions attending *Mrs Dalloway*'s conception suggest some likely motive on the part of the author – psychically frail herself, dependent on a husband for comfort and stability, perhaps not eager to court society's scorn as a radical in every way – for supporting marriage on both pragmatic and moral grounds.

THE VALUE OF MARRIAGE

In the 1920s, the nuclear family emerged as a social norm, yet it was a difficult time for such families. The war left one-third of England's young men deranged or dead. Divorce rates rose for familiar war-related reasons.[39] Popular presses responded to these disturbing facets of post-war life with a vigorous defense of conservative, family values. Gender discourses, even within feminism, tended to exaggerate, rather than downplay, differences between the sexes.[40] On a political extreme, eugenics movements declared the protection of marriage to be a primary goal.[41] Among more conventional forms of activism, motherhood campaigns sprang up in answer to declining population growth.[42]

Given the broad resurgence of traditional values, the 1920s were not a propitious time for a writer – particularly one associated with Bloomsbury – to be perceived as hostile to marriage and family.[43] Such an environment was better suited to the non-radical, even pro-establishment, strains in Woolf's temperament. For her as for Forster, the political did not necessarily equal the personal: categories including "suffragette," "homosexual," "feminist," and perhaps even "woman," with whatever crude accuracy they may have described someone's sympathy with a cause, were nevertheless felt as impositions on the imaginations of iconoclastic artists who "[did] not believe in Belief."[44] In place of "Belief" in impersonal causes, however enlightened, Forster and Woolf – and characters of theirs, from Rickie Elliot and Margaret Schlegel to Orlando and Clarissa – substituted "personal relations"[45] and self-narration, with its inevitable psychosexual lacunae.

With the expansion of economic and educational opportunities, Victorian families evolved from large, materially beleaguered groups toward the modern nuclear family. Since the 1880s, use of contraception had expanded and the influence of evangelism had waned; English women married in 1925 – the year of *Mrs Dalloway*'s publication – had, on average, 2.21 children. They had space and time, such as their mothers and grandmothers could not have conceived, to make their married, their private and intimate lives, a subject of free speculation, self-assertion, doubt, and reconsideration.[46] As the bourgeoisie more often graduated to rooms of its own, it developed a desperate commitment to privacy[47] – even while sex gradually became a topic of wider public discussion. Introspective late-Victorians and moderns came face to face with sexual desires – including perverse ones – as defining features of self.

Admittedly, much suggests that Woolf's sexually ambiguous heroine is beleaguered, that her self-narration is no tale of liberation. The novel's opening sentence – "Mrs Dalloway said she would buy the flowers herself"[48] – introduces her as a married subject. Only three sentences later is "Clarissa" supplied as the name of the missing self beneath the wife. Her name indicates not only to the reader, but to Clarissa herself, how insubstantial, in her married state, her own identity has become. The heroine ponders herself "being . . . invisible," her "being Mrs Dalloway; not even Clarissa any more; this being Mrs Richard Dalloway."[49] Three decades prior to this episode of de-realization, her father Justin Parry had hovered over her adolescent – and life-altering – adventures in intimacy, parrying Sally's charm with his disapproval of her improprieties, and also warding off his daughter's first male suitor. "I often wish I'd got on better with your father," the older Peter ominously tells Clarissa. She replies, biting her tongue for saying it, "But he never liked anyone who – our friends," suggesting the full extent of the blocking role played by the father.[50] The given name "Justin" – perhaps an ironic play on the justice he did not mete out to Clarissa – appears in conjunction with "Parry," but the first and last names "Clarissa Parry" never appear together. At the level of her name, the heroine has been exiled from a family in whose identity she never fully shared, into a marriage that subsumes her into its corporate whole.

Clarissa, furthermore, is riddled with blind spots and evasions, suggesting her weaknesses and withdrawals to be both physical and psychic. Peter's absence from her household has not left him absent from her thoughts; she has never ceased pondering the life she might have lived with him. Thus, "she would still find herself arguing in St. James's Park, still making out that she had been right – and she had too – not to marry him."[51] The curious interjection of support ("and she had too") – from the omniscient narrator? speaking on behalf of the community? from a different part of Clarissa's mind than the rest of the sentence describes? – serves more to highlight the fragmentary nature of her internal argument than to suggest its hope of being resolved.

Therefore, married though she be, she is not beyond jealousy at the thought of losing Peter to another woman: "she had borne about with her for years like an arrow sticking in her heart the grief, the anguish; and then the horror" of the news of his marriage.[52] That his own (rumored) betrothal, so many years after hers, should strike her as a violent assault upon her heart says more about her emotional susceptibility than about his recklessness. Therefore, she treats him with a combination of effrontery and affection (the former reminiscent of Millicent Bruton), mentioning her party "Which I shan't ask you to," then addressing him as "My dear Peter," and achieving the "delicious" effect for which the salutation is intended.[53] Her confusing treatment of him mirrors her internal confusion and forgetfulness: "Now I remember how impossible it was ever to make up my mind – and why did I make up my mind – not to marry him?"[54]

Nor is she forgetful only where such large questions are concerned. When the door first opens on Peter's visit, "for a single second she could not remember what he was called! so surprised she was to see him, so glad, so shy . . . to have [him come] unexpectedly."[55] How could she have forgotten the name of a man who haunts her thoughts, and whom even Sally thought she should have married? Claims to have been "surprised" and "shy" at his arrival are transparently disingenuous. Peter's visit is "unexpected" only because "she had not read his letter."[56] That the precise moment of his visit catches her off guard is plausible, but that the existence of his letter fails to warn her of his likely and imminent visit is not. Her avoidance of his letter reveals her forgetting of his name to be far from innocent. Beleaguered by external forces, Clarissa is also a victim of her own repression.

She dissociates not only from the man who would have been her husband, but also from the daily life of the man who is her husband. "She cared much more for her roses than for the Armenians,"[57] reports the narrator, in a satirical tone reminiscent of "Mrs Dalloway in Bond Street" – but a satire that retains affection for a heroine who loves her husband for his "adorable, divine simplicity." The affection dissipates, however, and Clarissa comes to seem more deserving of the appellative "simple" than her spouse: "Hunted out of existence, maimed, frozen . . . no, she could feel nothing for the Albanians, or was it the Armenians? but she loved her roses (didn't that help the Armenians?)"[58] At times, the novel's satirical treatment of Clarissa justifies Millicent Bruton's condescending attitude toward her. *Mrs Dalloway* suggests that Doris Kilman may be correct to interpret Clarissa's weaknesses of character sociologically, to assign the hostess to "the most worthless of all classes – the rich, with a smattering of culture . . . expensive things everywhere."[59]

The heroine, in other words, does not deserve credit for confronting her own crises of intimacy, and negotiating her familial and social role, with clairvoyant introspection and heroic political awareness. But a reading that focused only on her satirical treatment, and not her valorization, would be incomplete. Clarissa's determined pursuit of joy, her compassion for herself and others, her capacity for self-examination and philosophical wonder, and her ability to feel a range of emotions, even painful ones, all confer nobility upon her self-conceptions – despite their blind spots and dissociations. Since these character strengths flourish within the context of her marriage, they also suggest a positive answer to the question Sally poses to Peter at the party, the question upon which so much of the novel's moral weight rests: "And the marriage had been . . . a success?"[60] Though Septimus's union with Rezia, by contrast, does not achieve equal long-term success, this fact need not amount to a negative authorial judgment on marriage per se. It may instead be an admission that marriage can only perform so much of a pragmatic function, contain and help heal so much grief.

AN INDEPENDENT WIFE

The heroine's determination to live joyously announces itself at the beginning of her adventure. "Mrs Dalloway said she would buy the flowers herself," opens the novel. Her first act is not merely physical, but one of self-description, of saying what she will do. So she "plunge[s]" – a verb of great adventurous spirit – into her day.[61] Her own doors being unhinged in preparation for her current party remind her of door hinges at Bourton squeaking, and intimate the danger of Clarissa herself becoming unhinged.[62] Her plunge is all the braver because it entails psychological risk. The mobile narrator begins the novel largely in Clarissa's mind, making no ironic interjections; but implicitly endorsing and ennobling Clarissa's venture.[63] The heroine's self-fashioning, in the opening scene, is marked by her ecstasy, a response to daily experience at once poignant and admirable for its willed quality, its suggestion of Clarissa's psychic complexity, with one part of her encouraging another into joy.

Her determination to celebrate her marriage and her life reaches philosophical – nearly religious – proportions on multiple occasions. In a moment of self-doubt, wondering whether she should have married Peter, she imagines herself a child and grown woman at once, "coming to her parents . . . holding her life in her arms which, as she neared them, grew larger and larger in her arms, until it became a whole life, a complete life, which she put down by them and said 'This is what I have made of it! This!'"[64] Her sense that her life is not merely a given, but something to be "made," secures her footing as a modern heroine, an artist of more than just the hostess's realm.

Nor is her life-artistry lacking in intellectual rigor, whatever the deficiencies of her geographical knowledge. In a moment of super-personal doubt, she determines "to go deeper, beneath what people said (and their judgments, how superficial, how fragmentary they are!)." She shows her determination to be not only emotional (her willed ecstasy) but also intellectual (skeptical, iconoclastic): "in her own mind now, what did it mean to her, this thing she called life? . . . Here was So-and-so in South Kensington; some one up in Bayswater; and somebody else, say, in Mayfair. And she felt quite continuously a sense of their existence . . . and she felt only if they could be brought together; so she did it. And it was an offering . . . for the sake of offering, perhaps."[65]

The "life" motif in Clarissa's thinking links her to her author. From her diary entries to her long and short fiction, Woolf continually returns to the elusive subject of "life." For her it is no meaningless abstraction, but the energy, or principle, which it is the novelist's duty to capture; the failure of modern fiction lies, as much as anything, in its insufficient interest in this subject.[66] Clarissa seeks directly what Woolf seeks – as a matter of high aesthetic–moral principle – to represent. Moreover, Clarissa seeks it in a manner deserving of rich approbation, by Bloomsburian lights.

She seeks life, first of all, on atheistic grounds. As she bows her head "beneath the influence [of life]," she refuses false ontology: "not for a moment did she believe in God; but all the more, she thought . . . must one repay in daily life."[67] Atheism was central to Bloomsbury; not only as a dogma but as a sensibility, it separated them from their pious but – in their view – less spiritually sensitive ancestors. Numerous studies have noted Bloomsburians' paradoxical unworldly worldliness – with their atheism and hard work as artists constituting their worldliness, but their mysticism, their commitment to the private and intimate, marking them as unworldly. Many Victorians, by contrast, including some of Bloomsbury's parents, were marked by worldly unworldliness, with their protestations of religiosity (glum and largely hypocritical, in their children's eyes) constituting their would-be unworldliness, and their keen interest in politics and social position – combined with their obliviousness to aesthetic values – revealing their deep-set, imaginatively impoverished worldliness.[68] In her capacity for religious sentiment – in its most rapturous sense, before the physical splendors of London and daily life – without the comfort of false dogma, Clarissa demonstrates a worldly unworldliness that would make any Bloomsburian proud. "What she loved," says the narrator, "was this, here, now, in front of her,"[69] the sequence of deictics demonstrating Clarissa's power to immerse herself in the present.

Her resolution to make offerings for the sake of offerings, or in Peter's words, to do good for the sake of goodness (see the first epigraph to this chapter), echoes G. E. Moore. *Principia*'s final chapter, despite the absence of philosophical foundations, confidently promotes friendship and art as two of life's greatest goods. Although Clarissa also lacks the support of a foundation or dogma, theological or personal, she feels impelled to "repay,"[70] indicating – at least at the level of impulse – how generous her approach to life can be.

Clarissa also seeks life, to her further credit, in the otherness of others. "There she was," concludes the novel, in a celebration of Clarissa's radiance in the eyes of Sally and especially Peter.[71] She radiates otherness to onlookers: she is wholly herself, extant beyond category. "It is Clarissa," Peter says, and there is nothing more for the omniscient narrator to say, other than to concur with Peter's appreciation of Clarissa's irreducibility.[72] How fitting, given her power to inspire such a reaction in Peter and Sally, that Clarissa should apprehend other people with a generous awareness of their uniqueness. She feels "quite continuously a sense of [the] existence" of people in Bayswater and elsewhere.[73] At her party, she sees her guests and thinks "there was Professor Brierly" or "there was old Aunt Helena,"[74] foreshadowing the language with which Peter will note her appearance soon later. The Dalloway marriage enables both partners to flourish in their separateness, as a Walsh marriage likely would not; Clarissa's approach to life grants the same boon to many.

For her such an approach stems not only from instinct, but from principle. "Why creeds and prayers," she wonders, watching her neighbor move away from the window, "when . . . that's the miracle, that's the mystery; that old lady, she meant, whom she could see going from chest of drawers to dressing table . . . The supreme mystery which Kilman might say she had solved . . . was simply this: here was one room, there another."[75] Clarissa's atheism, in keeping with Bloomsbury's ethos, aims to encompass a greater sense of mystery, a greater sensitivity to a variety of traditionally religious sensations and insights, than institutional religion would often encourage. Existence, precisely in its diversity, strikes her as miraculous, in a way no fossilized creed could express. The "rooms" that she and her neighbor separately occupy stand for the unique importance inherent in each of their lives.

So morally conscientious is this atheist-heroine that she battles against her own dislike of Kilman and her sanctimonious "creed." Clarissa accuses herself harshly: "It rasped her, though, to have stirring about in her this brutal monster . . . this hatred, which . . . made all pleasure in beauty, in friendship, in being well . . . quiver."[76] She recognizes how moral attitudes (dislike) and aesthetic possibilities (for pleasure, beauty) interpenetrate. So she redirects her thought patterns, in the manner of an Austen or Eliot protagonist engaged in the noblest self-reckoning. "For it was not her [Kilman] one hated," muses Woolf's conscientious heroine, "but the idea of her, which undoubtedly had gathered into itself a great deal that was not Miss Kilman."[77] Given Doris's unappealing qualities, and the threat she represents to Clarissa's relationship with Elizabeth, such self-correction on Clarissa's part – separating her judgment of an individual from the individual in question – demonstrates an impressive moral composure.

The large number of judgmental characters in the novel – Sally and Peter, Kilman and Bruton, Holmes, Justin Parry, even passers-by on the street, guests at the party – reveals the rarity of Clarissa's virtue, and suggests Richard's virtue as well. One of the novel's least judgmental characters, Richard suits his conscientious wife well as a mate. On the rare occasion when he takes a strong dislike, he reveals his perspicacity, as well as his agreement with his wife's and the novel's moral attitude: Clarissa "did not know what it was – about Sir William [Bradshaw]; what exactly she disliked. Only Richard agreed with her, 'didn't like his taste, didn't like his smell.'"[78] The convergence of perceptions between husband and wife, where such a crucial villain as Bradshaw is concerned, speaks well for their marriage, and confirms the gift Clarissa claims of "knowing people almost by instinct."[79]

Her combination of accurate instinct and the capacity for self-correction largely mitigates her snobbery, and suggests that her decisions pertaining to human relations – such as her choice of husband – may well be wise, whatever her difficulty in articulating their rationale. In fact, though she may struggle to recall why she did not marry Peter – much as she "[does] not know" what disturbs her about Bradshaw – Peter confirms the fitness of her decision.[80] "But it would not have been a success, their marriage," he thinks in his hotel room. "The other thing, after all, came so much more naturally" – i.e., his attractiveness to women and the ease with which "some girl without a grain of sense could twist him round her finger."[81] The whiff of scandal attached to Peter's pursuit of a divorce for Daisy only intensifies, by contrast, the respectability of the Dalloways' marriage.

Whatever the value of Clarissa's inarticulate instincts, her self-definition requires skills of introspection and articulation. The attic scene, already discussed, reveals her range of curiosity about herself, others, and the meanings of her interactions with them. Among the many movements of her mind in the attic, the following seven – three concerning Sally, two concerning Peter, and two concerning herself – reveal her introspective rigor. Clarissa struggles to define love by reference to specific experience. "Had not that . . . been love?" she wonders.[82] She attempts to recall what Sally was really like, with her "amazing gift . . . personality."[83] She struggles to define the nature of her "love" – if that was indeed her feeling – for Sally. Was it actually as "disinterested" as Clarissa claims? Was it a clue – is it still a clue – to the different nature of Clarissa's feelings for men and for women? That Clarissa does not answer these questions points more to their insolubility than to her incapacity. Moving to the subject of Peter, Clarissa begins by resenting his intrusion on the Sally kiss. But then she immediately recalls how much she "owe[s]" her erstwhile suitor.[84] Her mind revolves, characteristically, from judgment of another – even where that other has been in the wrong – to compassion and gratitude. Likewise, in the novel's initial scene, the heroine thinks that she and Peter "might be parted for hundreds of years," but still "some days, some sights" could "bring him back to her calmly, without . . . bitterness."[85] From alienation to connection with others – and back again to separation – Clarissa's mind moves, as she moves, an individual in society, largely constituted by her relations with others, but at the same time irreducibly herself. Finally, in the attic, having given thought to Sally and Peter, she gives thought to herself. Looking in the mirror, she acknowledges – bravely, perceptively – how fictional her social self is, "how incompatible and composed so for the world only into one center."[86] Having made an effort to compose her reflected self, she wonders "Now where was her dress?"[87] She proceeds to mend the garment, a symbolic act of repairing into a coherent whole the social self that she knows to be a fiction. Without the comfort of a false ontology – a belief in a unified psyche – she bravely descends the stairs to greet the world again.

The attic scene encapsulates the heroine's intelligence as a self-authoring, morally responsible lover and woman. She regards Sally, Peter, and herself kindly, but without being uncritical. Sally, she thinks, was once, but is no longer, an object of her desire. Peter can be rude and egotistical – even to the point of "horror" – but has taught her much. Clarissa lacks a unified mind, perhaps also "something central which permeates," but is nonetheless – according to her own (accurate) testimony – "a radiancy no doubt in some [people's] lives . . . she had helped young people, who were grateful to her."[88]

As such a "radiancy," capable of balancing compassion for her friends with just appraisal of their limitations, Clarissa allows herself to experience negative feelings in their full force. A death wish circulates through her – understandably, given her illness, and given the preoccupation with mortality endemic to a war-torn society[89] – but does not cancel her *joie de vivre*. Immediately after comforting the weeping Peter, she imagines – falsely, of course – that Richard's lunch with Lady Bruton signals an abandonment: "He has left me; I am alone forever."[90] This notion is no more permanent in Clarissa's mind than true objectively: instinctively wise, she allows the feeling to rise, then pass away. The sorrow enriches her experience, but because it passes, does not unduly weigh her down.

Mrs Dalloway's philosophical radicalism, I said, lies in two areas: its broadly Freudian picture of sexuality, and its representation of the heroine's decentered self-authorship. Clarissa's mind exceeds what *A Room of One's Own* terms a "single state of being":[91] it revolves from judgment to compassion, from sorrow to joy, weariness to vibrancy, alienated independence to a sense of connection and social obligation. Whether Clarissa herself narrates these revolutions, or the third-person voice that renders her indirectly, is sometimes hard to discern. In these two interwoven textual strands – the inseparability of narrator from character, and the non-unity of said character – *Mrs Dalloway* expresses its psychological–philosophical radicalism. All the while, Clarissa's effort to narrate her own "incompatible" self into being gains dignity by resisting Peter's condescending narration of her life. Interdependent narratives and counter-narratives about the heroine dramatize the complexities and opacities of her humanness. Just as *Civilization and Its Discontents* accepts neuroses as the price of life in civilization, so *Mrs Dalloway* accepts multiple "states of being" as the necessary price of an androgynous-minded individual's life in a gender-bound body, in a complex society.

CLARISSA'S SUCCESS AS A HOSTESS

Because it combines a radical skepticism about sexuality and selfhood with a hard-won social pragmatism, particularly where marriage is concerned, the novel ends by emphasizing the successes of Clarissa's party – a married hostess's "offering for the sake of offering."[92] A large occasion, the party encompasses a range of effects and affects. News of Septimus's death temporarily darkens the affair, but Clarissa comes to feel connected to her alter ego, speculating "There was an embrace in death."[93] The Prime Minister – a unifying national symbol – graces the party. But then he departs, leaving an imprint in the chair, his vanished presence a physical reminder of the mortality shared by all guests. (The party assumes greater sobriety, even profundity – belying Peter's protestations of its triviality – for including such reminders.)

Nonetheless, the party can feel artificial even to its hostess. Clarissa "had this feeling of being something not herself."[94] Fortunately, though, such artificiality offers access to typically inaccessible realities: "every one was unreal in one way; much more real in another . . . being taken out of their ordinary ways . . . it was possible to say things you couldn't say anyhow else . . . to go much deeper."[95] Lady Bruton's smaller gathering (replete with its own artificialities) had already signaled this happy possibility: it prompted Richard to surprise his wife with roses, to "go much deeper" than he might otherwise have done, upon returning home. Clarissa's party, too, achieves her goal of "[bringing] together," and "creat[ing]"[96] connections between people: Peter and Sally, long linked by their mutual regard for the hostess, revel in one another's presence amid so many strangers, and go "deeper" in conversation than they might in a less formal, crowded setting.

Finally, what could better demonstrate the power of Clarissa's party to "combine"[97] than Richard's mystical apprehension of his daughter? "Her father had been looking at [Elizabeth]," begins one of the novel's final paragraphs, "and he had thought to himself, Who is that lovely girl? And suddenly he realized that it was his Elizabeth."[98] His de-familiarization – likely a function of the "unreality" that Clarissa notes as inherent to such gatherings – permits him to appreciate Elizabeth's otherness as a more routine encounter with her would not. Richard experiences something of

Peter's quasi-religious insight in sensing "there she [Clarissa] was," or of Clarissa's insight in observing her neighbor turn off her lights, in her separate room. This de-familiarization results in Richard's redoubled love for his daughter: "he had not meant to tell her, but he could not help telling her . . . he had wondered, Who is that lovely girl? And it was his daughter!" On the crest of his second wave of familial affection, Richard is more articulate with Elizabeth than he was with Clarissa. His articulation of his feelings does indeed "make her [Elizabeth] happy."[99] In ways that Clarissa could neither have predicted nor controlled, her party and family reinforce one another's value. The party creates an occasion for tenderness between father and daughter; its expression confers a crowning achievement on the party.

By setting up opportunities for de-familiarization, uncommon combinations of people, and even unpleasant reminders of mortality, the party generates philosophical dynamism. Likewise, Clarissa's marriage – in the face of another, very different marriage that she might have made – establishes opportunities for her self-questioning, her psychic dynamism: her full humanity, as conceived in a post-foundational milieu. In the modern vein, she exercises her freedom of choice, opting for one imperfect life rather than another, never losing sight of the fact that her choice entails sacrifice, never taking refuge in the false comfort of a philosophy of inevitability or of religion.

She stares in the face her modern intellectual–moral predicament – her lack of foundations, the certainty of her death – and, unlike Septimus, maintains her radiance amid her periods of depression. She eschews even the false comforts, the platitudes, of a celebrated contemporary "priest of science."[100] "Perhaps, after all, there is no God," muses Sir William Bradshaw. "He shrugged his shoulders . . . Sir William had a friend in Surrey where they taught . . . a sense of proportion. There were, moreover, family affection; honour; courage; and a brilliant career."[101] Bradshaw lazily cites an unspecified acquaintance – perhaps a highly fallible "specialist" like himself – whereas Clarissa reaches her own conclusions. Bradshaw invokes "proportion"; Clarissa honestly experiences feelings from joy to terror. Bradshaw invokes "honour" while maintaining a heartless practice, too swamped with patients to attend to any as individuals; Clarissa quietly incarnates honor by subjecting her hatred of Doris Kilman to severe introspection. Bradshaw invokes "family affection" while subjecting his wife, most likely without even realizing he does so, to "the slow sinking, water-logged, of her will into his."[102] The Dalloways, by contrast, achieve moments of genuine affection – amid their difficulties and differences –

between husband and wife, father and daughter. No Dalloway sinks, "water-logged," into the will of another.

Bradshaw, in other words, offers hollow, merely rhetorical solutions to the problem of lost foundations. Septimus, in stark contrast, can find no philosophical or psychological balm – apart from his fitful messianic delusions – for the complex wounds he has endured. But his alter ego, Clarissa, finds a happy medium between the doctor's pretensions and the patient's disintegration. She fashions a workable marriage and household, and a party that brings disparate people together, out of the potential chaos of her complex sexuality and her recognition that she might have lived a very different life. Of the numerous forms of intimacy around which she might have structured her life – at a time when the idea of intimacy was being radically reconceived – Clarissa chooses a marriage with clear limitations, but one that helps her to retain her individual integrity, her grace, her material well-being. The novel, on balance, celebrates her for doing so. *Mrs Dalloway* revises Freud's and Conrad's combinations of anti-foundationalism and pragmatism, at times stepping beyond even Conrad's skepticism, by suggesting that Clarissa's and Septimus's marriages have been self-betrayals. But the novel retains a pragmatic sense of the efficacy of marriage, and articulates its own prayerful gratitude – in Clarissa's moment-by-moment rapture at ordinary experience – for the merely human, merely temporary significance of such experience.

CHAPTER 6

A return to essences

The essentialism in *Howards End* (1910) – its retrenchment in Victorian gender roles and its skeptical, even unfriendly attitude toward androgynous Soul-material – is perplexing, given Bloomsbury's politics as a group, Forster's biography, and the array of "intermediates" in Forster's other novels. Bloomsbury's œuvre, frequently recognizable for embracing androgyny and critiquing ideals such as female angelic domesticity, is rendered less harmonious, but ultimately richer, by the presence of such dissonant notes as this retrenchment.

A similar essentialism – perplexing, and also anomalous among its author's works – colors the pages of Vita Sackville-West's 1931 *All Passion Spent*. As in *Howards End*, the conservative handling of gender in *All Passion Spent* counteracts its vigorous rejection of Victorian marriage, which is consistent with the BBC radio broadcasts that Sackville-West and her husband Harold Nicolson did at this time, on the topic of female independence. Having exposed, in narrative form, the limitations that such a matrimonial paradigm imposes on the wife, why not rethink the masculine and feminine Soul-material from which different domestic partnerships might be constituted in the coming decades? In her life Sackville-West did so, and other of her works (like others of Forster's) do so,[1] but *All Passion Spent* (like *Howards End*) only begins to do so, before slipping back into more familiar psychological contours.

The paradox of this retrenchment is deepened because *All Passion Spent* pays meticulous tribute to *Mrs Dalloway*, a novel as remarkable as any Bloomsburian writing for the rigor of its sexual anti-essentialism. Sackville-West's novel is an elegiac feminist homage to Woolf's masterpiece. Uncovering the Woolfian examples it follows, and those it eschews, reveals a tangle of theoretical questions (about *what men and women are like*), practical questions (about *how they can couple successfully*), and aesthetic questions (about *which authorial techniques*, ranging from realism and exposition to free indirect style and oblique suggestion, best *capture the challenges of intimate life*, as it unfolds over decades). The elegiac notes sounded in *Mrs Dalloway*, often by Big Ben, for the losses of the war, and for the lives Clarissa did not lead with Sally or Peter, are transformed in *All Passion Spent* into elegies for the lives that its heroine Lady Slane did not live, either by defying her prescribed role and following her adolescent dream of becoming an artist, or by partnering with FitzGeorge, the novel's Peter-Walsh analogue. Sackville-West's novel not only recapitulates – with differences – Woolf's elegiac tone, heightened by extensive comparisons of the heroine's past and present lives and by ruminations on the passage of time, but it also responds to Woolf's far-reaching analysis of the virtues and drawbacks of marriage. In addition to these tonal and thematic debts, Sackville-West also borrows character types from *Mrs Dalloway*. Peter has his analogue; so too do both Dalloways and Septimus.

Given these many borrowings, it is no surprise that *All Passion Spent* was composed in the shadow of an influence anxiety – one that has been insufficiently explored (though the two novelists' mutual influence on one another has been duly noted). Their years as acquaintances, lovers, and fellow artists were always informed by Sackville-West's sense of Woolf's greater gifts. Given this authorial anxiety, it is worth noting not only where *All Passion Spent* parallels *Mrs Dalloway*, but especially where its technique "swerves"[2] away from its precursor's, and how these swerves bear on its essentialist treatment of gender.

Woolf puts two major techniques in the service of her anti-essentialist themes; the comparative absence of these techniques from *All Passion Spent* provides one possible explanation for why its anti-essentialist potential is only barely exploited. First, Woolf's use of free indirect discourse for rendering interiority, and for moving gracefully between Clarissa's past and present, is absent in *All Passion Spent*. Why is this tactical difference important? Woolf's skill as a technician enables her development of subtle and difficult-to-render ideas: that time is fluid; that elements of Clarissa's past life affect her present experience in surprising ways; and hence that Clarissa's self, including her sense of her marriage, is also fluid and shifting, subject to the revisions of a passing mood, an unbidden memory, an unexpected event. By contrast, Sackville-West's competence – but lesser skill – as a technician leaves her unable to develop such essence-dissolving ideas, unable to move so fluidly between Victorian and contemporary moments of being (though the importance of the past to the present is one of the novel's main concerns), unable to render Lady Slane's selfhood in the shimmering way that Woolf renders Clarissa (though she shares Woolf's interests in freedom and contingency).

A second major difference between the novels' techniques lies in their use of the alter ego. Septimus is woven throughout *Mrs Dalloway*, whereas the young Deborah Holland, namesake of the heroine, appears only at the end of *All Passion Spent*. Just as past and present are more clearly separate in Sackville-West's novel, hindering its potential to dissolve the heroine's self across time, so the heroine's symbolic second self is effectively segregated from the bulk of the narrative, allowing for less exchange between the two figures, in the way that Clarissa and Septimus's bisexualities illuminate one another. This lack of interchange with her alter ego also explains Lady Slane's comparative solidity as a character, relative to Clarissa – the theoretical implication that she has a specifiable essence (including a sexual one). This implication poses problems for the novel's critique of marriage.

Finally, two additional, minor strategies contribute to the clarity and directness of Sackville-West's novel where *Mrs Dalloway* is vague and indirect. *All Passion Spent* asserts its heroine's positive and tender feelings about her past (which endows the feelings with a fixed quality), whereas *Mrs Dalloway* dramatizes Clarissa's nostalgia, without so baldly explicating it (which lends it an impermanent quality, as of one among many tendencies that emerge and recede within her consciousness). Not only are ideas about the past rendered clearly in *All Passion Spent*; so too are ideas about death, which Sackville-West's characters discuss openly and at length – unlike Woolf's characters, who shy away from mentioning the topic, though it weighs on their minds. These four ways, then, in which Sackville-West draws clearer lines than Woolf – her temporal divisions between past and present, her dramatic divisions between alter egos, her expository handling of nostalgia, and her explicit handling of death – together give *All Passion Spent* a determinacy of meaning that Woolf's novel studiously avoids.

Although conservative techniques, essentialist themes, and determinate meaning are not logically necessary partners, they function in tandem in *All Passion Spent*, and make it a fitting bookend to Bloomsburian treatments of modern intimacy. As the wind of experimental modernism ceases to puff Bloomsbury's sails, so too the skeptical renderings of selfhood, and the dogged application of doubt to all ideas – the qualities that endow *Women in Love* and *Mrs Dalloway* with much of their piquancy – give way to a different mode of character depiction.[3] While Bloomsbury did produce more novels – including several experimental ones by Woolf – subsequent to *All Passion Spent*, nonetheless Sackville-West's homage marks the waning of high modernism within the group, as within literary history. It is fitting, perhaps, that the homage should lack some of the trademark qualities of the text – and by extension, the literary era – that it memorializes. But before tracing the complex intersections of technique and theme in Sackville-West's homage, a review of the women's personal and artistic exchanges reveals that they learned much from one another before the composition of *All Passion Spent.*

PERSONAL AND ARTISTIC INTIMACIES

The women's personal attachment developed almost as soon as they met, and in its intensity it presaged what would become their aesthetic entanglement. Woolf, aged 40, and Sackville-West, aged 30, met at a 1922 dinner party given by Clive Bell, then Sackville-West's only connection to Bloomsbury. Woolf's diaries record Sackville-West as "the new apparition."[4] Five years later, in the category-defying character of Sally Seton, Woolf would pay thinly disguised tribute to the young Vita. Sally has French blood in her veins as Sackville-West had Spanish blood in hers,[5] each figure embodying, for Woolf, freedom from English inhibitions. A letter from Sackville-West to her husband calls Woolf "my darling" and concludes "I love [her] with a sick passion."[6]

The "sickness" of this passion – the ambivalences and dangers it entailed – were multiplied by the blending of aesthetic with personal admiration. "Darling, it makes me afraid of you," Sackville-West wrote of *To the Lighthouse*. "Afraid of your penetration and loveliness and genius."[7] Even before *To the Lighthouse* appeared, Sackville-West wrote in a letter to Woolf, "I don't know whether to be dejected or encouraged when I read the works of Virginia Woolf," addressing her mentor in the third person, as if "Virginia Woolf" were both an individual and an institution. "Dejected because I shall never be able to write like that, or encouraged because someone else can?"[8] The accomplishments and limitations of *All Passion Spent* and other works by Sackville-West are conditioned by her emulation of Woolf.[9] Sackville-West's sense that she never became a great writer was one of her two lifelong disappointments,[10] but it led to her creative alliance with Woolf, of whom she said in January 1927 "you have had infinitely more influence on me intellectually than anyone, and for this alone I love you."[11]

Woolf, then, was an inspiring and disturbing presence in the personal and creative life of a woman who was already flamboyant, energetic, and accomplished. Sackville-West married the diplomat and author Harold Nicolson in 1913, a union that lasted until her 1962 death, and that proved tranquil as she grew reclusive in middle age.[12] But their early marriage was troubled. Both partners had homosexual affairs;

Sackville-West also had an affair with a man. Their marriage exemplified traditions (and pitfalls) of sexual freedom within the leisured classes. While monogamy was not universal in the middle classes – as *Dora* amply demonstrates – social respectability did govern the *appearance* of middle-class intimacies, which is part of what makes Bloomsbury a site of controversy. With its de rigueur bisexualities and infidelities, the group made aristocratic sexual habits visible among the educated middle classes. Woolf and Sackville-West's romance[13] crystallizes this inter-class connection, and the dialogue they carried on in multiple published writings extends and aestheticizes it, in ways that would inspire subsequent novelists, feminists, and queer theorists.[14]

Sackville-West's sexual iconoclasm predates her relationship with Woolf,[15] and provides literary material for both writers. As a young woman, she changed her name to Julian, dressed as a man, and traveled through Europe with her lover Violet Trefusis. She said that "the extraordinary thing" about her cross-dressing was "how natural it all was."[16] She represents "Julian" and Trefusis as the hero and heroine of her romantic novel *Challenge* (1923). With greater subtlety, Woolf's *Orlando* (1928) recaptures these convention-flaunting women, with Sackville-West in the guise of the hero and Trefusis as the Russian princess Sasha. As much as any Bloomsburian text, *Orlando* blurs boundaries between biography and fiction. This generic experiment is indebted to Sackville-West's biography *Aphra Behn: The Incomparable Astrea* (1927), which includes numerous meditations, Bloomsburian in their playful spirit, on the epistemological difficulties faced by the biographer.

By 1931, Sackville-West and Woolf had learned in tandem how to enrich biographical and novelistic materials by blending them.[17] Though also biographically inspired, *All Passion Spent* is less confessional than *Challenge*. Benefiting from the examples of indirection in *Mrs Dalloway*, *To the Lighthouse*, and *Orlando*, it is more successful as a result. Lady Slane shares some circumstances with her author, but more fully recalls Lady Carnock, a mother-in-law whom Sackville-West had wished would assert her independence as Lady Slane does, once this heroine is widowed.[18] Prior to *All Passion Spent*, Woolf recast her mother as Mrs Ramsay in *To the Lighthouse*, and her friend Kitty Maxse as Clarissa Dalloway.[19] These heroines provided Woolf opportunities to transform personal observations into feminist critiques of her mother's generation, as Sackville-West does in *All Passion Spent*. Bloomsburians developed numerous strategies, in fiction and biography, for indirect exploration of themselves, their families, and their social roles.[20] Sackville-West's maturation as a writer, between her more direct treatment of autobiographical material in *Challenge*, and her more oblique treatment of it in *All Passion Spent*, reflects Woolf's and Bloomsbury's sophisticated lessons.

As a testament to Woolf's creative mentorship, *All Passion Spent* – excepting not even *Orlando* – is the richest homage that either novelist composed to her friend. More than any work by either woman, it risks being "contained" in the act of paying tribute to its precursor, as Sackville-West's May 26, 1925 letter to Woolf inadvertently divulges. Woolf's *Common Reader* had been published on April 23, and *Mrs Dalloway* on May 14, of that year. In *The Common Reader*, says Sackville-West, "there are passages that I should like to know by heart . . . [it] grows into a guide, philosopher and friend, while *Mrs Dalloway* remains a will-of-the-wisp, a dazzling and lovely acquaintance." In response to this craftily introduced criticism, Woolf writes, "Hah ha! I thought you wouldn't like *Mrs Dalloway*." Woolf's response may seem to misrepresent her friend's reaction. After all, Sackville-West nowhere claims to dislike *Mrs Dalloway*; in fact she says that it "illuminates and reveals" and that "the whole of London is contained in [its] first score of pages."[21] But Woolf is right to read these compliments as backhanded: critics frequently accused her fiction of insubstantiality.[22] Sackville-West borrows this tactic in calling *Mrs Dalloway* a "will-of-the-wisp," despite her emulation of Woolf's skill at capturing the protean qualities of consciousness. She dedicated to Woolf her 1924 novel *Seducers in Ecuador*, which employs unmistakably Bloomsburian – especially Woolfian – techniques of perspectivalism and temporal interruption. Louise DeSalvo speculates that Woolf's criticism of *Seducers* may partly explain why Sackville-West produced no novels for the next six years, until *The Edwardians* renewed her popular success in 1930.[23] Sackville-West was able, however, to repay Woolf's criticism one year later with her "will-of-the-wisp" comment.

But Sackville-West undermines her own criticism by writing of a "guide" and "philosopher." In attributing these influences to the essays in *The Common Reader*, she displaces them from their more prominent sources in Woolf's novels. Emulating *Mrs Dalloway* as an ambivalent feminist elegy that employs temporal layering and an alter ego, *All Passion Spent* could not more clearly honor Woolf's 1925 novel as its "guide." Finding a path that diverges from the one marked out by this guide becomes an implicit challenge for Sackville-West's 1931 work. How, for example, might *All Passion Spent* avoid becoming a "will-of-the-wisp?" By endowing its figures, as *Seducers in Ecuador* does not, with Victorian solidity? Whatever its benefits, such a strategy incurs a philosophical cost: *Mrs Dalloway*'s dextrous use of free indirect discourse, and its knack for depicting consciousness fluidly, help it to dissolve boundaries between maleness and femaleness. The same techniques that expose Woolf's novel to charges of insubstantiality also contribute to its philosophical rigor.

In eschewing such techniques, *All Passion Spent* swerves toward gender essentialism. Clarissa's romance with Sally, and her time in bed with military – i.e., "masculine" – memoirs, indicate that sexually "perverse"[24] energies circulate through her psyche. They are more than a passing whim. Conversely, if Lady Slane's adolescent dream is no more than a whim, then *All Passion Spent* offers a different – less "androgynous"[25] – account of female sexuality. The move toward psychological solidity holds the promise of freedom from Woolf's example, but threatens to relegate *All Passion Spent* to a museum of pre-modernist pictures of gender. A critique of the Victorian marriage paradigm is sure to be hindered if it reproduces the assumptions about sexual selfhood upon which such marriages largely depended. What happens, then, to Sackville-West's pointed attack on marriage – which distinguishes her novel from *Mrs Dalloway* – as a result of her theoretical timidity, and does this timidity indicate any influence anxiety?

AN ELEGIAC FEMINIST HOMAGE

Mrs Dalloway deftly combines its examination of marriage with an elegiac invocation of a possible life that its heroine did not live, and of a war-torn nation's recent past.[26] Clarissa unites with a successful Conservative politician for whom her feelings were never passionate, rather than with a woman who once captivated her, or a less successful man whom she continues to love decades later. The novel weighs the sacrifices entailed by her marriage against its benefits, as the heroine remains aware that her life might have been different, and struggles against psychic disintegration. Her marriage is not perfect, and one sign of its limitations is the spouses' scant knowledge of each other's interior lives. Richard's political life is largely unknown to Clarissa, including his lunch with Lady Bruton, to which she is not invited. Correspondingly, Clarissa's experience is unknown to Richard, as she lies awake in her "narrower and narrower" bed, with the candle "half burnt down," reading Marbot's *Memoirs*.[27] Nonetheless, she expends considerable energy convincing herself of his fitness as a mate. "One must repay," she thinks, "above all to Richard her husband, who was the foundation of it – of the gay sounds, of the green lights, of the cook even whistling."[28] Such thoughts may represent her unbidden feelings, or they may be attempts to talk herself into a fuller appreciation of Richard. His imperfections notwithstanding, she does appreciate the life they have made for themselves. She is helped to this conclusion by recalling Peter's officiousness. *Mrs Dalloway* nowhere indicates that Richard suspects what occupies his wife while he engages with the outside world, whether her gratitude to him or her struggle with her continued longing for Peter. But by the same token, the novel never deplores Richard's lack of such knowledge. Woolf is cagey in depicting relationships, indicating that healthy intimacy requires a measure of privacy, and that even some degree of isolation between spouses – things they will never know about one another – may be useful.

With comparable persuasiveness, if less delicacy, *All Passion Spent* combines its critique of marriage with an elegiac invocation of a past that its heroine did not live, and of an aristocracy's passing way of life.[29] Lady Slane is widowed at 88 by an earl and former prime minister for whom her feelings were never passionate. Such a force for tradition was the earl, until his death at 94, that "time seemed to have made a little jump forward," the narrator comments, "now that the figure of old Slane was no longer there with outstretched arms to dam it back."[30] Over the course of her "seventy years' association" with him,[31] Lady Slane has sacrificed her youthful artistic ambitions to an unsatisfying life of public ritual and a family largely driven by the desire for wealth and status. "All her life long," explains the narrator, "gracious and gentle, [Lady Slane] had been wholly submissive."[32] An additional lost possibility is brought to her attention shortly into her widowhood. The art collector FitzGeorge – who made no lasting conscious impression on her when they met fifty years earlier – announces that he has loved her ever since then,[33] which leads her to reflect, without bitterness, on how different her life might have been. Thus *All Passion Spent* echoes the nostalgic note of *Mrs Dalloway*.

Lady Slane's life could have differed most profoundly had her spouse and family been attuned to her inner experience: here *All Passion Spent* revisits one of Woolf's sharpest psychological insights, although it *explains* the dynamic of intra-familial isolation that Woolf *dramatizes*. Only after the earl passes away does it "dawn upon" Edith, the most perceptive of the Slane children, "that her mother might have lived a full private life, all these years, behind the shelter of her affectionate watchfulness."[34] Such a "full private life" was necessary to Lady Slane, because, as FitzGeorge helps her realize, her husband – in spite of his formidable social charm – never found fascination in her, or anyone's, interior existence. "You yourself," FitzGeorge asks her, "must often have suffered from his charm?" His sly question leads her to recall how she "had often watched Henry bending his brows in interest over some human question which could not really interest him at all, withdrawn as he was into a world where human interests shrank to insignificance, and nothing but a cold, sardonic ambition lay."[35] There is no exploration in *All Passion Spent*, as in *Mrs Dalloway*, of how a wife's full private life – and some degree of unknownness to one's spouse – might contribute to a healthy intimacy. Sackville-West leaves no doubt that the Slanes' lack of intimacy was damaging to the wife. Perhaps because Lady Slane has no familial audience for her deep thoughts or feelings, her "affection" manifests itself as a "shelter of . . . watchfulness." The narrator's language suggests that self-protection, including protection *from* her family, motivates this "shelter." From within her shelter, therefore, she learns to "hate" her husband for his "Jovian detachment and superiority" well before her discussion with FitzGeorge.[36] Henry Holland's charm was pure pretense, his widow sees when she contrasts "human interests" to "ambition," in one of the novel's characteristic binaries.

Given the earl's domineering power and indifference to others, and as the pun in Lady Slane's name suggests, her lifelong "submission" meant the slaying of her own ambition, in addition to decades of emotional isolation. Her name, comprising the title "Lady" and the location of her husband's earldom, carries further evidence of the patriarchy's power to erase female identity, as a wife's hands become physically oppressed, "loaded with rings."[37] At a previous moment of identity crisis, she remembered herself as a young woman, before assuming the "Slane" mantle. "She saw herself as a young girl walking beside the lake . . .. Yes, that was she, Deborah Lee, not Deborah Holland, not Deborah Slane; the old woman closed her eyes, the better to hold the vision."[38] The heroine's conviction that "that was she" – emphatically stated, with the help of a deictic – locates her true self prior to her marriage. Of course, even the name "Lee," being her father's, carries a patriarchal taint. But the main targets of Sackville-West's critique are marriage and wifehood, not daughterhood. Thus, the progression – or retrogression – of Deborah's last name, from "Lee" to "Holland" to "Slane," enacts the swallowing of her identity, her transformation from herself, into a wife, into a public figure's wife. Lady Slane suspects that "in a trice," upon accepting her husband's marriage proposal, "she had been changed from the person she was into somebody completely different."[39] Again, Sackville-West draws a sharp binary, whereas Woolf (comparing Clarissa Parry to Clarissa Dalloway, for example) draws a blurrier one.

Whatever the writers' differences, however, Sackville-West learned many lessons from Woolf: *All Passion Spent* combines ideas from both *Mrs Dalloway* and *To the Lighthouse* about the elusiveness of self-knowledge.

Mrs Dalloway encodes a tale of shifting identity in the changing of the heroine's name from "Clarissa" to "Mrs Richard Dalloway."[40] Clarissa Dalloway, like Deborah Holland, née Lee, feels her first and last names tug toward two separate versions of self. Her internal monologue anticipates Lady Slane's, in Clarissa's sense of the "nothing[ness]" that lies behind her married self. But contrary to Clarissa, when Lady Slane wonders "what, precisely, had been herself,"[41] she sometimes finds a satisfactory answer. On one occasion, she enjoys the "fortunate position of seeing into the heart of the girl who had been herself . . . not only the lingering step . . . [but also] the thoughts which accompanied this solitary ramble."[42] Conversely, on another introspective occasion, her anti-essentialist intimations resemble Clarissa's. Lady Slane feels that "there were many selves. She could never be the same self with [Henry] as when she was alone; and even that solitary self which she pursued, shifted, changed, melted away as she approached it."[43] She finds some clarity in distinguishing "the woman in her" from "the artist in her."[44] The former signifies her presumably false, socially constrained identity, and the latter hints at her hidden, instinctual self.

Sackville-West's heroine wavers, in other words, between conceiving of herself in essentialist and anti-essentialist ways – which is not a bad authorial strategy for treating such an imponderable question. And to the novel's possible further benefit, because Lady Slane never produces a work of art (at least the novel never says that she does), her sense of a thwarted calling is open to question. Perhaps the "artist" she imagines is a fantasy, not a genuine self who was slain by the patriarchy. Her "woman"–"artist" distinction supplies no permanent solution to the riddle of what constitutes her "solitary self," although it provides her with a greater degree of comfort than Clarissa finds. Though Clarissa is more unsettled by her Sartrean intuition of nothingness than Lady Slane is by her sense of "many selves," and though Lady Slane recovers her psychic equilibrium to a degree that Clarissa does not, their experiences nonetheless illuminate one another. Each novel deepens its critique by linking marriage to its heroine's alienation from present reality and to her lost sense of identity, rather than – as in a Jane Austen novel – to her assuming a mature and stable identity *as* a wife. Lady Slane's alienation, of course, is more thorough than that of Clarissa, who takes pleasure in hostessing: for Clarissa *what is* and *what might have been* are never clearly separated, but interpenetrate continually as a result of her memories and imaginings.

For Lady Slane, on the other hand, distinctions are sharper: between "artist" and "woman," between "the person she was" and "somebody completely different" whom she became, between the "ambition" harbored by her husband and the "human interests" she values. The clarity of her distinctions, echoed by the narrator, reinforces the novel's main themes. So vigorous are the heroine's attacks on conventional values that even "love" seems to her a version of self abnegation. "The stress had been constant," says the narrator, indirectly rendering Lady Slane's thoughts about her marriage. "Her love for [her husband] had been a straight black line drawn right through her life. It had hurt her, it had damaged her, it had diminished her, but she had been unable to curve away from it."[45] One of the novel's richer images, the "line" is ominous not only because of its color, archetypally associated with death – a recurring motif in *All Passion Spent*, as in *Mrs Dalloway*. The line is menacing also because of its phallic "straightness," which suggests that Lady Slane's feelings have been colonized by masculine interests – an image of psychic androgyny rarer in *All Passion Spent* than in other Sackville-West novels. The "curve" that Lady Slane could not execute suggests an unrealized feminine independence. That the "straight line" has "hurt" and "damaged" her associates masculinity with violent effects, even where violent intent may be absent. Thus, Lady Slane's "love" can encompass its opposite: she can "hate" her detached spouse while remaining emotionally connected to him. In reaching so heterodox a conclusion about so celebrated a virtue as love, Lady Slane's private musings follow a path similar to Clarissa's. "Love and religion!" thinks Clarissa, with Peter Walsh and Doris Kilman in mind. "How detestable they are!"[46] For Clarissa too, love is never so pure as to exclude negative feelings.

Sackville-West derives yet further lessons, as a critic of marriage, from Woolf's portrayal of wifely solicitude in the face of a husband's imperceptiveness. Distinct as the male and female spheres – psychological and social – may be, Lady Slane, Mrs Ramsay, and Clarissa are nonetheless burdened with the duty of perceiving their husbands' moments of self-doubt, and of subtly providing succor at such times. Lady Slane, explains the narrator, "must be swift to detect" Henry Holland's

> need for reassurance when a momentary discouragement overcame him . . . yet it must all be done without a word directly spoken; she must restore his belief that the obstructiveness of his Government or the opposition of his rivals was due to their short-sightedness or envy, and to no deficiency within himself, yet must not allow him to know that she guessed at his mood of self-mistrust or the whole fabric of her comfort would be undone.[47]

This wifely role recalls Mrs Ramsay, who repeatedly soothes her husband's ego, in part for her own "comfort" – although Woolf's narrator never explicates the heroine's strategy as Sackville-West's narrator does.

"Women have served all these centuries," laments *A Room of One's Own* – with the explicitness that Woolf's fiction generally avoids – "as looking glasses possessing the magic and delicious power of reflecting the figure of man at twice its natural size."[48] For his part, Richard Dalloway requires less propping up than Mr Ramsay, and seeks his wife's affection, when he needs it, less clumsily. Nonetheless, his inarticulateness – when he presents Clarissa with flowers but cannot bring himself to pronounce the words "I love you"[49] – recalls Henry Holland's need for "reassurance . . . without a word directly spoken." Though Woolf does not relish the function of "reflecting" men at "twice [their] natural size," her fiction expresses admiration for women's "art of life," and distaste for men's lack of skill, as she saw it, in that area.

Sackville-West saw, in *To the Lighthouse* and *Mrs Dalloway*, how a critique of marriage can depict both the large sacrifices that the institution demands of women as citizens and potential intellectuals, and the smaller spousal interactions by which "male" and "female" personality traits are perpetuated. Lady Slane's inability to "write out a cheque correctly," and her confusion about "what people meant" by "the Irish Question or the Women's Movement [or] Free Trade and Protection,"[50] like Clarissa's inability to distinguish Albanians from Armenians,[51] results not from an innate incapacity, but from her exclusion from the "masculine" world of finance and politics.[52] Marriage makes Lady Slane an "appendage" to her husband's career,[53] closing off whatever opportunities and ambitions she had to define her social position on her own terms. Sackville-West saw that a critique of marriage gains poignancy by evoking what might have been – the experiences a wife might have enjoyed (or endured) had she made different choices. She perceived, that is, how elegy complements polemics. And she perceived how elegy is enhanced by ambivalence, how a heroine's memories gain aesthetic potency by blending tones of pleasure and displeasure.

Contemplating scenes from the past, including life-altering choices, at times alienates Sackville-West's and Woolf's heroines from the present. But such contemplations can be "exquisite" as well as unsettling. Just as Lady Slane attempts to "hold [onto] the vision" of her past walk "beside the lake,"[54] so Clarissa treasures "the most exquisite moment of her whole life," when Sally Seton "picked a flower; kissed her on the lips."[55] The natural imagery of the lake and the garden flower – emblems of lives unlived – indicates that the paths actually followed were not inevitable, especially in Clarissa's more historically recent case.[56] Both heroines see their lives as contingent, knowledge that marks them as modern protagonists. Each demonstrates a measure of heroism in making peace with the life she is living, and the possibilities that her choices have foreclosed, though Clarissa's peace is troubled.

Each heroine makes peace with the present by remembering the past fully, not only its "exquisite" dimensions, but also its disturbing ones. When Clarissa recalls Sally's kiss, she also recalls Peter's interruption. The evocation of one life that might have been (including intimacy with Sally) immediately calls to mind another possible life with Peter. Thus, although Clarissa thinks of her memory of Sally's kiss as "a present, wrapped up . . . not to look at,"[57] she does unwrap and examine the gift. It provides her no simple escape from her present situation with Richard, nor a key to her "real" self, but an opportunity for a complex and pleasing meditation. Lady Slane glimpses, in a past moment as "Deborah Lee," what she considers her authentic self, but Clarissa – heroine of a more philosophically skeptical novel – experiences no such clarity.

Lady Slane enjoys such clarity because her widowhood provides her "plenty of leisure . . . to survey her life as a tract of country traversed . . . a unity."[58] In her retrospection, as in Clarissa's, however, even "exquisite" moments contain unpleasant associations.

> She remembered how, crossing the Persian desert with Henry, their cart had been escorted by flocks of butterflies, white and yellow, which danced on either side and overhead and all around them . . . but Henry, who was traveling on a tour of investigation, could only say "Terrible, the ophthalmia among these people – I must really do something about it," and knowing that he was right . . . she had transferred [her attention] to her duty . . . and would make arrangements for a further supply of boracic acid to be sent out from England.
>
> But, perversely, the fluttering of the butterflies had always seemed more important.[59]

The heroine's memory of a colonial scene encompasses a Bloomsburian combination of details, from her mystical–aesthetic apprehension of the butterflies to her husband's and her own awareness of human suffering and its possibility of being ameliorated politically.[60] Just as Clarissa's treasured memories are complex enough to embrace contradictory details (Sally's kiss and its interruption, Peter in both his charming and cantankerous moods), so too Lady Slane's spot of time encompasses both beauty and duty, neither canceling the other.

Sackville-West's and Woolf's heroines share ambivalent relationships to their personal pasts, and each negotiates this relationship in part by pondering the man she did not marry. Typically for the novels, Lady Slane reaches a greater degree of clarity about her past (FitzGeorge represents a golden missed opportunity) than Clarissa does (Peter's case is more ambiguous). In the years since FitzGeorge first saw Lady Slane, he has become the regular lunch partner of her son, Kay. Through Kay as surrogate, FitzGeorge maintains his affection for her, a tactic of which Kay has no idea, as the two men share an interest in antiques, and have been friends "for some thirty years," but share "no personal intimacy."[61] "Their relationship," says the narrator, "was beautifully detached."[62] This version of detachment, while lacking the menace of Henry Holland's Jovian attitude, also lacks the nobility of FitzGeorge's freedom from convention. It betokens the norm of human estrangement throughout the novel, in contrast to which Lady Slane's connections with several old men at Hampstead – discussed below – seem precious. FitzGeorge first saw Lady Slane in India (which recalls Peter Walsh's employment there).[63] Peter, like FitzGeorge, has for many years scarcely stopped thinking about the object of his youthful attraction, judging from his troubled obsession with the thought of Clarissa throughout the day of her dinner party. The two men differ, though, in the state of their affections while apart from the heroines. Peter claims to be "in love" with the wife of a Major in the Indian Army. "Love" itself may, as Clarissa momentarily thinks, be a "monster";[64] Peter's new attachment may be scandalous, given the woman's marital status; or the depth of his feelings for her may be questionable (he may mention her to make Clarissa jealous). Regardless, Peter's passion has been maintained in one form or another. Like his anxiety, this emotional predilection has not abated over the years. The intensity of his personality is at once attractive and repellent; Clarissa confronts this paradox every time she evaluates her decision to reject him for Richard. FitzGeorge, by contrast, has spent, sublimated, his passion in the process of ageing and acquiring antiques, which increases his attractiveness without raising concern. His equanimity and freedom from scandal suggest that he would have made a finer husband for Deborah Lee than Henry Holland did, especially as FitzGeorge aged. He does not confront Lady Slane with the sort of emotional paradox that Peter entails for Clarissa.

Despite these differences, the way the heroines respond to the reintroduction of these men into their lives further betrays Woolf's influence on Sackville-West. Clarissa forgets Peter's name, and Lady Slane forgets FitzGeorge's name, in ways that suggest unconscious motives. Peter first enters Clarissa's home soon after sending her a letter warning of his arrival. Yet his appearance catches her so much by surprise that "for a single second, she could not remember what he was called."[65] The nonchalant mention of her forgetfulness obscures its psychological significance. After all, when

Clarissa asks him the question – conventional after so long a separation – "Well, and what's happened to you?" she begins a "battle" between them. The old friends, "sitting side by side on the sofa, challenged each other."[66] The "old bitterness"[67] flares up immediately upon their reacquaintance. It is doubtful that Clarissa could ever forget the name of a man for whom her feelings are so powerfully ambivalent that – bitterness notwithstanding – the love of him might "suddenly . . . come over her" even if they had been "parted for hundreds of years."[68] Admittedly, Peter's appearance at Clarissa's house on the morning of her party is "unexpected" for a reason: "(she had not read his letter)."[69] But her failure to read the letter, far from being accidental, reveals her difficulty in contemplating Peter equanimously. That the narrator mentions her failure in parenthesis underscores her failed struggle to compartmentalize, and thereby to suppress, the thought of him.

Lady Slane experiences a similarly motivated forgetting throughout most of an extended discussion, in her Hampstead home, with FitzGeorge, "that stray young traveler whose name her consciousness had scarcely registered"[70] – as the narrator misleadingly explains. Only after FitzGeorge describes the details of their half-century-old trip together does the narrator comment "Mr FitzGeorge. The name came back to her now. It was not surprising that, among so many thousands of names, she should have forgotten it."[71] The narrator's protestations in support of her forgetfulness contradict all that immediately precedes, and all that immediately follows, this moment in their discussion. When FitzGeorge met and fell in love with Lady Slane a half century earlier, the encounter was not fleeting. Henry Holland, then Viceroy of India, invited FitzGeorge to join him and the Vicereine on a trip to Fatihpur Sikhri.[72] Although FitzGeorge assumed the invitation to be a matter of form, and that the Viceroy expected it to be refused, he accepted, in eagerness to spend time with Deborah Holland. In the uninhabited city, while the Viceroy is away inspecting a mosque, Lady Slane tells FitzGeorge that the ring-doves should appropriately inherit the buildings that people have left behind. FitzGeorge underscores the sexual significance of their conversation, mentioning that he "would like to see . . . a cobra coiling its length neatly in the council chamber."[73] The narrator has left no doubt as to the symbolic significance of this snake, by commenting, earlier in their discussion, that Lady Slane "was eighty-eight, but the man-to-woman mainspring still coiled like a cobra between them. Innumerable years had elapsed since she had felt that stimulus."[74] The repeated mention of the cobra indicates that FitzGeorge stimulates her passion in a way that Henry Holland failed to do. That she could innocently forget his name, even after so long a passage of time, seems doubtful, considering her powers of retention. With no difficulty, and to the consternation of her children, she recalls "the name of the agent" – Bucktrout – thirty years after last seeing the Hampstead house that she purchases upon the earl's death.[75] Her ability to "detect in herself a lie"[76] suggests that she will not continue "forgetting" FitzGeorge's name for long. As it happens, their discussion, far from being unmemorable, develops into a mellower version of the "battle" between Peter and Clarissa. FitzGeorge describes it as "a sequel to the conversation" in Fatihpur Sikhri,[77] and prods Lady Slane – to her enjoyment – with the question "What would you have done with your life . . . had you not married that very delightful and disconcerting charlatan?"[78]

Sackville-West is a keen disciple, who finds models for character portrayal in ways as broad as Woolf's depiction of a woman's ambivalent memories, and as specific as Woolf's depiction of disingenuous forgetfulness. But disciples cannot merely follow their teachers' paths; they must chart their own courses, and *All Passion Spent* does so, in part, by clarifying what *Mrs Dalloway* leaves vague, by asserting what *Mrs Dalloway* evokes. Whether this greater explicitness amounts to an aesthetic loss is a question of some complexity.

FREE INDIRECT DISCOURSE AND THE HANDLING OF TIME

Against the background of their shared examinations of spousal unknownness, their shared skepticism about the value and meaning of "love," the temporal lacuna each evokes between the heroine's past and present, the heroines' similar ambivalence about their pasts, and the novels' many other parallels, their differences stand in sharper relief – including the way Sackville-West draws a clear line between past and present, whereas Woolf's techniques enable her to blur this line. Because *All Passion Spent* begins with the death of Henry Holland, it can view Lady Slane's marriage only in retrospect, not while it unfolds, as is the case in *Mrs Dalloway*. Because of the limited penetration of its free indirect discourse, it is spare with details about what the union was like. Few temporal "hinges" open doors from Lady Slane's day-to-day experiences with her spouse onto her premarital apprehensions of Henry and of other people. Admittedly, the narrator comments at one point that Lady Slane's "foreign memories and her English present played at *chassé-croisé* often now in her mind, mingling and superimposing"[79] – a sign that Sackville-West admires the usefulness in novels such as *Mrs Dalloway* of such temporal superimpositions. But *All Passion Spent* merely gestures toward such "mingling" as *Mrs Dalloway* enacts in the structure of its sentences that zigzag between Westminster and Bourton. "What a plunge!" says Woolf's narrator of Clarissa's entrance into the Westminster day. "For so it had always seemed to her, when, with a little squeak of the hinges, which she could hear now, she had burst open the French windows . . ." at Bourton. "How fresh, how calm" it was at Bourton, continues the narrator, whose perspective blends with the protagonist's, "stiller than this" at Westminster – thereby dramatizing the *chassé-croisé* that *All Passion Spent* posits. Admittedly, Woolf's narrator differentiates the climate at Bourton and Westminster (the former was "stiller"), but this clarity dissolves at the level of aural detail. The "hinges" on the door at Bourton are something Clarissa can "hear now"[80] in Westminster, says the narrator, but it is not clear whether the Westminster hinges also squeak (and the verb "hear" refers to a present sensation), or whether *only* the Bourton hinges squeaked in their time, and this aural memory of long ago "mingles" with and is "superimposed" upon her present experience. This confusion is part of the psychological point: the literal hinges are also temporal hinges between past and present, and Woolf's syntax makes it impossible for the reader to separate the two cleanly, just as it can be difficult to separate the consciousness of the narrator from that of the heroine. Sackville-West's narrator asserts such a process to be occurring, but only begins to merge with the heroine's consciousness, and thus to endow the "mingling" with dramatic reality, before lapsing into a general, third-person description of the widow's memories. "Was she on a hillside near Pekin with Henry," asks the narrator about Lady Slane, "or was she alone, old, and dressed in black, resting on a bench on Hampstead Heath?"[81] The widow's confusion is effectively described from without, but less effectively evoked from within. Readers know the answer to the narrator's question – of course Lady Slane is at Hampstead Heath, not near Pekin – in a way that Woolf's reader does not know what Clarissa "hears."

This readerly uncertainty, this indeterminacy of meaning, expands throughout *Mrs Dalloway*, from a question as small as what Clarissa hears to mysteries as large as which love interest – Sally, Peter, or Richard – would have been best for her, and whether any standard (Clarissa's ongoing passion for Peter, the lesbian desire that only Sally can fulfill, the safety that only Richard can offer) can be used to adjudicate among them. Clarissa's ambivalence is our uncertainty, and this uncertainty is central to our pleasure as readers.

Lady Slane, of course, is also an ambivalent heroine – ambivalent, like Clarissa, both about her personal past (what her adolescent dreams of escape signify today) and about the historical past (what value Victorian life held).

But the means by which this ambivalence is conveyed distinguishes the authors from one another: concerning historical even more than personal matters, Woolf dramatizes the ambivalence that Sackville-West asserts. *Mrs Dalloway*, like *To the Lighthouse*, depicts a gulf between two generations of women: between the Angels in the House of Clarissa and Mrs Ramsay's time and the more self-assertive young women of Elizabeth Dalloway and Lily Briscoe's emerging century. But these novels draw blurrier distinctions than *All Passion Spent*. Though different from her mother, Elizabeth is not an icon of liberated womanhood. Any hope that *Mrs Dalloway* evinces of a utopian feminist future – perhaps of a society in which Clarissa and Sally's attraction might bloom more freely – is sparing. Clarissa's experience reading Marbot suggests that "masculine" impulses dwell in women's minds, just as Septimus's hat-making suggests the presence of "feminine" energies in men's minds. But this theoretical undermining of gender distinctions and inequities implies nothing particular about what institutions, or what types of male and female personalities, the future holds for England.

To the Lighthouse, on the other hand, does depict a liberated woman artist in Lily Briscoe. But this 1927 novel does not reject Victorian forms of "femininity" to the degree that *All Passion Spent* does. Admittedly, Lily's completion of her painting lends *To the Lighthouse* a feeling of completeness, of accomplished artistic expression. Despite the triumphal overtones in Lily's completion of her painting, however, even she demonstrates Woolf's penchant for softening distinctions. As different – even alienated – from Mrs Ramsay as Lily is in many ways, she nonetheless admires the matron.[82] In part through Lily's consciousness, *To the Lighthouse* looks back on Mrs Ramsay and her generation – the generation of Woolf's mother – with a mixture of fondness and judgment. In performing her wifely and motherly duties, Mrs Ramsay embodies a form of femininity that has definite virtues: it benefits others and provides women like her with a sense of purpose and satisfaction. The same can be said for Clarissa, performing her duties as hostess. While *Mrs Dalloway* expresses no hope that future generations of women will face the same limited horizon of choices as Clarissa, it nonetheless admires the way she fulfills her role – and thereby acknowledges some use for the role, some sympathy for the way Victorians lived.

All Passion Spent, by contrast, describes without dramatizing a feeling of ambivalence about the way English life used to be. Lady Slane wonders whether women, "in their new Protestant spirit" – their spirit of feminist revolt – are "defrauding the world of some poor remnant of enchantment, some illusion, foolish perhaps, but lovely?"[83] Victorian life strikes her in retrospect as "foolish" but "lovely." These few words sum up her feeling of judgment tinged with nostalgia, and her judgment is supported elsewhere in the novel. The "foolishness" of Victorian values, including patriarchal ones, is attested to by the author's harsh treatment of Henry Holland and unsparing satire of four of his six children. But Lady Slane's nostalgia is not so well supported. Her long-ago walk "beside the lake" explains her personal ambivalence about her sexuality, but not her (nor the novel's avowed) historical ambivalence about the time. It fails to evoke the "loveliness" of Victorian life, of which the world might conceivably be "defrauded" by women's "new Protestant spirit." The reader wonders what "enchantment" or "illusion" from her childhood, or especially from her marriage, Lady Slane feels was "lovely." Did she once take comfort in being a sheltered female, despite her eagerness at 88 to escape from her patronizing family? In comparison to Mrs Ramsay's and Clarissa's hosting, the role that Lady Slane performed in her family and in political ceremonies was hollow and lacking in dignity, let alone "enchantment." Arguably, the writers' different techniques for introducing ambivalence into their generally critical attitudes toward Victorian gender roles – Woolf's evocation and dramatization versus Sackville-West's comparatively bald assertions of vanished beauty – provide alternative routes to one destination. On the other hand, different routes could lead to different destinations: how one recuperates Victorian loveliness could determine what loveliness, if any, one recuperates.

THE UNMENTIONABLE

A similar question hovers about the two death-soaked novels' divergent strategies for treating mortality. Sackville-West's characters discuss death openly and derive clear ethical values from the thought of it, while Woolf evokes the topic indirectly (though constantly), and her characters – no matter how surely they feel the brush of death's wing – are still bereft of ultimate answers. After the Earl of Slane passes away, the newly liberated heroine of *All Passion Spent* refuses to submit to her children's selfishly motivated plans for her care-taking, instead moving into the small Hampstead house. Only two of her six children support the decision. The reclusive Kay "could understand [the] desire for retirement."[84] Edith, "now living in ... a state of bliss in her own flat" at age 60,[85] more enthusiastically supports her mother's independence. Only at Hampstead is Lady Slane able to "survey her life as ... a unity." There, to borrow a term from G. E. Moore, she pursues "ideal goods," searching for the same kind of heightened experience that she remembers from the Persian desert. "Personal affection and the appreciation of what is beautiful in Art or Nature, are good in themselves," Moore writes.[86] At Hampstead, Lady Slane extricates herself not just from her family, but from all her old, affection-less connections. She prepares for death by pursuing mellow personal intimacies, enjoying works of art (primarily literature), and communing with nature.[87]

Her focus on dying is emblematic of *All Passion Spent*, which transpires between the Earl's and Lady Slane's demises, a brief period during which FitzGeorge dies too. Sackville-West's novel, like Woolf's, looks simultaneously toward the past (including its unrealized possibilities) and the future, as it measures the heroine's fluctuating sense of present reality. The difference between their treatments of death lies in their techniques: indirection in Woolf's case, open discussion in Sackville-West's. Woolf achieves her thematic effect with the help of intricate patterns of imagery and Septimus's mad, but perhaps clairvoyant, visions. "Leaden circles" dissolve in the air,[88] as Big Ben marks off the day's inexorable progress. Clarissa repeatedly recalls the line from *Cymbeline* "Fear no more the heat of the sun,"[89] as she prepares for her eventual passing, as if her own "passion" were "spent." The shadow of war looms over the narrative, not merely as a reminder of universal mortality. Just as the war's survivors may have feelings of historical belatedness, likewise the ageing, recently ill hostess labors under a sense of personal belatedness. "The late age of the world's experience," says the narrator, "had bred in them all, all men and women, a well of tears."[90] Clarissa and Septimus's illnesses (out of which the novel emerges) and his suicide (toward which it moves) enhance the saturation effect: death is everywhere palpable. From Septimus's memories of Evans being killed to his injunction not to cut down the trees,[91] he cannot escape the thought of mortality. From Clarissa's illness to her reaction to Septimus's death, she remains acutely sensitive to human vulnerability.

In *All Passion Spent*, death is as omnipresent, though not as ominous, as in *Mrs Dalloway*. Lady Slane and her friends contemplate it with impressive serenity. No equivalents of "leaden circles" nor the "heat of the sun" haunt her hour-by-hour experience at Hampstead; only her family at Elm Park Gardens pesters her, and she is happiest when free to meditate on mortality. No character in *All Passion Spent* degenerates mentally like Septimus, although its various elderly characters do degenerate physically. While none rages against the destruction of trees, Bucktrout does frequently elaborate upon what Woolf's narrator calls "the late age of the world's experience." When Lady Slane first moves in at Hampstead, they discuss possible changes to her new residence:

> Courteous though he was, Mr. Bucktrout ... [made] no bones about the fact that Lady Slane would require the house for a short period only. Whenever he discouraged her from unnecessary expenditure, he did so on the grounds that it was scarcely worth her while. When she mentioned central heating, he reminded her that she would spend but few winters, if any, in this her last abode.[92]

The nonchalance with which he discusses her imminent passing encapsulates the novel's attitude. Ubiquitous as death is in *All Passion Spent*, it results neither from tragic illnesses nor war, as in *Mrs Dalloway*, but from old age. The "central heating" of the Hampstead house, rather like the passion of Lady Slane and her gentlemen friends, has long been spent.

In the process of readying themselves to die, Sackville-West's sympathetic elderly figures articulate the novel's ethical values, with a clarity that *Mrs Dalloway* – by design – never achieves. At Hampstead, tranquil contemplativeness and detachment reign in place of sexual anxiety, feverish activity, and ambition. "The pleasures of contemplation" says Bucktrout, "are greater than the pleasures of activity."[93] FitzGeorge is described as "genuinely detached from ... social conventions."[94] In a moment when they demonstrate keen perceptiveness, Bucktrout and his friend Mr Gosheron appear to Lady Slane's mean-spirited daughter Carrie as "detached figures ... figures of justice."[95] Unlike the superciliousness of Henry Holland (who was unjust to his spouse), the detachment of the elderly Hampstead figures from competitiveness and conventional falsehoods does establish them as "figures of justice" – according to the novel's gently subversive conception of justice.

Unconcerned though it is with World War One and its aftermath, *All Passion Spent* shares with *Mrs Dalloway* a sense of historical belatedness. Bucktrout raises this theme for his author, though she does not endorse all his theories. The old agent defies the convention dictating that "people do not willingly speak in plain English of death, however fixedly its imminence may weigh on their hearts."[96] A short way into his initial meeting with Lady Slane, he shares his idea that "the end of the world is due in two years' time."[97] Soon later he expands on his theory:

> "As you may know," he said, standing in an unfinished room while painters suspended their brushes in order to listen, "there are at least four theories presaging the end of the world. Flame, flood, frost, and collision ... In so far as I believe numbers to be a basic part of the eternal harmonies, I am a convinced Pythagorean ... I do not mean by this that I hold with ... the Babylonians ... nor [with the claim] that the world would end on March 21, 1843. No, I have worked out my own system, Lady Slane, and I can assure you that, though distressing, it is irrefutable. The great annihilation is close at hand ..."

Lady Slane had never taken so much pleasure in anybody's company.[98]

Bucktrout's visions faintly recall those of Septimus, who also imagines the general end to be near. But *All Passion Spent* treats the old agent with gentle and affectionate irony. His notions are not to be taken seriously: that Lady Slane finds such pleasure in his unselfconscious musings neutralizes any specter of "annihilation" raised by his use of the word. Bucktrout theorizes about "the end of the world," the novel implies, in part because his own end, like that of Lady Slane, is near.

But the agent, although an eccentric, is not without ethical insight. "The world," he tells Lady Slane, "is pitiably horrible . . . because it is based upon competitive struggle." He asks rhetorically whether such struggle is "convention" or "necessity," "extraordinary delusion" or a "law of life." He demonstrates a combination of savvy, in recognizing the world's horror, and compassion, in finding the horror "pitiable." In implying that struggle results from "convention" and "delusion" rather than "necessity," he aligns himself with those in *All Passion Spent* – especially Lady Slane – who recognize the contingency of their own individual lives, and of society's collective life. Lady Slane helps him to elaborate one of the novel's central arguments – its paean to non-conformism – by asking whether "anyone who goes against this extraordinary delusion is helping civilization on?" Her question implies that acts such as her move to Hampstead serve not only her personal interests, but the broader interests of civilization. Bucktrout answers in the affirmative, adding however that as the world is "presently constituted," only "poets" or "people of advanced age" can afford the "luxury" of such non-conformism.[99] In Bucktrout's answer, *All Passion Spent* acknowledges the idealism of its vision of life at Hampstead, reminiscent of existence on the Howards End farm at the conclusion of Forster's novel. Bucktrout prefers poets and art collectors to politicians, and "people of advanced age" to the young – clean binaries of just the sort that Woolf complicates. *All Passion Spent* marks a return to Bloomsburian essentialism most prominently in its representation of selfhood, particularly sexual selfhood; but the clarity of these binaries furthers the project of retrenchment, of shoring up an array of concepts – ontological, epistemological, ethical – that skeptical modernist texts such as *Mrs Dalloway* systematically undermine.

Lady Slane's experiences recall Clarissa's in each of her Moorean Hampstead communions – with nature, art, and friends (the third being Moore's "greatest good").[100] The widow enjoys nature by walking on Hampstead Heath, as Clarissa finds bliss in walking through London to buy flowers. Lady Slane derives even greater pleasure from reading

Shakespeare, the only writer she feels it necessary to read in her advanced age.[101] Shakespeare is, for Lady Slane, the rough equivalent of Marbot for Clarissa. Each heroine reads in order to explore private ontological depths. But they seek and discover different things. Clarissa reads to de-compose herself, not by neutralizing her sexuality but by problematizing it. She does not seek comfort in received wisdom, but revels in fluctuation and uncertainty. Lady Slane reads Shakespeare, by contrast, to find repose in eternal truths, not uncertainty in a maze of sexuality. One heroine finds the "deep truth" of dis-unity; the other, the "deep truth" of unity, in her chosen writer. For each heroine, her privately discovered truth stands in opposition to social falsity: the fiction of the unified self that Clarissa must present to her dinner guests, or of the "extraordinary delusion" of struggle and dis-unity that Lady Slane and Bucktrout perceive in the "world."[102] The anti-essentialism of Woolf's novel (which treats unity as a fiction, albeit a necessary one) transforms into the essentialism of Sackville-West's novel (which treats dis-unity as a delusion, albeit a pervasive and intractable one).

The widow's greatest pleasures at Hampstead are her relationships with Bucktrout, Gosheron, and FitzGeorge, who reject the competitive greed that motivates this "world," including most of Lady Slane's family. These treasured friendships are her equivalent of Clarissa's dinner party, venues for the widow's interpersonal artistry. But there are differences between Clarissa's "offering" – as she describes her party[103] – and Lady Slane's small-scale intimacies at Hampstead, just as there are differences between the heroines' reading experiences. Because Clarissa's party gathers together both distant and close acquaintances, it creates moments of de-familiarization for the Dalloways. Like reading Marbot, the experience of meeting Peter and Sally after many years – and of hearing about Septimus's death – throws Clarissa into a state of intellectually productive perplexity. The artificiality of her party helps it guide its hostess toward usually hidden aspects of reality – one of many instances of *Mrs Dalloway* softening a binary. In Lady Slane's case, her intimate moments with Bucktrout and others are valuable precisely because there is nothing artificial about them. *All Passion Spent* lambastes pretentious social rituals, and Henry Holland for his indifference to "human" questions; it links "reality"[104] to privacy and interiority. *Mrs Dalloway* derides the humbuggery of Dr Bradshaw and more gently satirizes Hugh Whitbread, but depicts routes to "reality" as being less direct than those in *All Passion Spent.*

Sackville-West's novel states its moral most directly when FitzGeorge castigates Lady Slane for having lived an inauthentic life, married to a man incapable of loving her, burdened by public rituals for which she never cared. He insists that her family life "defrauded [her] of the one thing that mattered. Nothing matters to an artist except the fulfillment of his gift."[105] She pretends to resist his loving rebuke, but admits that she had once dreamed of becoming a painter, and consents "I know you are right."[106] FitzGeorge delivers the speech to his beloved, and elicits the response, of which Peter Walsh could only hope. *Mrs Dalloway* denies its characters such communicative success. Clarissa may intuit some of what Peter thinks as he fiddles with his knife, and much of what her husband feels as he presents her with flowers, but in both cases, the man fails to articulate his feelings as transparently as FitzGeorge does. Clarissa must compensate, in her silent interpretations, for the men's indirection or incompleteness of meaning. By contrast, FitzGeorge's genius as a communicator extends beyond the verbal realm, and even beyond his own grave.

Soon after admonishing Lady Slane about her "gift" (a term that, thanks to his generosity, takes on a double meaning), FitzGeorge dies and bequeaths to her all his possessions.[107] His family money and skill as a collector have made his estate extremely valuable, and the estate provides the heroine both a material boon (that she might keep, to her own harm) and a spiritual boon (the chance to divest herself of the estate, and thus to prove her independence to herself). Her children, wealthier in property than cash, scheme for their material shares. They are satirized throughout the novel, but never more acidly than when her son William laments the possibility of being financially disappointed. Mother "seems to have no idea of value, no idea of responsibility," he says. "For all we know, she may hand over the whole collection to the nation."[108] That a former prime minister's son should see a gift to the nation as "irresponsible" indicates the narrow-minded pecuniary motives behind the Holland family's corporate idea of "value." His hypocrisy illustrates the relish with which *All Passion Spent* exposes conventional principles such as "responsibility" – much as *Mrs Dalloway* exposes the hollowness of Dr Bradshaw's ideals of "proportion," "honour," "courage," and "career,"[109] although Woolf's novel lacks the stable foundation of values, articulated at Hampstead, against which to measure the false ones.

Happy with her modest existence at Hampstead, and in possession (eventually) of just such a core of values as Clarissa never discovers, Lady Slane does what William fears. In her evolving understanding of her own action lies one of the novel's central moral arguments. Her initial motive for bequeathing FitzGeorge's collection to England is to exact revenge, not to establish her freedom from the need for wealth. "Think how much I shall annoy my children!" she tells Bucktrout.[110] But then she recalls FitzGeorge's personal integrity, and justifies her bequest on grounds more political than personal. Contrary to her conservative family, she has grown sympathetic to socialism in her advanced years: "It had seemed wrong to her that private people should own such possessions."[111] She decides that FitzGeorge's gift to her had really been a test. She "understood why FitzGeorge had tempted her with this fortune . . . in order that she should find the strength to reject it. He had offered her . . . a chance to be true to herself."[112] She feels that, in making her gift to England, she both redeems her own integrity and does right by a man who loved her. Whereas Clarissa's party is her "offering" merely "for the sake of offering,"[113] FitzGeorge and Lady Slane's bequeathals result in more easily measurable good, both for the nation and the heroine's sake.

FEMINISM WITH AN ESSENCE

The most important beneficiary of Lady Slane's bequest, however, is neither herself nor the nation. At novel's end, when a reincarnation of her young self appears, *All Passion Spent* glances joyously forward to a future in which women can be free to pursue the ambitions that were sacrificed in the heroine's case. Lady Slane has largely refused visitors at Hampstead, and flatly refused to see children. But her great-granddaughter and namesake – Deborah Holland – pays a surprise visit, just after breaking her marriage engagement to a duke's eldest son, and immediately launches into a deep confidence. While the old woman lovingly "allow[s] her fingers to ruffle Deborah's hair," Deborah confesses that she aspires to be a musician and never wanted to marry her fiancé.[114] Sackville-West evinced some feminist sympathies over the course of her career and during her iconoclastic sexual exploits – political instincts that balanced, sometimes uneasily, with her aristocratic values. Her life's second great disappointment was her inability, as a woman, to inherit the family estate at Knole – a deprivation that Woolf helped her to recognize as political and that put Sackville-West's feminism and class allegiance squarely in conflict with one another.[115] The pointed feminism of *All Passion Spent*, including its refusal to allow a second artistically inclined Deborah to become an "appendage" to a spouse's career, is inspired in part by Woolf's *A Room of One's Own* (1929),[116] with its lament for Shakespeare's forgotten sister, and for all female artists denied the opportunity for the "fulfillment of [their] gifts" – to repeat FitzGeorge's words.[117]

Lady Slane not only comes to understand the importance of such "gifts," thanks to FitzGeorge, but she also articulates – both for her own and the readers' sakes – her connection with her alter ego, whereas Clarissa only intuits her connection with Septimus. Recognizing the parallels between the young Deborah's current, and her own former, dilemma, Lady Slane tells her "go on, my darling, you might be myself speaking."[118] She admires her alter ego's resolution – "This child, this Deborah, this self, this other self, this projection of herself, was firm and certain"[119] – noting two character traits that are negatively connoted in *Mrs Dalloway* (Doris Kilman and Millicent Bruton are unattractively "certain" of themselves), but more positively connoted in Sackville-West's novel. But Lady Slane had not anticipated that her bequest, by reducing the net worth of the entire Slane family, would make Deborah a less attractive fiancée, and would thus free Deborah to break her engagement. Deborah visits the old woman to express her gratitude for being liberated to pursue her ambitions. When it appears that Lady Slane has fallen asleep, Deborah quietly leaves the house. In fact the old woman has blissfully passed away, having bequeathed to Deborah both freedom from an unwanted marriage, and also, metaphorically speaking, a youthful artistic spirit that was "thwarted" in the old woman's case,[120] but that now gets a second chance for expression. Sackville-West's novel refigures Clarissa's frustration with her contrary-minded daughter by granting Lady Slane a like-minded daughter figure, to compensate for her four disagreeable offspring.

The young Deborah also refigures Septimus Smith, and in so doing illustrates an essentialist technique of *All Passion Spent* as surely as she clarifies its feminist sympathies. Woolf's early ideas for *Mrs Dalloway* included no Septimus figure, and ended with Clarissa killing herself.[121] But in the published version, Septimus's death suggests that the self-destructive side of Clarissa's mind has been laid to rest, at least for the time being. *All Passion Spent* reverses *Mrs Dalloway*'s use of the alter ego: its heroine dies so that a secondary character may live more fully, rather than vice versa. But the more important difference lies in how Septimus and the young Deborah are functionally deployed: the first in an anti-essential way, to dissolve boundaries between characters, and the second to establish conceptual distinctions. Septimus and Clarissa alternate appearances throughout *Mrs Dalloway*, and they are aesthetically blended, almost into one, as Big Ben strikes noon (the chronological and symbolic mid-point of the novel), when "Clarissa Dalloway" and "the Warren Smiths" are mentioned in the same sentence.[122] Not just at this moment, but throughout the novel, the identity of one seeps into the other: her compromised bisexuality (her affair with Sally relegated to a precious memory) and her tenuous hold on psychic stability scarcely differ from Septimus's obliterated bisexuality

(Evans dies a gruesome death) and loss of psychic stability. The narrative does not merely imply that *there, but for the grace of good fortune, goes Clarissa*, in itself an unsettling suggestion. The narrative goes further, implying that Clarissa *has already gone there*, i.e., she has already endured the same kinds of traumas (though not exactly the same ones) and wrung from them the same kinds of insights as Septimus: they differ only in degree. The heroine and her alter ego can be viewed as two characters, or as two aspects of one character.

The two Deborah Hollands, for their part, are conceptually distinct in ways that Woolf's doubles are not. One enters the tale as the other passes from it and passes away. One represents an unlived life of open possibilities; the other, a life lived, with opportunities missed. One might fulfill ambition, the other has not. One embodies twentieth-century femininity; the other, Victorian femininity. Because Lady Slane does not meet the young Deborah early in the novel, her memory of herself as a young woman does not "mingle" with images of this aspiring musician.

The same lack of blurring applies to the young Deborah's sexuality. In *Mrs Dalloway*, Clarissa's bisexuality roughly mirrors that of Septimus; she has male traits and he has female ones; categories are confounded. But in *All Passion Spent*, the young Deborah is not ambiguously gendered: she represents (with vague promise) fresh possibilities for women in the social matrix, but her character is not a vehicle for rethinking the definition of "woman." It goes without saying that she is under no requirement to be such a vehicle, and that, its essentialism notwithstanding, *All Passion Spent* pursues its themes in its own rigorous ways, not least among them its feminist assault on Victorian spousal roles.

Nonetheless, its relationship to *Mrs Dalloway* is, quite clearly, fraught with emulation and anxiety. That such particular thematic concerns could migrate between novels of such radically different techniques is a fact of salutary aesthetic surprise to one who reads the texts consecutively. While Woolf's formal experimentalism, anti-essentialism, and complex signification produced works (as the same qualities did for Freud) of rare aesthetic power, *All Passion Spent* too deserves a prominent place among Bloomsburian critiques of intimacy. Lawrence's roots enable him to depict sons and daughters of the working class struggling over the meaning of "love"; Woolf's social circles enable her to imagine a dinner party which a prime minister attends and from which he quickly vanishes; Sackville-West's more patrician experiences enable her to draw back the veil from a prime minister's family and reveal it to be fraught with much of the interpersonal alienation, ennui, and lack of freedom that people of other classes confront, as they negotiate their intimacies and reflect on their sexual careers.

No matrix of twentieth-century personalities bequeathed to Anglo-American culture as many unsettling and inspiring examples of intimacy as the Bloomsburians. Whether by constantly falling in and out of love, by remaining married through difficulties, by simultaneously pursuing intimacies with partners of both sexes, by meditating on the value of intimacy in public and private writings, by composing elaborate love letters in the guise of literature, or by providing biographical fodder for a prurient press, members of this group and its satellites challenged a new century to think beyond received Victorian notions about sexuality, desire, and affection. They were no less reverent toward love than their ancestors, different though their morality was. With its sharp insights into the social construction of "feminine" intellectual limitations, its halting ruminations on what a rival definition of womanhood might be like, and its stern repudiation of the Victorian marriage paradigm, Sackville-West's novel distinguishes itself from its precursor – imperfectly and yet impressively – as only the work of a loving disciple could do.

Conclusion: the prescience of the two Bloomsburies

There are of course more than two Bloomsburies: future critics will formulate other accounts of the group and its relations to modernism, modernity, and post-World War Two culture than I do, with my categories of *anti-essentialist accommodations* and *essentialist disenchantments.* By gathering, under the *anti-essentialist* heading, texts associated both with the group's inner circle (Moore, Woolf) and with its satellites (Freud, Lawrence), and by doing the same under the *essentialist* heading (Forster the inner-circle member, Sackville-West the satellite), I aim to evoke a few of the many ways in which Bloomsbury and modernism exert gravitational influences on one another.

By applying these labels to texts rather than writers, I emphasize how multifaceted each of these writers was. Lawrence expressed essentialist ideas in his essays and anti-essentialist ones in his fiction; these tensions make all his works more exciting. Nowhere do Forster and Sackville-West treat sexuality in quite such Victorian ways as in *Howards End* and *All Passion Spent*, which makes these two works illustrative of the group's ambivalence about the reinvention of intimacy. Without an essentialist counterpoint to its Freudian and Woolfian essence-dissolving points, this set of six writers – one possible sample of Bloomsbury and its extensions – would make a blander music. It is because they conjure, both individually and in tandem, the paradoxes of modern couplehood, love, and friendship that these compositions have an uncanny prescience.

From one point of view, the anti-essentialist texts seem the more prescient ones, with their *avant-garde* means for depicting how new kinds of people adapt themselves to inherited institutions. In keeping with Virginia Woolf's comment about human character changing,[1] I said in the Introduction that the "spouses" and "friends" of 1930 inhabited those roles differently than their grandparents did. Woolf's free indirect style both recorded and provoked the transformations of the psyches that inhabit these roles. And even today, generations after 1930, people continue accommodating to marriage, and altering it from within. Sometimes we feel more like prisoners than like agents of marriage, as "mass divorce" suggests – a psychological malady that Russell and Lawrence diagnosed in spouses of their time. Nonetheless, we continue rethinking what maleness and femaleness mean, and adjusting our expectations of intimacy to a transforming economy and culture.

In comparison to avant-garde anti-essentialist works by Woolf and Freud, with their subtle attention to changing mores, *Howards End* and *All Passion Spent* can seem antique. Their Victorian narrative voices and their amber-encased male and female personalities – Henrys Wilcox and Holland with their "hard" Soul-material and spousal "appendages" – depict paradigms of matrimonial imprisonment that numerous demographic facts suggest have been superceded. First, there are more single people now (see Table 2 in Appendix). The 2005 US census indicated that for the first time more than half of American females over the age of 15 were living without husbands.[2] Women are not stigmatized for being "spinsters" as they were in the Victorian era; the independent joys of Lady Slane's post-marital life, though difficult for several of her children to understand in the early twentieth century, are today savored by millions of divorced, widowed, and never-married women in Britain, America, and Europe. Second, couples from advanced democratic nations continue to have fewer offspring than Victorian households such as the Stracheys (Lytton and James were among thirteen children, ten of whom survived childhood), suggesting that, thanks to such forces as contraception and female emancipation, families are increasingly planned to meet the personal and professional desires of both spouses. Clarissa Dalloway may be unlike many of today's middle-class mothers in her lack of professional ambition and her retinue of servants, but she mirrors them in the small size of her nuclear family. Finally, the kinds of couples in today's sexual landscape differ from those of the past. "Cohabiting couple families" are an important enough (rapidly growing) phenomenon that they comprise their own category on the 2001 British census. The growing numbers of mixed-race couples, especially in the United States, testify to the possibilities and perils of a post-civil rights era sexual culture, as Zadie Smith chronicles in *On Beauty* (2005). Dual-career couples test the rigidity of contemporary professions, the creativity of small and geographically isolated families, and the lingering association of masculinity with superiority.[3] Most pertinently to this study, Lawrence's "other kind of love" comes decreasingly to be seen as a "perversion." Moore's obfuscations of male–male desire in his 1903 treatise remind us of the homophobic atmosphere that led Forster, even into the late-twentieth century, to disguise his sexual orientation; but they also illustrate how radically different today's post-Stonewall culture is for gay members of elite campus communities such as Cambridge's. Off of campus, in some nations and some American states, same-sex marriage is legal; in others it is recognized though not performed; in others yet, civil unions or unregistered cohabitations are legally recognized, as the patchwork of gay and lesbian civil rights expands (see Table 11 in Appendix). From a perspective of Freudian-inspired anti-essentialism, marriage seems very able to bend with the times, to be reconstituted by the same people who accommodate themselves to it, and who in some cases agitate for the right to wed.

But from an equally compelling perspective, Forster and Sackville-West's more stylistically Victorian and psychologically essentialist novels, which pull no punches in their depictions of marital strife and inequity, can seem the more prescient ones. Perhaps today's mass divorce and large number of singles tell us that some marriages cannot or should not be salvaged, and that for many people marriage is not necessary to a happy life. *All Passion Spent* placidly suggests as much with its heroine's joyous widowhood; and *Howards End* more violently suggests as much when events as good as nullify its heroine's first marriage, and enable her remarriage to a man who – now physically and emotionally defeated – is the same in name only as the erstwhile self-assured patriarch. These novels tell tales of trapped wives (Forster's concludes with a sort of trapped husband), of spouses unable to meet as equal companions or husbands uninterested in doing so. Evidence of Forster's and Sackville-West's prescience may lie particularly in the disproportionate numbers of divorce-seeking wives in our era, for whom marriage has apparently not transformed enough since the Victorian years. Perhaps more of Lady Slane's contemporaries would have divorced, had the taboo against it not remained so strong prior to World War Two. (See Table 13 in Appendix, for divorce rates across time; Table 14 in Appendix, entry on "1923," for wives.) Sackville-West captures the power dynamics of a Victorian marriage (and some twenty-first-century unions) with the terse clarity and god's-eye perspective of sentences such as "All her life long, gracious and gentle, [Lady Slane] had been wholly submissive."[4]

Such sentences evoke a world of stable truths and easily diagnosed familial dysfunction; what they lack in psychological subtlety, they compensate for with the clarity of radical social critique. By contrast, the free indirect style of *Mrs Dalloway* and the sophisticated narrative techniques in

Dora evoke, at a more minute level, the psychic fluctuations of a wife in an imperfect marriage, a daughter in an imperfect family. But what these texts gain from their dazzling inward turns,[5] they lose in the level of potency that *Howards End* and *All Passion Spent* share as indictments of a marital paradigm that women can only accommodate through submission.

While twenty-first-century citizens struggle to understand their marriages, the legacy of the anti-essentialist Bloomsbury is open to question. Classical Freudian analysts are a dwindling band, and the epistemological value of Freud's and Woolf's stylistic innovations is more apparent to scholars of modernism than to general readers. Carpenter's celebration of emergent intermediate male Soul-material can seem premature, and Lawrence's more essentialist talk of "polarisation" can seem astute, as theories of gender dimorphism abound in books such as John Gray's 1992 *Men Are from Mars, Women Are from Venus*. For Gray, acknowledging these innate differences is necessary to cultivating happy marriages. Admittedly, he does not use such supposed differences to justify political discrimination: he never refers to "henny" women "laying" votes. Nonetheless, beyond the admonitions of today's advice manuals about sex and love, sociological and psychological scholarship demonstrates the persistence of sexual divisions in the allocation of household work. Wives continue to do more than their share of it, often at the cost of depression; and even husbands of working wives contribute little more domestic labor than husbands of stay-at-home wives.[6] The "democratization" of intimacy that Giddens trumpets, that Lawrence regards warily, and of which Forster and Sackville-West's novels offer scant evidence, remains an unfinished enterprise.

THE SEXOLOGICAL PROJECT

But even as gender dimorphism continues to structure household labor, sexology goes on redefining human sexuality, with each development in research raising new questions and provoking new (and old) criticisms, from both the right and the left. After Bloomsbury's time, just as in its time, avant-garde sexual theories have sometimes but not always accompanied liberationist politics. With his two "Reports," the 1948 *Sexual Behavior in the Human Male* and the 1953 *Sexual Behavior in the Human Female*, Alfred Kinsey attacked the notion of sexual essences in several ways. For one, he resisted the binary terms "heterosexual" and "homosexual," proposing in their place a seven-point scale, on which individuals could rate themselves a "0" if exclusively heterosexual, a "6" if exclusively homosexual, one of five gradations between if their sexual preferences were mixed, or an "X" if they were asexual. Second, he recorded people's placements on the scale according to different age groups, leaving open the possibility that their sexuality could be fluid over time. "Males," he wrote in the first Report, "do not represent two discrete populations, heterosexual and homosexual. The world is not to be divided into sheep and goats . . . It is a fundamental of taxonomy that nature rarely deals with discrete categories."[7] His rhetoric recalls Carpenter's, combining the confidence of an objective scientist with the passion of a social reformer. If anything, with talk of "sheep and goats," he is more polemical than Carpenter tended to be, more openly scornful of contemporary prejudice and Puritanism, as Freud sometimes was.

Not surprisingly, this made him enemies. His first Report has been on more than one conservative list of the worst books of modern times. He was accused of child sexual abuse and of collaboration with a child molester, charges designed to discredit both him and his work, and that he and his Institute vigorously rebutted. His methodology was criticized on more scholarly grounds for being colored by his personal motives (his own sexuality moved from the hetero- to the homo- end of his scale over the course of his life), and for failing to utilize random samples, specifically for overrepresenting prisoners and male prostitutes. But Paul Gebhard, his successor as director of the Kinsey Institute for Sex Research, claimed in his 1979 *Kinsey Data* that after "cleaning" methodological contaminants from Kinsey's original estimates (e.g., of men who had at least one homosexual orgasm), he found that no data were significantly affected. The six main authors in this study, of course, did not engage in the intensive statistical research associated with Kinsey's Institute, but nonetheless in the decades between Havelock Ellis's first published works and Kinsey's first Report, Freud, Lawrence, and Woolf used path-breaking authorial techniques to put complex human faces (fictional, though clinically and autobiographically derived) on the data that sexologists established with the help of methods specific to their discipline.

The husband-and-wife team of William Masters (an obstetrician) and Virginia Johnson (a psychologist and sex therapist) built on Kinsey's work and went in directions he did not, in their widely translated *Human Sexual Response* (1966) and *Human Sexual Inadequacy* (1970). Using such methods as laboratory observations of thousands of hours of coitus, they researched the physiology of human sex. They describe a four-phase sexual response in people; their distinction between "plateau" and orgasm inspired many subsequent sex-advice books and articles. Research at the Masters and Johnson Institute advanced scientific understanding of the physiology of female sexual arousal and established that sexual responsiveness persists, though in diminished ways, throughout human life. In all these ways, Masters and Johnson challenged taboos, aimed to combat ignorance, and promoted the idea that sex is natural and healthy, linking them to a tradition including Kinsey, Ellis, and other precursors.[8] Though Freud was among these precursors, they rejected Freudian assumptions they found erroneous. Their rapid (two-week) treatment for sexual dysfunction was a radical alternative to the protracted Freudian talking cure, for example. And to the delight of many feminists, they overturned a Freudian idea in asserting that there is no physiological difference between orgasms achieved by vaginal and clitoral stimulation.

But whereas their attitudes toward female sexuality excited many on the counter-cultural left, their approaches to homosexuality did not. From 1968 to 1977, their Institute administered a program to convert homosexuals to heterosexuality. Their 1979 book *Homosexuality in Perspective* touts their success rate, though Johnson and co-author Robert Kolodny were skeptical of Masters's data.[9] Forster's *Maurice* was prescient in portraying collusion – which permeated psychiatry for decades – between heteronormativity and the post-Freudian medicalization of sexual dysfunction. Nonetheless, the psychiatric profession preceded Masters in the evolution of its diagnostic attitude toward same-sex attraction. *Homosexuality in Perspective* appeared six years after the American Psychiatric Association repealed its classification of homosexuality as a psychological "disorder." In convoluted ways, sexology (like psychoanalysis) has for decades undermined some sexual norms, reinforced others, and wavered in its own ethical attitudes.

THE AESTHETIC LEGACY

It seems, then, that both the anti-essentialist and essentialist, both the accommodationist and the radically disaffected texts in this study anticipate the work of subsequent literary and scientific figures. Today's husbands and wives both are and are not like their Wilcoxian ancestors. The institution of marriage both is and is not the same now as it was in the Dalloways' milieu, and it continues both to elicit compromises and inspire rejections. Religious and secular, conservative and liberal polemicists continue to wrestle with the implications of non-normal sexualities, though rarely with the same spirit of mutual regard that Birkin and Gerald bring to their wrestling match.

High Modernism may or may not be a closed chapter in literary history. Perhaps modernist Bloomsbury's nexus of technical avant-gardism and reimagining of human sexuality was a one-time perfect storm of crises in artistic method and social ideology. Nonetheless, the complex relations between psychosexual experimentation and technical experimentation are still playing out, as Bloomsbury's progeny pick and choose from among the group's techniques. Norman Mailer took inspiration from Lawrence's romantic vitalism, sex worship, and antifeminism in a range of works that respond to the legacy of modernists' formal experiments with their own deft blends of journalistic, historiographic, and novelistic techniques. Marleen Gorris's skillfully directed *Mrs Dalloway* (1997) underscores the continued relevance of the novel's feminist themes, but as Rebecca Walkowitz explains, largely drains the tale of its modernism in adapting it to a linear narrative for the screen.[10] Michael Cunningham's *The Hours* (2000), on the other hand, not only finds *Mrs Dalloway* relevant to post-AIDS New York, but also interweaves scenes from different decades and locales in ways that, without replicating Woolf's methods, share her commitment to a non-realist, non-linear examination of sexual psychology.

I have argued that *Howards End* is more Victorian than *Mrs Dalloway*, especially in its sexual themes, and to a lesser degree in its narrative techniques. But its afterlife, like that of Forster's other novels, suggests that its importance stretches far beyond Victorian and Edwardian boundaries. Five of Forster's six novels have been adapted for the screen, by filmmakers as distinguished as David Lean and the Merchant–Ivory team. As novelist and theorist, Zadie Smith has shown Forster's humanist values, ironies, and liberal self-critiques to be highly refined instruments for analyzing many of contemporary Transatlantic society's contradictions and achievements, including the aforementioned phenomenon of mixed-race couples.[11] While I pointed earlier to the capacity for radical critique shared by *Howards End* and *All Passion Spent*, Smith describes Forster as walking a "middling line." She admires his avoidance of ideological extremes even as she notes his capacity for "disingenuousness" as a closeted homosexual. Though not a High Modernist, Forster, the man and the artist, can be as suggestive an example as Woolf to today's politically astute, technically meticulous citizen-novelists.

It is not only critics, but also storytellers literary and filmic, as well as artists in other media associated with Bloomsbury, who explain why the group mattered to its time and determine why it matters to ours. Prescience, of course, is constructed as much as discovered in past cultural figures, and other critics may construct three or even four Bloomsburies to capture how widely suggestive the group has been to its various successors. But whatever number of Bloomsburies the six main works in this study represent, with their various attitudes toward sexual essences, the ambiguities of marriage, and the epistemological value of formal experimentation, it is a testament to their dynamism that thinkers a century later – enmeshed in the contradictions of our own intimate lives and political struggles – can find so many resonances in their pages.

Appendix

Table 1 *Percentage of adults ever married (currently married, widowed, or divorced)*

Year	Men (%)	Women (%)
1851	83.8	83.7[1]
1861	85.8	84.1
1871	86.3	84.4
1881	86.2	84.6
1891	85.3	83.6
1911	83.1	80.4
1921	85.0	80.8
1931	87.8	80.6
1941	88.8	82.7[2]
1946	88.1	83.6
1951	89.1	85.8
1956	89.7	89.5
1960	89.0	91.3

[1] For the years 1851 to 1931 (which cover the 35- to 44-year-old age group), see Office of Population Censuses and Surveys, *Census 1931: General Tables, England and Wales*, Table 21: Ages (grouped) and marital conditions at successive censuses (England and Wales), 150. Tracking marriage rates by an age bracket, particularly one in the prime of life, is a standard method of tabulation. Data are uncertain before 1851, when the Census began recording marital status.

[2] For the years 1941 to 1960 (which cover the 40- to 44-year-old age group), see Busfield and Paddon, *Thinking about Children*, Table 1:5 Proportion of persons ever married (out of 1,000) in England and Wales, 1881–1960, 9.

Table 2 *Married couples as percentage of adult population (age 16 or over)*[1]

Year	Percentage of population
1971	67
1981	64
1991	55
2001	50.7

[1] Statistics are for England and Wales. See www.statistics.gov.uk/census2001/profiles/commentaries/family.asp

Table 3 *Urban population as percentage of total population (England and Wales)*[1]

Year	Census	R. Price-Williams	T. A. Welton	C. M. Law
1801	24.2	40.1	39.1	33.8
1811	25.6	42.8	46.3	36.6
1821	27.1	43.4	48.2	40.0
1831	29.5	46.0	51.5	44.3
1841	31.9	48.3	54.0	48.3
1851	50.2	51.4	57.4	54.0
1861	54.6	51.9	60.7	58.7
1871	61.6	55.6	65.0	65.2
1881	67.9	–	67.1	70.0
1891	72.0	–	68.8	74.5
1901	77.0	–	79.4	78.0
1911	78.1	–	80.7	78.9
1921	79.4	–	–	–
1931	82.4 (80.0)[2]			
1941	No census due to the war			
1951	80.7			

The census's earlier estimates differ significantly from those of the three researchers because its "Urban Districts" only include districts that contain London and 62 other "Principal Towns." The census did not begin trying systematically to measure rural versus urban population until 1851, and its methods developed over the decades. I include the researchers for a study in contrasting data that, by the twentieth century, give way to consensus.

[1] Saville, *Rural Depopulation*, 61, from England and Wales' *Census of 1911: General Report* (35); *Census of 1931: General Report* (39); *Census of 1951: Preliminary Report* (Table E, xvii). For a fuller discussion of increases and decreases in percentages, see Saville, *Rural Depopulation*, 61–3, including his table on 62. For a definition of "urban" and other types of populations, see Lawton, "Census data," 114–20, esp. 115. See Lawton, "Census data," 83, nn. 2–5 for citations of these other three researchers.
[2] The parenthetical figure for 1931 is the original tabulation. The first figure is amended from boundary changes under the Local Government Act of 1929 (not completed until after 1931). These boundary changes finally began to count newly suburban areas as urban – "urban overspill into the rural areas" (Saville, *Rural Depopulation*, 63).

Table 4 *Population density in England*[1]

Year	Inhabitants per square km
1871	163
1881	187
1891	209
1901	234

Table 4 (*cont.*)

Year	Inhabitants per square km
1911	255
1921	270
1931	287

The populations of London and each of three categories of large towns (those with populations over 100,000; between 50,000 and 100,000; and between 20,000 and 50,000) all grew as a portion of the total combined population of England and Wales for each census year 1801–1911.[2]

[1] Rothenbacher, *European Population 1850–1945*, 723, Table UK3.
[2] See Lawton, "Census data," 112, Fig. 11, who bases his data on (and cites) Law's work.

Table 5 *Population of suburbs as raw number and as percentage of national population*

	Tunbridge Wells town,[1] in Kent (county)	Richmond-upon-Thames,[2] borough of London	Greenwich,[3] borough of London	Pop. of England[4]
1801: .201	15,586 (.201)	14,560 (.188)	16,866 (.218)	7,754,875
1811: .200	17,545 (.200)	16,748 (.191)	20,900 (.239)	8,762,178
1821: .204	21,187 (.204)	19,908 (.191)	25,208 (.242)	10,402,143
1831: .191	22,947 (.191)	22,752 (.189)	30,113 (.251)	12,011,830
1841: .236	32,218 (.236)	25,224 (.185)	38,284 (.280)	13,654,914
1851: .230	35,163 (.230)	28,769 (.188)	52,190 (.341)	15,288,885
1861: .216	39,544 (.216)	40,194 (.219)	74,801 (.408)	18,325,052
1871: .206	43,925 (.206)	51,619 (.242)	97,413 (.456)	21,361,235
1881: .198	48,306 (.198)	63,045 (.258)	120,024 (.492)	24,397,385
1891: .189	51,410 (.189)	79,854 (.293)	174,316 (.640)	27,231,229
1901: .199	59,846 (.199)	103,720 (.345)	185,062 (.615)	30,072,180
1911: .208	69,710 (.208)	134,729 (.401)	196,471 (.585)	33,561,235
1921: .198	69,691 (.198)	152,968 (.434)	213,562 (.606)	35,230,225
1931: .186	69,672 (.186)	173,683 (.464)	232,142 (.621)	37,359,045
1941: .189	73,158 (.189)	187,420 (.485)	227,864 (.589)	38,668,830
1951: .187	76,817 (.187)	202,246 (.491)	223,674 (.543)	41,159,213
1961: .195	84,857 (.195)	187,923 (.432)	220,305 (.507)	43,460,525
1971: .204	93,773 (.204)	174,640 (.380)	216,993 (.472)	45,978,080
1981: .208	95,254 (.218)	157,298 (.344)	209,868 (.459)	45,767,974

Table 5 (*cont.*)

	Tunbridge Wells town,[1] in Kent (county)	Richmond-upon-Thames,[2] borough of London	Greenwich,[3] borough of London	Pop. of England[4]
1991: .212	102,035 (.212)	164,235 (.341)	213,488 (.443)	48,197,672
2001: .212	104,030 (.212)	172,327 (.351)	214,540 (.437)	49,138,831

[1] "Tunbridge Wells through time," University of Portsmouth, *A Vision of Britain through Time.* Tunbridge Wells was popular for its mineral spas (the town and its wells were built around a mineral spring in the seventeenth century) and wooden crafts (Tunbridge Ware was manufactured until the 1920s). The town built a theater in the early nineteenth century, the railway reached it in 1846, sewers came in the early 1870s, a technical institute opened in 1897, and (after boundary extensions) a council house estate was built in the 1920s (Lambert, "A brief history").

[2] Urban growth reached Richmond after 1850, along with areas such as Acton, Chiswick, Brentford, Twickenham, Ealing, Willesden, Hampstead, Hornsey, Tottenham, Putnam, Wimbledon, Streatham, Dulwich, Catford, Lewisham, Greenwich, Charlton. See Lambert, "London in the 19th century." Richmond has had several names over the decades – it is now Richmond-upon-Thames – but by "*redistrict*[*ing*] the historical statistics to the modern units" ("Richmond upon Thames," University of Portsmouth , *A Vision of Britain through Time*; see "Population") we see a clear growth pattern to the mid-twentieth century, then a drop.

[3] "Greenwich through Time" (the borough of Greenwich contains Woolwich), University of Portsmouth, *A Vision of Britain through Time.* During the "era of mandatory marriage 1850–1960," Gillis writes, "in Greenwich and Woolwich, the highly paid engineering and shipbuilding workers separated themselves from the casually employed of the dockside" (*For Better, for Worse*, 247). In 1915, "the greatest of the government-built housing developments" was built "to accommodate munitions workers at Woolwich Arsenal. Over one thousand houses were constructed on . . . streets [laid out] in a low-density, garden suburb manner, which was to prove highly influential with local authorities across the country after the Armistice ("Greenwich," *London Suburbs*, 195).

[4] "England: total population," University of Portsmouth, *A Vision of Britain through Time.*

Table 6 *Family sizes, 1861–1939*

Marriage cohort (England and Wales)[1]	Family size
1861–9	6.16
1871	5.94
1876	5.62
1881	5.27

Middle classes increasingly begin family planning, coincident with early modes of contraception and the Great Depression of the 1880s. Fewer families have numbers of children that deviate greatly from the average.[2]

Table 6 (*cont.*)

Marriage cohort (England and Wales)[1]	Family size
1886	4.81
1900–9	3.30
1910–14	2.82
1915–19	2.46
1920–4	2.31
1925–9	2.11
Great Depression, *c.*1929–33	
1930–4	2.07
1935–9	2.03

[1] Busfield and Paddon, *Thinking about Children*, 9.
[2] British Family Research Council, *Families in Britain*, 78.

Table 7 *Live births per woman sorted by class, 1900–24*[1]

Date of first marriage	Non-manual group	Manual group
1900–9	2.81	3.96
1910–14	2.36	3.36
1915–19	2.07	2.94
1920–4	1.90	2.72

The ratio of children per woman of manual–non-manual groups remained roughly 1.4–1 between 1900 and 1924. By contrast, from 1851 to 1886 family size increasingly differentiated by class, as professional classes, industrial and retail employers, and some textile workers limited families at higher rates than groups such as miners and agricultural laborers.[2]

[1] McGregor, *Divorce in England*, 84.
[2] *Ibid.* 83.

Table 8 *Domestic service in England and Wales, 1851–1931*

Year	Number of servants[1]	Servants as % of population age 15+[2]	Number of charwomen[3]	Charwomen as % of servant class
1851	908,138	6.92	55,423	6.0
1861	1,123,428	8.70	65,273	6.3
1871	1,387,872	9.56	77,650	6.1
1881	1,453,175	8.80	92,474	7.0
1891[4]	1,549,502	8.23	104,808	7.0
1901	1,370,773	6.24	111,841	7.5
1911	1,314,024	5.25	126,061	9.1
1921	1,209,704	4.42	118,476	8.9
1931[5]	1,410,713	4.64	140,146	9.9

Two trends not directly reflected above are the overall feminization of domestic service, especially in the late-nineteenth century; and the disappearance of resident domestics, who occupied close to 5% of English homes in 1931, 1% of homes in 1951, and 0.6% of homes in 1961.[6]

[1] McBride, *Domestic Revolution*, Table 2.2 English servant population, 36; Table 7.1 Total servant populations in France and England, rates of increase and decrease, 1851–1931, 112 (*ibid*).

[2] Population statistics from Rothenbacher, *European Population 1850–1945*, Table EW.1 Population structure at census dates, England and Wales 1851–1931 (v.1, 720). This percentage will be slightly inflated, especially in Victorian years, because a small (but shrinking) portion of servants would be girls under 15.

[3] McBride, *Domestic Revolution*, Table 7.2 Charwomen in England and Wales, rates of increase and decrease, 113. I preserve the percentages in McBride's original chart (rather than recalculating them in accordance with the servant totals in the far-left column) to keep the integrity of that study (and regardless, the percentages vary by less than 1 percent).

[4] The 1891 census counts "women and girls working as 'servants' in their own families," thus artificially inflating the total (Horn, *Victorian*, 232).

[5] During the Depression, women reentered "the domestic labour force to supplement declining family incomes" (McBride, *Domestic Revolution*, 111).

[6] For feminization, see *ibid.*, and Horn, *Victorian*, Appendix G: "Servant numbers in Victorian England and Wales," 232–3. For disappearing resident domestics, see Horn, *Life Below*, 231.

Table 9 *Owner-occupied dwellings as percentage of all dwellings*[1]

Year	Percentage of dwellings occupied by owner	Area measured
1900	10[2]	Great Britain
1914	14–23 (estimate)[3]	England and Wales
1945	26[4]	England and Wales
1951	29	Great Britain

Table 9 (*cont.*)

Year	Percentage of dwellings occupied by owner	Area measured
1964	45	Great Britain
1979	52	England and Wales
1983	63	England and Wales
2000	68	England and Wales

[1] Pre-1900 data are minimal. O'Carroll's data ("Tenements to bungalows," 223) on Edinburgh (8.4% of dwellings occupied by owners in 1855) likely approximate trends in England and Wales, given the similarities between the three places' employment patterns and wages (*ibid.* 228, 229). Even after 1900, despite increasing home ownership being "one of the most important social changes" in Britain, figures on its "extent" are approximate and spotty, because the Census did not ask a question on tenure until 1961 (*ibid.* 221).
[2] Data for 1900/1, 1951, and 1964 are from "Stock of dwellings: by tenure," at *National Statistics Online.*
[3] Morris and Rodger, *Victorian City*, 25.
[4] Data for 1945, 1979, 1983, and 2000 are from Waller, *English Urban Landscape*, 23.

Table 10 *Married women in various classes using any form of birth control (as percentages)*[1]

Date of marriage	Class 1	Class 2	Class 3	Overall
Before 1910	26	18	4	15
1910–19	60	39	33	40
1920–4	–	–	–	58
1925–9	–	–	–	61
1930–4	–	–	–	63
1935–9	–	–	–	66
1940–7	–	–	–	55

Class 1: wives of non-manual workers
Class 2: wives of skilled manual workers
Class 3: wives of unskilled manual workers

[1] From Leathard, *Family Planning*, a combination of Tables 1.2 and 9.2.

Table 11 *Legalization of same-sex marriage*[1]

Date of legalization	Nation	US state
2001, April 1	*Netherlands* 2,500 marriages in 2001	
2003, January 30	*Belgium* 2,442 marriages by July 22, 2005	
2004, May 17		*Massachusetts* Defense of Marriage Act (September 21, 1996) prevents federal government from recognizing same-sex marriages
2005, July 3	*Spain* 4,500 marriages within first year	
2005, July 20	*Canada* 8 of 10 provinces and 1 of 3 territories had already legalized it	
2006, November 30	*South Africa*	
2008, June 16–November 4		*California* Same-sex marriage repealed with passage of Proposition 8
2008, November 12		*Connecticut*
2009, January 1	*Norway*	
2009, April 27		*Iowa*
2009, May 1	*Sweden*	
2009, September 1		*Vermont*
2009, September 14 (approx.)		*Maine* Pending a people's veto
2010, January 1		*New Hampshire*

[1] For information on US laws, see "Same-sex marriage, civil unions, and domestic partnerships." For the Netherlands, see Hundley, "Homosexual unions." For Belgium and other European nations, and European opinion on the issue, see "Same-sex marriage: re-defining marriage around the world." For Spain, see "Spain approves liberal gay marriage law." For Canada, see "Canada passes bill to legalize gay marriage." For South Africa, see "South Africa passes same-sex marriage bill." For Norway, see Grew, "Norway legalises gay marriage." For Sweden, see "Gays win marriage rights." For further data on European opinions, see "Eight EU countries back same-sex marriage."

Table 12 *Illegitimacy rates (England and Wales)*[1]

Year	Percent of unmarried women (age 15–44) who gave birth (in percentages)	Illegitimate births per 100 legitimate births
1851	1.88	7.3
1861	1.81	6.8
1871	1.70	5.9
1881	1.41	5.1
1891	1.06	4.4
1901	0.84	4.1
1911	0.80	4.5
1915	–	4.7
1918	–	6.7
1921	0.79	4.8
1931	0.57	4.7
1941	–	5.7
1945	–	10.3
1951	0.98	5.1
1961	1.66	6.4
1971	2.22	9.2
1981	1.99	14.6
1991	3.99	43.3

The 1891 to 1931 period, coincident with this study, shows a nadir in illegitimacy rates. The 1960s mark the start of the sexual revolution.

[1] Garrett, *Changing Family Size*, 212–13. See also Rothenbacher: Table EW.4 Demographic developments, England and Wales 1850–1945, v.1, 734–7; Table EW.4A Demographic developments, England and Wales 1946–1995 (absolute figures and rates), v.2, 880–3 (*European Population 1850–1945*). For a graph of this data for the entire UK, see Figure UK.5 Fertility and legitimacy, United Kingdom 1864–1939, v.1, 711; Figure UK.5 Fertility and legitimacy, United Kingdom 1946–1995, v.2, 855 (*ibid.*).

Table 13 *Three phases of increase in divorce rates*

Year	Divorces per 100 marriages performed[2]	Raw number of divorces[1]
Phase 1: 1857–WWI		
1858	0.0	24
1861	0.1	196
1871	0.1	166
1881	0.2	311
1891	0.2	369
1901	0.2	477
1911	0.2	580
Phase 2: WWI–1960		
1918	0.4	1,111

Table 13 (*cont.*)

Year	Divorces per 100 marriages performed[2]	Raw number of divorces[1]
1919	0.4	1.654
1920	0.8	3,090
1921	1.1	3,522
1931	1.2	3,764
1939	1.9	8,254
1941	1.6	6,368
1945	3.9	15,364
1947	15.0[3]	60,254
1951	8.0	28,767
Phase 3: 1960–present		
1961	7.3	25,394
1971	18.4	74,437
1981	41.4	145,713
1991	51.7	158,745
2001	–	143,818

[1] *Marriage, Divorce, and Adoption Statistics*, Dataset PVH41: "Divorces: 1858–2002, Numbers of couples divorcing, by party petitioning/granted decree."
[2] Derived from Rothenbacher, *European Population 1850–1945*, Table EW.4: Demographic developments, England and Wales 1850–1945 (v.1, 734–7) and Table EW.4A: Demographic developments, England and Wales 1946–1995 (absolute figures and rates) (v.2, 880–1).
[3] This year demonstrates a post-war "bump," as do 1920–1.

Table 14 *Divorce legislation since WWI*

1923: The Matrimonial Causes Act allowed wives to petition for divorce on the basis of adultery alone, as husbands could already do. From 1857 to 1922, a wife could only petition if her husband's adultery was accompanied by another transgression, and husbands sought more divorces.[1] Beginning in 1924, wives were more likely to seek divorce; by 1974, they did so twice as often as husbands.[2]

1938: The Divorce Act "extended the grounds on which divorce was admissible, to include desertion, cruelty and insanity."[3]

1969, 1973: The Divorce Reform Act and Matrimonial Causes Act sought to alter "the whole philosophy underlying . . . divorce. The concepts of the 'guilty party' and a 'matrimonial offence' were . . . replaced by a solitary ground for divorce: 'the irretrievable breakdown of marriage.'" A petitioner must prove "one or more of the five 'facts'" of "adultery, behaviour, desertion, two years' separation with respondent's consent to divorce, or five years' separation."[4]

Table 14 (*cont.*)

1984: The Matrimonial and Family Proceedings Act no longer required the courts to try to place the divorced spouses in the financial position they would have enjoyed, had the marriage not broken down. When considering orders for financial relief, courts are required to place greater emphasis on the desirability of the parties becoming self-sufficient.[5]

[1] "Legislation affecting official statistics on divorce in England and Wales," 6.
[2] See *Marriage, Divorce, and Adoption* Statistics, Dataset PVH41: "Divorces: 1858–2002, numbers of couples divorcing, by party petitioning/granted decree."
[3] "Legislation affecting official statistics on divorce in England and Wales," 6–7.
[4] *Ibid.*
[5] *Ibid.*

Table 15 *Legislation pertaining to homosexuality*[1]

1791: France decriminalizes all adult consensual sex. All legislation below applies to England, and illustrates its historical differences from France.
1828: Offences Against the Person Act[2] makes buggery (anal intercourse between men or sex between man and beast) easier to prove. Previously, both anal penetration and ejaculation had to be proved to secure conviction. Now proof of penetration is sufficient for conviction.
1861: Offences Against the Person Act reduces punishment for buggery, which Henry VIII had made a capital crime, to ten years to life in prison.
1885: Labouchère Amendment expands punishable offences to acts of "gross indecency," reduces maximum prison sentence to two years.
1891: 36-year-old Oscar Wilde meets 20-year-old Alfred Douglas at a tea party.
1895: The trials of Wilde. At the first trial, the prosecutor asks Wilde about the meaning of the phrase "The love that dare not speak its name," from a poem of Douglas's. Wilde defends the "love" as "pure," "perfect," and "misunderstood." The second trial returns a guilty verdict and two-year sentence against Wilde under Labouchère rules.
1967: Sexual Offences Act partly decriminalizes private homosexual acts between two men, both of whom must be 21.
1994: Criminal Justice and Public Order Act reduces age of consent for homosexual males to 18. (For heterosexuals it is 16.)
2000: Sexual Offences Amendment Act equalizes age of consent to 16 for homosexual and heterosexual behaviors.
2003: Sexual Offences Act deletes "gross indecency" and "buggery" from statutory law, decriminalizes sexual activity between more than two men.

[1] See Bedell, "Coming out of the dark ages;" Tatchell, *Europe in the Pink*.
[2] After the passage of this 1828 Act, "offences against the person" became a stock title used to name numerous other pieces of nineteenth-century legislation.

Notes

INTRODUCTION: NARRATING BLOOMSBURY

1. Cunningham's *The Hours* (1998) and Smith's *On Beauty* (2005) pay tribute to *Mrs Dalloway* and *Howards End* respectively. Important biographies include Hermione Lee's *Virginia Woolf* (1996) and Victoria Glendinning's *Leonard Woolf: A Biography* (2006). Work on Bloomsbury and philosophy includes Ann Banfield's 2000 study of Virginia Woolf's treatment of epistemological themes. On Bloomsbury and liberalism, see Brian May's 1997 study of Forster. Scholarship on Bloomsbury's feminism and gay politics is considerable; Christine Froula's 2005 study of Virginia Woolf examines pacifism.
2. Quoted in Regan, *Bloomsbury's Prophet*, 118–19.
3. Wittgenstein, *Philosophical Investigations* 66, 27.
4. On newness, see Bradbury and McFarlane, "The name and nature of modernism," and C. S. Lewis, "*De Descriptione Temporum*." On realism and subjectivity, see Lukács, "The ideology of modernism."
5. See Pericles Lewis, *Modernism*; Armstrong, *Modernism*.
6. Gillis, *For Better, for Worse*, 229–304.
7. Woolf's claim appears in *Mr Bennet and Mrs Brown*, 4–5. Stansky, *On or About December 1910*, discusses its motivation and context, 1–8.
8. Lawrence, *Letters vol. 2*, 286.
9. Bradbury and McFarlane, "Name and nature of modernism," 19–20.
10. "The challenge of our time," 54.
11. Strachey, "Does absence make the heart grow fonder?," xiii.
12. Feldman's 2002 *Victorian Modernism* distrusts notions of modernism as a "crisis" or "rupture," and proposes instead a coherent body of literature, that she calls "Victorian modernism," running from the mid-nineteenth through the mid-twentieth century and marked by pragmatism (an anti-dogmatic, anti-metaphysical, anti-systematic attitude). Ellis's 2007 *Virginia Woolf and the Victorians* shares Feldman's mistrust of scholarship that sees Victorians and moderns as polarized, describing Woolf instead as "post-Victorian": a committed yet anxious modernist, nostalgic for some aspects of Victorian culture. Joyce's 2007 *The Victorians in the Rearview Mirror* contests definitions imposed by Bloomsbury on "Victorianism," noting a broad Victorian influence on many aspects of British culture and politics from Bloomsbury's time to our own.

13. von-Hallberg and Laity, "Men, women and World War I," discuss World War One and modernism. Berman describes the dizzying loss of foundations in modern life, though the beginning of the "modernity" he examines antedates the "modernism" I interpret. Bradbury and McFarlane collect a number of writings that link historical modernity to literary modernism across Europe ("Name and nature of modernism"). Eliot's critique of modern life – "Ulysses, order, and myth," which first appeared upon the publication of *Ulysses* in book form, in 1922 – also links history to aesthetics, and employs language of cataclysm.
14. McBride, *Domestic Revolution*, 114–18.
15. McGregor, *Divorce in England*, examines marriage; Phillips, *Untying the Knot*, treats divorce; and Davidoff and Hall, *Family Fortunes*, discuss gender issues within families.
16. Published posthumously in *Death of the Moth and Other Essays* (1942).
17. Leathard, *Family Planning*, 72–3, 76.
18. Bertrand Russell. "Marriage and the population question." *International Journal of Ethics* 26:4 (July 1916), 443–61.
19. *Ibid.* 458.
20. *Women in Love*, 352: 5.
21. Bertrand Russell. "Education without sex taboos." *New Republic* 52 (Nov. 16, 1927): 346–8.
22. *Autobiography of Bertrand Russell: The Middle Years: 1914–44*, 320.
23. For more on the "Bertrand Russell Case," see John Dewey and Horace M. Kallen, eds. *The Bertrand Russell Case* (New York: Da Capo Press, 1972). See also Thom Weidlich, *Appointment Denied: The Inquisition of Bertrand Russell* (Amherst, NY: Prometheus Books, 2000).
24. Celia Marshik's *British Modernism and Censorship* (Cambridge University Press, 2006) argues that official and unofficial forms of censorship affected modernist writing (both for better and for worse), modernist writers' public images, and the shape of canonical "modernism."
25. *Study of Thomas Hardy and Other Essays*, 175, 16.
26. Robinson discusses the history, over numerous decades, of what he dubs the "Freudian Left" – European and American thinkers who find Freud's social conservatism at odds with his theoretical radicalism, and who invoke Freudian theories of selfhood to support their own radical social politics.
27. See Freud's *Three Essays* for an elaboration of this concept that neither male nor female sexual curiosity is confined to the other sex nor to the genitals.
28. See his autobiography, *My Life* (Boston: Houghton Mifflin Co., 1939)
29. *A Passage to India*, 362.
30. Froula, *Virginia Woolf*, xi, 2.
31. Berlant, *Intimacy*, 3; Kipnis, *Against Love*, 10.
32. See "Is modern marriage a failure?" a 1930 debate between Russell and John Cowper Powys in which Russell argued for the affirmative and argued that perfect fidelity is not to be expected in most marriages (Seckel, *Bertrand Russell*, 271–300).

33. *Women in Love*, 352: 23.
34. C. Vogler, in L. Berlant (ed.), *Intimacy: A Special Issue*, 24(2) (winter 1998), 328–65.
35. *Women in Love*, 201: 17.
36. Haralson, *Henry James*, 1–26 (esp. 18–20), 173–213.
37. Levy, *Moore*, 14. Raymond Williams takes issue with the notion of Bloomsbury as an "intellectual aristocracy," which Levy borrows from Noel Annan.
38. Ardis, *New Women, New Novels*, 12, 169.
39. Pines, *Marriage Paradox*, 1–18, 55–75.
40. *A Room of One's Own*, 57, 99.
41. Lawrence, *Sex, Literature and Censorship*, 49–50.
42. Ardis cites this, borrowing from the scholarship of Ellen Jordan (*New Women, New Novels*, 11).
43. Giddens, *Transformation of Intimacy*, 155.
44. See Poovey, *Uneven Development*, 1–4 for a discussion of mid-nineteenth-century attitudes toward the large number of England's unwed young women, as documented by the 1851 census.
45. *Women in Love*, 2: 3.
46. Davidoff and Hall, *Family Fortunes*, 385.
47. See Gay, *Bourgeois Experience*, vol. 1: 445ff., for a discussion of the interplay between privacy and surveillance in Victorian households. In my narrative, as twentieth-century households grew less crowded with staff and family, surveillance waned and privacy expanded.
48. See McGregor, *Divorce in England*, 83–5, for data about family sizes; Hynes, *Edwardian Turn of Mind*, 197, on England's fear over falling birthrates circa 1870–1910; and Davidoff, 328–9, on family politics.
49. *Women in Love*, 9: 24–5, *Howards End*, 353.
50. Horstman, *Victorian Divorce*, 22.
51. *Ibid.* 37–9, 88–9, 97–9.
52. Graff, *What is Marriage For?*, 3.
53. Phillips, *Untying the Knot*, 185–223.
54. While homosexual behavior is of course age-old, the first emergence of gay and lesbian identity categories is a matter of historical debate. Depending on the historical narrative, such categories emerged only after Stonewall, or around the turn of the twentieth century, or in London's early-eighteenth-century molly houses. For a description of the latter, see Bray, *Homosexuality*, 81–118, esp. 88–9. For Bray's discussion of the historical debate, see *ibid.* n. 8, 89. For Foucault's discussion of "reverse" discourse, see *History of Sexuality*, vol. 1, 101.
55. *Diaries* (16 June 1911). Locked Journal. Forster Collection, Modern Archive Centre, King's College Library, Cambridge. Quoted in Armstrong, *Howards End*, 275.
56. *A Room of One's Own*, 82.
57. See Bristow, *Sexuality*, 4, 13.
58. Regan elaborates this idea (*Bloomsbury's Prophet*).

59. See Meisel and Kendrick (eds.), *Bloomsbury/Freud*; Bell, *Bloomsbury Recalled*, 149–50.
60. *Downhill All the Way: An Autobiography of the Years 1919–1939* (London: Hogarth Press, 1967), 166.
61. *Letters*, vol. 2, 321.
62. See Seymour, *Ottoline Morrell*.
63. A 1992 collection of essays edited by Richard Rorty and entitled *The Linguistic Turn* popularized this term. In his introduction (9), Rorty credits Gustav Bergmann – a contributor to the collection – with its coinage.
64. "The sexual enlightenment of children," 132.
65. *Women in Love*, 149: 31.
66. *Ibid.* 352: 23.
67. *Mrs Dalloway*, 35.

CHAPTER 1 YELLOWY GOODNESS IN BLOOMSBURY'S BIBLE

1. *Principia*, 58, 59, 237.
2. See n. 63 to the Introduction.
3. *Principia*, 57.
4. *Ibid.* 94, 213, 219.
5. *Ibid.* 48, 208–9.
6. *Ethics* (1912) continues Moore's dialogue with the utilitarian tradition. He remains a critic of utilitarianism, which he finds overconfident in its own epistemology. But as he eschews the metaphysical attitudes that influence *Principia*, his positions hew more closely to Mill's.
7. *Principia*, 91, 116–26.
8. Although the term does not appear in *Principia*, it was current at the time. Regan, *Bloomsbury's Prophet*, 39 discusses Moore's disgust at the thought of literal sodomy.
9. See Rorty's Introduction (esp. 18 and 26–7); Bergmann, "Logical positivism," 63–71; and Malcolm, "Moore and ordinary language," 111–24. Moore also features in other essays in this collection.
10. Hare, *Language*, 83–4, follows Moore's lead in attacking naturalism, though he thinks that Moore misunderstands what he attacks. Nakhnikian, "Naturalistic fallacy," 64, echoes Hare, claiming that Moore's attack on the "naturalistic fallacy" is poorly formulated, but that *Principia* issues "perfectly correct warnings against certain mistakes in moral philosophy." Frankena, "Naturalistic fallacy," 30, groups Moore with other "philosophical controversialists of the first quarter of [the twentieth] century" who employed the "ingenious trick . . . of labeling their opponents' views 'fallacies.'"
11. See "Metaphysics and ethics" and the opening pages of "The idea of perfection," in *Existentialists and Mystics* (Birmingham: Delos Press, 1993).
12. See *Victorian Bloomsbury*, 214–38.

13. Levy, *Moore*, 8, argues that Moore's "shining innocence," far from being a potential detriment to his philosophy, was one of the "striking traits of character" that earned Moore – a "great man," in Leonard Woolf's estimation (*ibid.* 1) – the love and admiration of numerous Bloomsburians.
14. See Haralson, "'Thinking about homosex.'"
15. Jackson, *Eighteen Nineties*, 139.
16. The magazine debuted on April 1, 1894, and published both the literary vanguard (Max Beerbohm, Arthur Symons, George Moore) and the old guard (Henry James, Edmund Gosse). Weintraub has collected its issues into one volume (*Yellow Book*).
17. Jackson, *Eighteen Nineties*, 46.
18. Hynes, *Edwardian Turn of Mind*, 309.
19. Levy, *Moore*, 234; Ayer, *Russell and Moore*; Coates, *Claims of Common Sense*.
20. *Principia*, 58.
21. Ayer, *Russell and* Moore, 3.
22. *Principia*, 72.
23. *Ibid.* 73–5.
24. *Ibid.* 58.
25. See, e.g., his discussion of the requisite features of an "ideal language" in his introduction to Wittgenstein's *Tractatus*, x. Russell acknowledges that no such language exists in reality, but holds with Wittgenstein that such a hypothetical language and its purely functioning "simples" provide useful standards against which to measure the effectiveness of actual language.
26. Tredwell flatly disagrees with every part of Moore's claim that "goodness," as Tredwell restates the claim, is "an indefinable, nonnatural property known by direct intuition" ("Moore's analysis of goodness," 53).
27. *Principia*, 58.
28. *Ibid.* 40, 67.
29. *Ibid.* 61–2 (my emphases).
30. *Principia*, 59.
31. Dean is one critic of Moore's reasoning who does discuss aesthetics, including the inspiration that Clive Bell – perhaps Bloomsbury's most polemical aesthete – found in Moore. Dean explains that Bell was not "wholly justified in basing his rather extravagant claims about the moral significance of art on Moore's aesthetics." Nonetheless, "Bell, like the rest of Bloomsbury, owed much to the spirit of Moore's methodology" ("Clive Bell and G. E. Moore," 135).
32. *Principia*, 36.
33. "My early beliefs," 94.
34. Cavarnos, *Dialogue*, 21.
35. Heine, Introduction, xxxii; see also Levy, *Moore*, 3 and endnote 3.
36. In this discussion of Moore and Plato, I am deeply indebted to Iris Murdoch, a champion of Moore's and one of his most perceptive readers. See, e.g., "Idea," 4, where she says that "on almost every point I agree with Moore and not with his critics." *Fire and the Sun* explains her aesthetic–moral interpretation of

Plato. Her idiosyncratic reading of Plato's "good" as unknowable is crucial to her importance as a Cambridge successor of Moore's.

37. Forster discusses Dickinson's desire to found such a club, presumably modeled on the Apostles, in *Goldsworthy Lowes Dickinson*, 93.
38. Forster explains that, while "it would be too much to say that Moore dethroned McTaggart . . . Moore's steady questioning as to What *is* good? . . . [tore] some large holes in the McTaggartian heaven. More care . . . had evidently to be taken as to what one said and how one said it, and intuition seemed less than ever enough" (*ibid.* 92).
39. Levy, *Moore*, 277–9.
40. *Ibid.* 234.
41. Russell 95.
42. Levy, *Moore*, 277.
43. Schlipp, *Philosophy of G. E. Moore*, 24.
44. Interview with Leonard Woolf, quoted in Levy, *Moore*, 212.
45. *Ibid.* 215ff. makes a provocative argument that Moore's intimacy with Ainsworth and a conversation he had with H. O. Meredith immediately before he began composing "The ideal," together gave him the needed impetus to treat friendship as an "intrinsic good."
46. *Principia*, 237.
47. The last of these three targets is the title of Moore's chapter 4.
48. *Principia*, 232–3.
49. *Goldsworthy*, 59–60.
50. *Principia*, 235.
51. "What I believe," 66.
52. *Principia*, 237.
53. *Ibid.* 238.
54. Coleridge, *Selected Poetry*, 79.
55. *Principia*, 241.
56. *Ibid.*
57. *Ibid.*
58. Heine, Introduction, xvi and xxxi describes Ansell as a composite of Moore (in the days of his youthful Hegelian idealism) and H. O. Meredith.
59. *Principia*, 241.
60. *Longest Journey*, 17.
61. *Principia*, 242.
62. *Howards End*, 22.
63. *Principia*, 251–2.
64. *Ibid.* 249.
65. Throughout this paragraph I am indebted to Levy, *Moore*, esp. 245.
66. Keynes, "My early beliefs," 99.
67. Dangerfield (*Strange Death*) and Hynes (*Edwardian Turn of Mind*) evoke the calmness of English garden life in the decades prior to World War One.
68. "Foreword," 486.
69. *Ibid.* 252.

70. *Ibid.*
71. *Ibid.* (my emphasis).
72. Levy, *Moore*, 238–9, 259.
73. See Warner, "Introduction," xxi–xxv, for a discussion of this concept.

CHAPTER 2 FREUD'S DENIAL OF INNOCENCE

1. In the Standard Edition of Freud's writings (VII, 7–122), this case history is entitled *Fragment of an Analysis of a Case of Hysteria*, but I refer to it throughout by the eponymous title by which it is commonly known: *Dora*.
2. See Rieff's "Introduction" to *Dora*, and Marcus's "Freud and Dora," for two admiring discussions of Freud's stylistic innovations.
3. See Cravens, "Historical context," 177; Ross, *G. Stanley Hall*, 309–94.
4. Himmelfarb discusses the variety of ways that Victorians imagined themselves, and imagined femininity (see, e.g., *Demoralization*, 88–124).
5. Hall, *Adolescence*, vol. II, 301; Cravens, "Historical context," 183–4.
6. In 1909, Hall brought Freud and Jung to lecture at Clark University, where he was the first president, providing Freud his first academic audience. Hall thus played a key role in Freud's gaining wide recognition in the English-speaking world. See Ross, *G. Stanley Hall*, xiii.
7. *Dora*, 57.
8. Erikson, "Reality and actuality," 49.
9. In *Freud*, Rieff depicts the "moral" side of Freud's imagination in much the way I depict its "pragmatic–conservative" side.
10. "Resistances to psychoanalysis," Standard Edition, 19, 219.
11. Sprengnether, "Enforcing Oedipus," 254–75.
12. Marcus, "Freud and Dora," 87.
13. Poovey, *Uneven Development*, discusses the Victorian ideology of "separate spheres" for the genders, and the ways in which it was challenged. Foucault's critique of the opposition between "madness" and "civilization" evokes the longstanding intellectual background against which the efforts of Freud and others, to blur the normal–pathological distinction, can be measured. Canguilhem, *Normal and Pathological*, also situates Freud's work historically.
14. Freud's *Three Essays*, discussed below, develop his concept of polymorphous perversity. Their engagement with Havelock Ellis and Krafft-Ebing reveals Freud's indebtedness to sexology. *Dora* alludes to *Psychopathia Sexualis*, dismissing "simple-minded" readers who blame Krafft-Ebing's work for "the production of perverse tendencies" (50).
15. Robinson, *Freudian Left*, explains how this group of thinkers highlighted what they saw as Freud's implicit political radicalism.
16. "Psychotherapy of hysteria," 305.
17. *Three Essays*, 221.
18. "Some psychical consequences," 257–8.
19. "Sexual enlightenment of children."
20. "'Civilized' sexual morality," 201–4.

21. *Ibid.* 204.
22. Freud not only passes this judgment on "introversion" elsewhere, but also repeats the metaphor of a misdirected, or "dammed-up," libido. See "Paths to symptom formation," 374.
23. "'Civilized' sexual morality," 198–201.
24. As old-fashioned as some of these attitudes, such as the condemnation of masturbation, can sound today, they were extremely common around the turn of the twentieth century. See Arnett, "G. Stanley Hall's *Adolescence*," 192–3.
25. "'Civilized' sexual morality," 202–4.
26. See Thompson and Himmelfarb (esp. 31–52), for discussions of "respectability."
27. See Graff, *What Is Marriage For?*, 3 on popular anxiety. Gillis provides a broad historical discussion of British marriage (*For Better, for Worse*). McGregor (*Divorce in England*) does the same for divorce in England, and Phillips (*Untying the Knot*) for divorce in various nations. Horstman (*Victorian Divorce*) offers a more historically focused study of divorce – as well as respectability, hypocrisy, and other related topics – in nineteenth-century England. Thompson (*Rise of Respectable Society*, 85–6) argues that, with the benefit of hindsight after the latter quarter of the twentieth century – when rates of divorce and children living in broken homes spiked – it is easy to see turn-of-the-twentieth century anxieties about familial disintegration as excessive.
28. *Dora*, 49.
29. See McGregor, *Divorce in England*, 80–90 for statistical analyses, Davidoff and Hall on domestic space and privacy (*Family Fortunes*, 375), and Walvin (*A Child's World*) for a discussion of the hardships faced by large, poor families.
30. This point is debatable: critics including McClintock (*Imperial Leather*, 182–202) criticize Freud for underestimating the importance of the governess to Dora's psychosexual development.
31. For example, Angelica Garnett, née Bell, daughter of Vanessa, believed until age 18 that she was the daughter of Clive Bell, her siblings' father, and not of Duncan Grant, her mother's lover. The truth was a source of lasting bitterness to Angelica, who may have preferred a more typical bourgeois childhood to the bohemian one she knew. (See her autobiography, *Deceived with Kindness*.) Nonetheless, Angelica had the distinction of eventually marrying a man – David Garnett – who had previously been her (biological) father's lover, as the web of Bloomsburian homo- and heterosexual interconnections continued weaving itself into a subsequent generation.
32. To speak of "gay" and "lesbian" culture in the early twentieth century is somewhat anachronistic, as these identity categories had not fully emerged. See Bristow for a discussion of how various sexologists challenged contemporary thinking (*Sexuality*, 20–44).
33. *Three Essays*, 160.
34. "Sexual enlightenment of children," 132.
35. *Dora*, 18.

36. *Ibid.* 23, 24.
37. On the accomplishments of Otto Bauer, brother of "Dora," see Bernheimer and Kahane, "Biographical note," 34; Deutsch, "Footnote," 42; and Rogow, "Dora's brother."
38. *Dora*, 18.
39. *Ibid.* 34, 46.
40. *Ibid.* 88.
41. *Ibid.* 22.
42. *Ibid.* 23.
43. *Ibid.* 29, fn. 3.
44. *Ibid.* 61.
45. *Ibid.* 25.
46. *Ibid.* 20.
47. *Ibid.* 24.
48. Marcus, "Freud and Dora," 58.
49. Numerous commentators discuss this antipathy, often in the context of analyzing Freud's counter-transference. See Rieff "Introduction," vii; Sprengnether, "Enforcing Oedipus," 262; Moi, "Representation," 188–92; and Marcus, "Freud and Dora," 89–90.
50. *Dora*, 46.
51. *Ibid.* 54.
52. *Ibid.* 26.
53. "'Civilized' Sexual Morality," 191–2.
54. Lawrence's assertion appears in the "Foreword" to *Women in Love*. Freud suggests that a woman's second marriage is likely to be more satisfying than her first in "Femininity," 133 and "Taboo of virginity," 206.
55. *Dora*, 39.
56. *Ibid.* 33.
57. *Ibid.* 23.
58. *Ibid.* 42.
59. *Ibid.* 44.
60. Somerville finds it ironic that literature frequently depicted children as martyrs of industrialism at a time when child mortality was on the wane: he sees the literature as motivated by Romantic ideas about children, which work against literary verisimilitude (*Rise and Fall*, 170). Walvin, on the other hand, sees literature about child exploitation as politically motivated, and suggests that it may have had some causal role in the reduction of factory deaths (*A Child's World*, 116–20, 161–9).
61. Somerville, *Rise and Fall*, 174.
62. See Taylor and Wakeling, *Lewis Carroll*, 61, 64 for an argument against reading this photograph sexually.
63. Comini, "Toys in Freud's attic," 177.
64. *Ibid.*
65. Walvin, acknowledging the arbitrariness of any cut-off point for childhood, chooses 14 as the transitional age. Adopting his scheme, one can read Dora's

kiss as an aptly timed rite of passage into adulthood – or into adolescence (*A Child's World*).

66. The full text for Figure 3 reads:

    Next to you and seeing your arm bending / a story such / that it ceases to exist / if you touch it / behind all words and all signs I see / oh how happy am I / that you resemble me / how you resemble me / do not come any closer / but live in my home and I will await the child-like shudder of your shoulders and I will see / how your mouth /without searching words / speaks for me /

    I was alone in my white room / but perhaps I carried you in just now and something remains and speaks to me as if out of heavy flowers / my room became something like another country / I enter the white woods / the hoof of a reindeer resounds and raises reflective snow-stars in all of the white woods / you seem surrounded by lacey gardens / you reindeer-rider / and the reindeer is a mountain / your dresses are snow covers / where flowers will bloom / the touch of your slender fingers / and the snowy woods stand around you like amazed boys / the snow melts into a lake and you sat on a red fish / I had only seen your naked neck in your hair /a branch is growing into the water / where the end of all being lies /out of your round breast goes your breath over the blue lake / how quiet is the working of all being. (Thanks to Fenna Wächter and Joshua Brazee for the translation.)

67. The full text for Figure 4 reads:

    I reach into the lake and dive into your hair / like one lost in thought I am in the love of all being/ and I fell down again and dreamt /

    I was overcome by heat in the night / because in the woods the mating snake rubbed her skin under the hot rocks, and the stag rubs his antlers on the cinnamon-bushes / when I smelled the animal's musk in all of the low growing shrubs /

    I feel lost / someone should respond to my calls / everything follows its own scent / and the singing mosquitoes drown out the screams /

    Who thinks of the gods' grinning faces and questions the singsong of wizards and wise men / when they accompany the ferrymen / who take women /

    And I was a crawling thing / as I was looking for the animals and held to them / little man / what did you want behind the wise men / when you visited the god-wizards / and I was staggering / when I recognized my flesh / and I was all-loving / as I spoke with a girl /. (Thanks to Fenna Wächter and Joshua Brazee for the translation.)

68. Timms, *Freud*, 56; Comini, "Toys in Freud's attic," 175.
69. Timms, *Freud*, 60.
70. *Die Fackel* also attempted to launch a cult of the courtesan in November 1905. See Timms, *Freud*, 168, fn. 9.
71. Timms, *Freud*, 73.
72. Deutsch's "Footnote to Freud's 'Fragment'" discusses the persistence of Ida Bauer's hysterical symptoms decades after her consultation with Freud.
73. *Dora*, 19, 21–2, 75.
74. Timms, *Freud*, 48–9.
75. For the "dreams," see *Interpretation of Dreams*, IV, 182, 183, and 188, and V, 420. For "jokes," see *Jokes and Their Relation to the Unconscious*, 90, 92. In the first volume of *Interpretation of Dreams*, Freud does describe childhood as "still innocent of sexual desires" (vol. IV, 130), although previous writings of

his contradict this idea. He added a corrective footnote to the text in 1911, a process Strachey discusses in his "Editor's note," 129.

76. The condemnation of "prudery" occurs in "Sexual aetiology of the neuroses," 264. The "clever men" are refuted in "Question of lay analysis," 209.
77. *Women in Love*, 30:13.
78. "Postscript" to *Analysis of a Phobia in a Five Year Old Boy*, 148.
79. Eysenck criticizes Freud's presentation of the "little Hans" material in his chapter on child development (*Decline and Fall*, 92–114), and also discusses Freud's other case studies, including *Dora* (*ibid.* 62–4). Magid, *Freud's Case Studies*, collects scholarship on each of Freud's case studies (Dora, little Hans, the Rat Man, the Wolf Man, and Schreber), on the Anna O. case (which Freud co-authored with Josef Breuer), and on "Psychogenesis of a case of homosexuality in a woman," a brief study of an unnamed subject.
80. *Dora*, 49.
81. *Ibid.* 57.
82. Deutsch discusses Bauer's pride, years later, at having been "written up as a famous case in psychiatric literature" ("Footnote to Freud's 'Fragment,'" 38).
83. *Three Essays*, 219, 222.
84. *Dora*, 28–9.
85. *Ibid.* 29.
86. *Ibid.* 49.
87. Marilyn Brown's *Picturing Children* collects a number of works that examine these (and related) thinkers' attitudes toward children. Linda Pollock's "Foreword" introduces these figures. Nancy Locke assigns Baudelaire a complicated role in this narrative of ideas; Comini mentions his continuities with Romantic ideals ("Toys in Freud's attic," 173); and Dimrock discusses his anathematization of them ("Children's studies," 195).
88. Himmelfarb, *Demoralization*, 73–4.
89. Kingsley, *Charles Kingsley*, vol. 2, 330.
90. Webb, *Diary*, vol. 2, 52. Also, Himmelfarb is very helpful in gathering together various quotations that represent a range of Victorian opinions, including those of Webb and Kingsley (see, *Demoralization*, 53–87).
91. "Femininity," 114–17.
92. Huxley, "Emancipation," 194–6.
93. Mill, *Enfranchisement*, 42.
94. Himmelfarb, *Demoralization*, 95–7; Caine, *Victorian Feminists*, 37–8.
95. *Dora*, 22.
96. *Ibid.* 18.
97. Bernheimer and Kahane, "Biographical note," collect several examples.
98. *Dora*, 36.
99. *Ibid.* 36–7.
100. See especially, "Dora: fragment of an analysis," 141–5.

CHAPTER 3 FORSTER'S MISSING FIGURES

1. *Aspects of the Novel*, 67.
2. See Bradshaw, "*Howards End*."
3. Barthes's *Pleasures of the Text* distinguishes between representation (as a pose of objectivity) and figuration. Ardis, *New Women, New Novels*, makes use of Barthes's notion of figuration throughout her book. See esp. 117–18.
4. In 1974, Armstrong read the novel in terms of "liberal crisis" ("Forster's *Howards End*"). Admirably, in 2001, he revised his reading in the light of queer theory and Forster's now-public biography ("Narrator"). Rosecrance, *Forster's Narrative Vision*, 131–2 discusses *Howards End*'s "personal" narrator. Roby discusses how more than one reviewer thought the narrator female ("Irony"). Cucullu reads the nostalgic note in *Howards End* as a veiled homoeroticism aimed at legitimizing men of Forster's class and sexual affinity ("Shepherds").
5. Ardis, *New Women, New Novels* is a major source for my discussion. Since Ardis's work, scholarship has examined New Womanliness in numerous national contexts, including America, Ireland, Germany, South Africa, and Japan; as well as in Islamic culture. New Women have been paired as topics with such things as music, painting, criminality and detective fiction, sexual inversion, cross-dressing, and socialism. For a small sample of scholarship on the New Woman, see Heilmann, "(Un)masking desire;" Cameron, "Grant Allen's *The Woman Who Did*;" Miller, *New Woman*; and Vorachek, "Rebellion."
6. Ardis, *New Women, New Novels*, 140 uses this evocative term to describe novels whose heroines choose against careers as political activists or artists, opting instead for motherhood. See also *ibid.* 93–8.
7. Dowling, *Bloomsbury*, sees Ruth Wilcox, along with Mrs Moore of *A Passage to India*, as a Forsterian type – a sympathetic matron of civilization – of which Clarissa Dalloway is a Woolfian variation.
8. George Moore referred to conventional fiction as "pulse-less" (Ardis, *New Women, New Novels*, 32). Such critiques of popular literature, and the corollary calls for more honest literature, were voiced also by Thomas Hardy, Olive Schreiner, and others. See Ardis, *New Women, New Novels*, 31–4, 62–6.
9. "Terminal note" to *Maurice*, 235.
10. For an analysis of how *Maurice* influenced *Chatterley*, see King, "Influences."
11. Forster's *Diaries* (June 16, 1908) record his sensation that, while he composed *Howards End*, Whitman's poetry "started speaking to me . . . convincing me that he knows me personally." Notebook Journal. Forster Collection, Modern Archive Centre, King's College Library, Cambridge. Quoted in Armstrong, "Forster's *Howards End*," 275.
12. *Selected Writings, vol. 1, Sex*, 233.
13. *Ibid.* 216–17.
14. *Ibid.* 187.
15. *Ibid.* 186.

16. *Ibid.* 209.
17. *Ibid.* 214, 210.
18. *Ibid.* 212
19. *Ibid.* 118.
20. *Ibid.* 195.
21. *Howards End*, 237.
22. See *Intermediate Sex* in *Selected Writings, vol. 1, Sex*, 191 for Carpenter's critical discussion of Ulrichs's metaphor.
23. *Ibid.* 186.
24. *Ibid.* 190.
25. *Ibid.* 196.
26. *Ibid.* 234.
27. *Ibid.* 241.
28. *Ibid.* 108.
29. *Ibid.* 113.
30. "Notes on English character," 4–5.
31. *Intermediate Types Among Primitive Folk* (1914) discusses homosexuals' roles as prophets, priests, wizards, witches, warriors, etc. in Greek, Judaic, Arabic, Chinese, Japanese, and other cultures. *Ioläus: An Anthology of Friendship* (London and Boston: C. E. Goodspeed, 1902), edited by Carpenter, traces the forms that friendship (which can shade into sexual love) has taken from classical antiquity through modern times.
32. Wilde speculates that the boy actor Willie Hughes was an object of the poet's affection and a subject of many of his sonnets, especially number 38.
33. *Intermediate Sex* in *Selected Writings, vol. 1, Sex*, 207–8.
34. *Ibid.* 241.
35. *Ibid.* 185–6.
36. *Howards End*, 238, 335.
37. *Mr Bennet and Mrs Brown*, 4–5.
38. *Howards End*, 305.
39. *Ibid.* 240.
40. *Intermediate Sex* in *Selected Writings, vol. 1, Sex*, 243–4.
41. Goldman provides a thoughtful discussion of Forster's depictions of women, and the reception history of this aspect of his fiction ("Forster and women"), 120–37.
42. With particular regard to *The Longest Journey* and *Maurice*, Martin formulates brilliant readings of Forster's use of "double structure" ("Edward Carpenter").
43. *Where Angels Fear to Tread*, 145.
44. "The whole effect is less satisfying than that of the much slighter but more beautifully harmonious *Where Angels Fear to Tread*" (*Death of the Moth*, 171).
45. Finkelstein, *Forster's Women*, 41 and 153 links anti-feminism in Forster's writing to "homosexual jealousy" of women. Heine, "Introduction," reads Rickie as Forster's negative alter ego, "a case of 'there but for my knowledge of myself go I.'" W. Stone, *Cave*, 213, describes Rickie as Forster's "ego character as well as

his anti-ego." Hodges and Hutter, *Downcast Gays*, bitterly accuse Forster of gay self-hatred.

46. Bristow, "*Fratrum*," 121, discusses the porous conceptual boundaries between literal "brotherhood" and passionate, extra-familial male bonds. In his reading, though, the "brotherhood" that Rickie pursues with Stephen is free from sexual taint, directly opposed to what Rickie begins to explore with Ansell.
47. Beauman (*Morgan*) and Furbank (*Forster*) each discuss Forster's legal predicament. Hodges and Hutter, *Downcast Gays*, credit *Longest Journey* with revealing more of Forster's heartfelt sentiments as a gay man than any of his subsequent novels, save the long-unpublished *Maurice*.
48. *Room with a View*, 209.
49. *Ibid.* 207.
50. *Ibid.* 203.
51. Haralson, "Thinking about homosex," 66–72.
52. Herz, "Double nature," deserves credit for this insight (87–8).
53. See Martin's essay on *Maurice* ("Edward Carpenter").
54. *Passage to India*, 69.
55. Beer, *Achievement*, 120 notes an Austenian echo in *Howards End.*
56. *Howards End*, 125.
57. *Ibid.* 28, 62, 77.
58. *Ibid.* 37, 75.
59. Goldman speaks to the question of Forster's feminism ("Forster and women").
60. Holroyd, *Lytton Strachey*, vol. 2, 392 and vol. 1, 305 recounts Strachey writing for *The Woman's Leader*, and discussing the merits and demerits of sapphism and sodomy with Harry Norton. When Philippa Strachey (*ibid.* vol.1, 302–3), a long-time feminist organizer, attempted to persuade her brothers Lytton and James to participate in a march for the Society for Women's Suffrage, Lytton – expressing a distaste for political activism shared by other Bloomsburians including Woolf – fled from Cambridge to London, sarcastically worrying that the women would criminalize prostitution. But Sanders describes how Lytton donated proceeds from his play *The Son of Heaven* to the London Society for Women's Service, where Philippa was secretary (C. R. Sanders, *Lytton Strachey, His Mind and Art*, New Haven: Yale University Press, 1957), 42.
61. Sedgwick, *Between Men*, 3 cautions against seeing feminist and anti-homophobic ideals as necessary allies. She describes male homosociality – homosexuality included – as a potential enemy of feminism. Woolf's portrait, in *A Room of One's Own*, 53, of Oscar Browning, a gay Cambridge don beloved by Forster – whose sexism Woolf does not neglect to link by implication to his obesity and lascivious desire for a stable boy – makes Sedgwick's point in a more vivid, personal manner.
62. *Room of One's Own*, 83.
63. *Ulysses*, 15, 1798–9.
64. *Mrs Dalloway*, 100.

65. Strachey, *Really Interesting Question*, 103.
66. Trilling helped set the parameters for much later criticism by perceiving a gender split beneath the appearance of "business class" versus "intellectual class" differences in Helen's initial conversation with the Wilcoxes (*Forster*). Lago discusses how Margaret subverts gender codes in differing from the fainting heroines of Victorian literature (*Forster*). Finkelstein sees Margaret as Forster's "quintessential androgynous hero," an implicit case for the acceptance of women (and, by extension, gays) in society (*Forster's Women*). Heilbrun says the novel demands "a new concept of identity, especially for women" (*Toward a Recognition*). Hardy dissents from feminist readings, arguing that the Schlegel sisters' feminist liberalism is sterile and that they need rescuing by something extrapersonal ("*Howards End*").
67. *Howards End*, 217, 215.
68. *Ibid.* 217.
69. *Ibid.* 15.
70. *Ibid.* 240.
71. *Ibid.* 105.
72. *Ibid.* 24, 23.
73. *Ibid.* 75.
74. *Ibid.* 41.
75. *Ibid.* 283.
76. *Ibid.* 148.
77. *Ibid.* 175.
78. *Ibid.* 19.
79. *Ibid.* 227.
80. *Ibid.* 183.
81. W. Stone (in "E. M. Forster's subversive individualism," 32–9 and *The Cave*, 250) subjects to critical examination, and ultimately vindicates, Forster's preference for "softness," as Forster expresses it in the post-World War Two essay "Challenge." Dangerfield discusses the death of the "liberal England" of Forster's boyhood with the onset of World War One.
82. *Howards End*, 243.
83. *Ibid.* 327.
84. *Ibid.* 340.
85. *Ibid.* 66.
86. *Ibid.* 73.
87. *Ibid.* 75.
88. *Ibid.* 74–5.
89. *Howards End*, 339.
90. *Ibid.* 332.
91. *Ibid.* 337.
92. *Ibid.* 338.
93. *Ibid.* 334.
94. *Ibid.* 300.
95. *Ibid.* 310–11.

96. *Ibid.* 264.
97. *Ibid.* 337.
98. *Ibid.* 328.
99. *Ibid.* 199.
100. *Ibid.* 36.
101. *Ibid.* 334.
102. Hardy, "*Howards End*," 120 and Widdowson, "*Howards End*," 131 discuss the novel's "problem ending" and uneasy mix of realistic and romantic styles.
103. *Longest Journey*, 171.
104. *Howards End*, 41.
105. *Ibid.* 41.
106. *Ibid.* 25, 23.
107. *Ibid.* 247.
108. *Ibid.* 31.
109. "What I believe," 65.
110. *Howards End*, 302.
111. *Ibid.* 323.
112. *Ibid.* 322.
113. *Ibid.* 232.
114. *Ibid.* 325.
115. See esp. 160–3.
116. *Ibid.* 35.
117. *Ibid.* 135.
118. *Ibid.* 301.
119. *Ibid.* 320.
120. See n. 31.
121. *Howards End*, 103.
122. *Ibid.* 2.
123. *Ibid.* 40, 249, 251.
124. *Ibid.* 40.
125. *Ibid.* 237, 241.
126. *Ibid.* 144.
127. *Ibid.* 142.
128. *Ibid.* 315.
129. *Ibid.* 316.
130. *Ibid.* 317.
131. *Ibid.* 313–14.
132. *Ibid.* 247.
133. *Ibid.*
134. *Ibid.* 296.
135. *Ibid.* 276.
136. *Ibid.* 308.
137. *Ibid.* 8.
138. *Ibid.* 63.
139. *Ibid.* 116.

140. *Ibid.*
141. *Ibid.*
142. *Ibid.* 103.
143. *Ibid.* 111.
144. *Ibid.* 108.
145. *Room with a View*, 96.
146. *Howards End*, 108.
147. According to the *OED*, use of the word "guy" to mean "man" or "fellow" developed in the mid-nineteenth century.
148. *Howards End*, 108.
149. *Ibid.* 103.
150. *Ibid.* 248.
151. *Ibid.* 247.
152. *Ibid.* 276.
153. Trilling (*Forster*, 98–116) reads *Howards End* as a novel about the question "Who shall inherit England?"
154. *Howards End*, 276.
155. *Ibid.*
156. *Ibid.* 183.
157. *Ibid.* 237.
158. *Ibid.* 75.
159. *Ibid.* 335.
160. *Ibid.* 238.
161. See Rosecrance, *Forster's Narrative Vision*, 131–42 on the novel's contradictions.
162. *Howards End*, 291. See Duckworth, Howards End, 81–3 for a discussion of the lesbian overtones in Monica's character.

CHAPTER 4 THE LOVE THAT CANNOT BE ESCAPED

1. "Foreword," *Women in Love*, 486.
2. *Women in Love*, 481: 27.
3. From a technical, sexological perspective, Ursula is accurate, "perverse" denoting "non-normal." See Freud's *Three Essays*, 160 .
4. For a different account than mine of how modernists balance continuity and change, see Levenson (*Modernism*). Whereas I see modernists portray polymorphously perverse selves encountering a world with residual Victorian social norms, such as monogamy and marriage, Levenson sees Lawrence and Woolf portray nineteenth-century selves (whole characters like those in Victorian works) who seek autonomy in fragmented twentieth-century milieux.
5. "Preface" to *Beyond Culture*, xvii. For a discussion of Trilling's account of modernism in relation to that of subsequent scholars, see Begam ("Making modernism matter"). For a reading of Lawrence as a "Gothic modernist" opposed to "classicist modernism," see Pinkney (*Lawrence and Modernism*).
6. *Women in Love*, 352: 23; Pines, *Marriage Paradox*, 1–18, 55–75.

7. *Women in Love*, 227: 30.
8. *Ibid.* 352: 34–9. For feminist criticism of Lawrence, see de Beauvoir, *Second Sex*; Millet, *Sexual Politics*; Nixon, *Lawrence's Leadership Politics*; and A. Smith, *Lawrence and Women*. For rejoinders to some of these criticisms, see Lerner, "Lawrence and the feminists."
9. *Women in Love*, 352: 31–3.
10. *Ibid.* 481: 28.
11. *Ibid.* 481: 34.
12. *Ibid.* 145: 23.
13. *Ibid.* 154: 23.
14. *Ibid.* 352: 6–7.
15. *Ibid.* 127: 9.
16. Graff, *What is Marriage For?*, 3 locates the "conception" of "modern" marriage at around 1850 and its "birth" at around 1920. I. Watt credits the novel, by the eighteenth century, with aiding the construction of modern psychological interiority (*Rise of the Novel*). Giddens, *Transformation of Intimacy*, 155, 43 says that "companionate marriage [on] a model of friendship" is a "late modern type" of marriage, and that prior to the late eighteenth century, any love spoken of in relation to marriage was anemic in comparison to *amour passion*.
17. See Hynes, *Edwardian Turn of Mind*, 168 for a discussion of these and other crusaders on behalf of sexual purity.
18. See Lindsey's 1927 book of the same title for a fuller exposition of the model.
19. Giddens, *Transformation of Intimacy*, 40–1.
20. The "conventional moralist" is discussed in "How to be free and happy" 328. Post World-War-One feminists' lack or prudery is discussed in *Marriage and Morals*, 68–71; premarital sex is discussed *ibid.* 99–101.
21. Russell's tirade against Pauline morals appears in *Marriage and Morals*, 40–53. He deplores mystifying language in these same pages, *ibid.* 77–95, and in a 1930 debate with John Cowper Powys (Seckel, *Bertrand Russell*, 271–99). Comments on monogamy and jealousy appear in *Marriage and Morals*, 9–24; "Education without sex taboos" (Seckel, *Bertrand Russell*, 201–6); and the debate with Powys (*ibid.* esp. 272–81).
22. *Love in the Western World*, 60.
23. *Ibid.* 19.
24. *Ibid.* 37
25. *Ibid.* 34–5.
26. *Ibid.* 21.
27. *Ibid.* 65.
28. *Ibid.* 16, 25.
29. *Ibid.* 67.
30. *Ibid.* 68.
31. *Ibid.* 68–9.
32. *Marriage and Morals* discusses Romantic love (54–64) and marriage (105–15).
33. *Conquest of Happiness*, 38–9.
34. See Warner, "Introduction," xxi–xxv for a discussion of this concept.

35. *Women in Love*, 270: 21–2, 7–9.
36. *Ibid.* 276: 17.
37. *Ibid.* 276: 10–11.
38. C. Ross provides a useful overview of the two novels' manuscript history, dating back to Lawrence's earlier working title of "The Sisters," and of the possible influence of censorship on their revisions (*Composition*). Worthen and Vasey's "Introduction" to their edition of *The First "Women in Love"* provides a meticulous history of the novel's composition.
39. Ford's 1963 "Introductory note," a landmark in textual scholarship on Lawrence, discusses Lawrence's yearning for intense "male friendship" evident in his life and writing, and the possibility that "fear of censorship" led him to strike from *Women in Love* its Prologue and some of the more homoerotically charged passages from its chapters.
40. *Appendix* III, 512.
41. Clarke *et al.*, "On 'Lawrence up-tight,'" 299
42. *Women in Love*, 481: 22.
43. *Mrs Dalloway*, 35.
44. *Women in Love*, 153: 14–17.
45. *Ibid.* 145: 33–7.
46. Since the 1970s, critics have grown particularly sensitive to the plurality of feminisms. A. Smith, *Lawrence and Women*, 47–8 introduces distinctions between the "equality feminists" and the "new feminists" of the 1920s.
47. *Women in Love*, 201: 17.
48. *Ibid.* 132: 25–9.
49. *Ibid.* 145: 15–17.
50. *Ibid.* 145: 29.
51. *Ibid.* 148: 13–14.
52. *Plumed Serpent*, 411: 13–14.
53. *Women in Love* 250: 28, 147: 33, 314: 24.
54. 146: 30–1
55. Lawrence, *Sex*, 48.
56. *Ibid.* 53.
57. *Women in Love*, 193: 27–9.
58. Lawrence, *Reflections*, 67: 39–40.
59. *Women in Love*, 226: 4.
60. *Ibid.* 26: 13.
61. *Ibid.* 232: 10–14.
62. *Ibid.* 232: 34.
63. *Ibid.* 72: 1.
64. *Ibid.* 296: 25–6.
65. Rieff provides a useful comparison and contrast of Lawrence and Freud (*Freud*).
66. See Clarke (*River*) and Davies ("Contexts") for two perceptive readings of *Women in Love* that focus on misogyny, misanthropy, and anti-nationalism.
67. *Women in Love*, 196: 11–36.

68. *Ibid.* 310: 1.
69. *Fantasia of the Unconscious*, 90–1.
70. *Women in Love*, 163: 33.
71. *Ibid.* 138: 36, 111: 3, 139: 7–8.
72. *Ibid.* 429: 2–431: 29.
73. *Ibid.* 231: 29–30.
74. In Adelman's reading of *The Rainbow* and *Women in Love*, Lawrence articulates a "psychology of industrialism" that blames a variety of modern pathologies on the combined effects of Christianity and industrialism (*Snow of Fire*).
75. *Women in Love*, 130: 13–14.
76. *Ibid.* 128: 15–129: 25.
77. *Ibid.* 193: 33–194: 3.
78. *Ibid.* 13: 16–17.
79. *Ibid.* 453: 18–20.
80. Holbrook, *Eighteen Nineties*, 187–8 says that the author participates strongly in this feeling, that Lawrence's admirers are "strangely indifferent" to this "strange psychopathological element" in his writing, "a certain gladness about the death of people he rejected or detested."
81. Kennedy, *Rise and Fall*, 195.
82. Spengler says that he conceived *Decline of the West* before 1914 and had it fully worked out by 1917: it depicts his view not of the war's aftermath but of civilization as the war found it. See Atkinson, "Preface," ix.
83. *Women in Love*, 33: 28.
84. *Ibid.* 61: 1–2.
85. *Ibid.* 226: 39–40.
86. *Ibid.* 428: 19–20.
87. *Ibid.* 30: 13–27.
88. *Ibid.* 299: 9–10.
89. *Ibid.* 249: 9.
90. Hostettler, *Lawrence*, discusses the "spell" cast by the Alps on Gerald and Gudrun, the symbolic role played by this landscape in *Women in Love*, and how this symbolism grew from Lawrence's travel writing, particularly his essay "Twilight in Italy."
91. Davies ("Contexts") discusses the symbolic importance of giving away the chair, but focuses more on what it means to Ursula, whereas I focus on what Ursula's act means to Birkin. See Gloversmith, *Theory*, 211–13.
92. *Selected Literary Criticism*, 112–13.
93. *Women in Love*, 355: 34–5.
94. *Ibid.* 356: 9–10
95. *Selected Literary Criticism*, 112.
96. *Women in Love*, 146: 28.
97. *Ibid.* 147: 38.
98. *Ibid.* 145: 8, 148: 19.
99. *Ibid.* 147: 3.

100. *Ibid.* 481: 23–7.
101. *Ibid.* 249: 15.

CHAPTER 5 WOOLF'S SANE WOMAN IN THE ATTIC

1. *Mrs Dalloway*, 77–8, 31–2, 86.
2. Conrad, *Heart of Darkness* 9, 77.
3. *Mrs Dalloway*, 77, 78.
4. Neuman, "Heart of darkness," 58; Henke, "*Mrs Dalloway*," 126; Froula, *Virginia Woolf*, 115.
5. Henke, "*Mrs Dalloway*," 126.
6. Froula and Henke also make use of the manuscript history of *Mrs Dalloway*; each reads Clarissa sympathetically. Henke sees Clarissa's parties – facilitated by her marriage to Richard – as elaborate and beautiful offerings to her deceased parents ("*Mrs Dalloway*," 127–8). Froula, following Freud's "On transience," reads *Mrs Dalloway* as expressing a desire to build up what the war (and other tragic events) have destroyed, in Clarissa's personal experience as well as in broader civilizational terms (*Virginia Woolf*).
7. See Abel, *Virginia Woolf*, 30–44; Neuman, "Heart of darkness," 60–2.
8. Phillips, *Untying the Knot*, 169–79; Bristow, *Sexuality*, 20–44.
9. See Branca, *Women*, for a broad examination of women's shifting social roles over the last several centuries; technological and transportation issues are covered (*ibid.* 100–10)
10. McGregor discusses marriages and their challenges (*Divorce in England*, 83–4). Davidoff and Hall discuss family and gender politics (*Family Fortunes*, 328–40).
11. See the first of Freud's *Three Essays*, "The sexual aberrations" (1–38).
12. For a helpful summary of all these thinkers' contributions, see Bristow, *Sexuality*, 20–44.
13. *Mrs Dalloway*, 4, 8, 10, 37, 76.
14. *Ibid.* 41, 44.
15. *Ibid.* 111, 180.
16. *Women in Love*, 481:27.
17. Lawrence, *Letters vol. 2*, 321.
18. Schlack's Freudian reading of *Mrs Dalloway* links the heroine's androgyny to her arrested development ("Freudian look").
19. *Mrs Dalloway*, 31.
20. *Ibid.* 8.
21. *Ibid.* 126.
22. *Room of One's Own*, 57.
23. *Mrs Dalloway*, 13.
24. *Ibid.* 34.
25. Minow-Pinkney explores psychic (in)stability in Woolf, in great depth (*Virginia Woolf*).

26. *Mrs Dalloway*, 31.
27. *Ibid.*
28. See Booth on George Eliot and Woolf (*Greatness Engendered*, 1–26, 168–284).
29. *Mrs Dalloway*, 34.
30. *Ibid.* 33.
31. *Ibid.* 35.
32. The *Three Essays* circle continually around this point.
33. *Mrs Dalloway*, 32.
34. *Ibid.* 35.
35. *Ibid.* 32.
36. *Ibid.* 35.
37. *Ibid.* 115–18.
38. See *Room of One's Own*, 4, 22–3, 38, 93.
39. Horstman describes the gradual emergence of divorce, first among the upper classes, after its legalization with the 1857 Divorce Act (*Victorian Divorce*, 85–112).
40. H. Smith, "Introduction," 2; *Room of One's Own*, 88.
41. Phillips, *Untying the Knot*, 179.
42. H. Smith, *British Feminism*, 47.
43. Kent, "Gender reconstruction," 66–70 discusses the conservative tone of much inter-war feminism.
44. Forster, "What I believe," 65.
45. *Howards End*, 28.
46. See McGregor, *Divorce in England*, 80–90, for statistical analyses; Davidoff and Hall for examinations of domestic spaces and privacy (*Family Fortunes*, 375).
47. See Gay, *Bourgeois Experience*, vol. 1, 445; and *ibid.* vol. 2, 3–4.
48. *Mrs Dalloway*, 3.
49. *Ibid.* 11.
50. *Ibid.* 42.
51. *Ibid.* 7.
52. *Ibid.* 8.
53. *Ibid.* 41.
54. *Ibid.*
55. *Ibid.* 40.
56. *Ibid.*
57. *Ibid.* 120.
58. *Ibid.*
59. *Ibid.* 123.
60. *Ibid.* 188.
61. *Ibid.* 3.
62. The *OED* traces the use of "unhinged," as a specifically psychological term, back to J. A. Noble in 1895, and as a general reference to confusion or disorder, back to Defoe's *Crusoe* (1719).
63. H. Miller discusses the role of omniscient narration, as the voice of the community, in Woolf's aesthetic ("Virginia Woolf's All Soul's Day").
64. *Mrs Dalloway*, 43.

65. *Ibid.* 122.
66. "Modern fiction" opposes the materialism of less accomplished English novelists to the spiritualism, or attention to "life," which marks the achievements of Joyce and the Russians.
67. *Mrs Dalloway*, 29.
68. I derive these paradoxes from various commentators on Bloomsbury and its prehistory, most notably from Levy (*Moore*, 19–27) and from Rosenbaum.
69. *Mrs Dalloway*, 9.
70. *Ibid.* 29.
71. *Ibid.* 194.
72. *Ibid.*
73. *Ibid.* 122.
74. *Ibid.* 176, 178.
75. *Ibid.* 127.
76. *Ibid.* 12.
77. *Ibid.*
78. *Ibid.* 183.
79. *Ibid.* 9.
80. *Ibid.* 183.
81. *Ibid.* 156.
82. *Ibid.* 32.
83. *Ibid.* 33.
84. *Ibid.* 36.
85. *Ibid.* 7.
86. *Ibid.* 37.
87. *Ibid.*
88. *Ibid.*
89. See Levenback on Woolf's treatment of war and its aftermath ("Virginia Woolf").
90. *Mrs Dalloway*, 47.
91. *Room of One's Own*, 97.
92. Froula thinks this "offering" has a specific object: not the "patriarchal Jehovah," but "a composite ancestral figure whose primary aspect is maternal" (*Virginia Woolf*, 127).
93. *Mrs Dalloway*, 184.
94. *Ibid.* 170–1.
95. *Ibid.* 171.
96. *Ibid.* 122.
97. *Ibid.* 122.
98. *Ibid.* 194.
99. *Ibid.*
100. *Ibid.* 94.
101. *Ibid.* 101–2.
102. *Ibid.* 100.

CHAPTER 6 A RETURN TO ESSENCES

1. I discuss the 1923 novel *Challenge* below. Sackville-West's 1921 novel *The Dragon in Shallow Waters*, and her 1936 biography *Saint Joan of Arc*, also examine the interaction of male and female traits in one person.
2. Harold Bloom ponders literary originality in many places, from *Anxiety of Influence* to the "Preface and prelude" of *Western Canon*, 4–9. In *Anxiety of Influence*, 14, he borrows the image of swerving atoms, or "Clinamen," from Lucretius, as one way of picturing the process by which writers escape from being contained, or dominated, by previous writers.
3. See Levenson, *Modernism*, for analyses of character depiction in Forster and Lawrence, and Chapter 4 in the present book for a discussion of his analyses.
4. Bell, *Diary of Virginia Woolf*, vol. 2, 225.
5. Through her mother Victoria, the illegitimate daughter of Lionel Sackville-West and "Pepita," the eponymous subject of a 1937 biography by Sackville-West (published by Hogarth). See Glendinning, *Vita: The Life*, xiv–xv and 285–91.
6. *Vita and Harold*, 119.
7. DeSalvo and Leaska, *Letters*, 196.
8. *Ibid.* 105.
9. Leonard Woolf sneeringly discusses the traits that made Sackville-West's writings such as *The Edwardians* popular (158–9). In 1925, on the other hand, the *New York Evening Post* ran reviews of *Seducers in Ecuador* and *Mrs Dalloway* on the same page, and greatly preferred *Seducers* (*Vita: The Life*, 141).
10. *Vita and Harold*, 101.
11. DeSalvo and Leaska, *Letters*, 165.
12. *Vita: The Life*, 286–90.
13. Numerous scholarly works analyze the historical determinations of female friendships. Smith-Rosenberg's historical study, though nineteenth-century America is its subject, sheds some light on the situation in England ("Female world"). Burke's discussion of Gertrude Stein *et al.*, is similarly useful ("Gertrude Stein"). Faderman covers a broader historical canvas (*Surpassing the Love of Men*). Abel discusses representations of female friendship in fiction (*Virginia Woolf*). See also essays collected by Cruikshank (*Lesbian Studies*); Ascher *et al.* (*Between Women*).
14. Various scholarship traces intersections between sexuality and class as evolving historical phenomena. Foucault establishes the theoretical terrain on which much subsequent work in sexuality has been carried out (*History*). Allen discusses the sexual prehistory of Bloomsbury (*Cambridge Apostles*). Ellman investigates the pre-Bloomsburian nexus of class privilege, artistic Bohemia, and male same-sex desire (*Oscar Wilde*). Sinfield dedicates a helpful chapter to sexuality and class relations (*Wilde Century*). Tsuzuki (*Edward Carpenter*), Bray (*Homosexuality*), Boucé (*Sexuality*), and Rousseau and Porter (*Sexual Underworlds*) examine sex and culture from various angles. Gay (*Bourgeois*

Experience), Macfarlane (*Marriage and Love*), and Davidoff and Hall (*Family Fortunes*) examine sexuality within familial contexts.

15. There is not sufficient space here to review all of Woolf's well-known life story, from her multiple suicide attempts to her molestation by her half-brother. Bell, *Diary of Virginia Woolf*, Lee, *Virginia Woolf* and DeSalvo, *Virginia Woolf*, supply useful biographies.
16. *Vita: The Life*, 95.
17. For a discussion of how Sackville-West's *Knole and the Sackvilles* (1922), a study of her Elizabethan ancestral home, inspired the Elizabethan portions of *Orlando*, see DeSalvo, *Virginia Woolf* and Schlack, "Freudian look". See Sproles, "Virginia Woolf," for a discussion of how Sackville-West's *Saint Joan of Arc* (1936) responded to *Orlando*'s treatment of the biographical genre, after *Orlando* had incorporated theoretical concerns of *Aphra Behn*.
18. *Vita: The Life*, 237.
19. Lee, *Virginia Woolf*, 161.
20. Forster's *Goldsworthy Lowes Dickinson* (1934), a biography of his friend and Cambridge mentor, is also an oblique examination of many of Forster's personality traits, including his homosexuality.
21. DeSalvo and Leaska, *Letters*, 65–6.
22. In particular, Woolf's method of characterization has drawn this criticism, even from commentators who admire other traits of her writing. Forster's essay "Virginia Woolf," originally delivered at Cambridge as the Rede Lecture, exemplifies this line of admiring but critical reaction. Latham collects responses to various writings by Woolf, of which Beach's excerpted "Her characters' limitations" articulates a similar criticism (14–16). Sprague provides a similar collection of responses (*Virginia Woolf*), among which Guiguet's "Characters" discusses this misgiving about Woolf's style among French critics (40–50). Beja (*Critical Essays*) collects a combination of contemporary reviews of Woolf's novels, and subsequent scholarship, including Bennet's "Characters," which responds to Forster's critique.
23. DeSalvo, *Virginia Woolf*, 203.
24. See Freud's *Three Essays* for a discussion of this clinical, and normative, term of classification (26 and elsewhere).
25. *Room of One's Own*, 99.
26. Levenback ("Virginia Woolf") and von-Hallberg and Laity (*Men*) discuss the novel in relation to World War One.
27. *Mrs Dalloway*, 31.
28. *Ibid.* 29.
29. Sackville-West's 1930 novel *The Edwardians* more lovingly elegizes the aristocracy and its author's aristocratic youth. See Hynes for a sociological description of the era that Sackville-West captures literarily (*Edwardian Turn of Mind*).
30. *All Passion Spent*, 18.
31. *Ibid.* 19.
32. *Ibid.* 23.

33. *Ibid.* 134.
34. *Ibid.* 49.
35. *Ibid.* 135.
36. *Ibid.* 104.
37. *Ibid.* 52.
38. *Ibid.* 94.
39. *Ibid.* 93.
40. *Mrs Dalloway*, 10–11.
41. *All Passion Spent*, 94.
42. *Ibid.* 95.
43. *Ibid.* 110.
44. *Ibid.* 111.
45. *Ibid.* 107.
46. *Mrs Dalloway*, 126.
47. *All Passion Spent*, 109–110.
48. *Room of One's Own*, 35.
49. *Mrs Dalloway*, 115.
50. *All Passion Spent*, 84–6.
51. *Mrs Dalloway*, 120.
52. Sackville-West's letter to her husband expresses similar feelings of alienation; see also Nigel Nicolson's editorial commentary (*Vita and Harold*, 277–8). Glendinning complains that Lady Slane's ineptitude in "masculine" matters squares poorly with her intelligent response to Shakespeare ("Introduction," 11–12).
53. *All Passion Spent*, 23.
54. *Ibid.* 94.
55. *Mrs Dalloway*, 35.
56. It can be inferred that Clarissa was born in the last third, and Lady Slane in the first third, of the nineteenth century.
57. *Mrs Dalloway*, 35.
58. *All Passion Spent*, 91.
59. *Ibid.* 88–9. See *Passenger to Teheran*, an account of the time she and Nicolson spent in Persia, on his diplomatic post, for the biographical source of this reverie.
60. Bloomsbury wrote frequently on colonialism, imperialism, and international relations. In the years before *All Passion Spent*, Forster wrote *A Passage to India* (1924). Leonard Woolf's writings included *Economic Imperialism* (1920), *Imperialism and Civilization* (1928), and *Empire and Commerce in Africa* (1919), originally a report for a committee of the Labour Research Department. In the years after *All Passion Spent*, Harold Nicolson's writings included *Diplomacy* (1939) and *Peacemaking, 1919* (1939).
61. *All Passion Spent*, 33.
62. *Ibid.* 34.
63. *Ibid.* 129.
64. *Mrs Dalloway*, 45.

65. *Ibid.* 40.
66. *Ibid.* 44.
67. *Ibid.* 7.
68. *Ibid.*
69. *Ibid.* 40.
70. *All Passion Spent*, 133.
71. *Ibid.*
72. *Ibid.* 132.
73. *Ibid.* 132–3.
74. *Ibid.* 125–6.
75. *Ibid.* 47.
76. *Ibid.* 127.
77. *Ibid.* 137.
78. *Ibid.* 135.
79. *Ibid.* 120.
80. *Mrs Dalloway*, 3.
81. *All Passion Spent*, 120.
82. Dowling, *Bloomsbury*, sees Clarissa Dalloway as a Woolfian variation of a character type common in Bloomsbury's writings, especially Forster's: the matron of civilization incarnated also in Ruth Wilcox and Mrs Moore of *A Passage to India*.
83. *All Passion Spent*, 111.
84. *Ibid.* 142.
85. *Ibid.* 119.
86. *Principia Ethica*, 188.
87. Lady Slane's order of pleasures is roughly analogous to Moore's: people first (the right ones), art second, and nature third. But Moore's extended attention to aesthetics undercuts his explicit rankings, and suggests that should come ahead of nature – at least as high as second on his list of "ideals" (see ch. 1). Rather like the final chapter of *Principia* anaesthetizes sexual passion by aestheticizing it, *All Passion Spent* neutralizes sex as a threat to its placid Hampstead community by populating the community with octogenarians.
88. *Mrs Dalloway*, 4, 48.
89. *Ibid.* 9, 30, 39, 139, 186.
90. *Ibid.* 9.
91. *Ibid.* 29.
92. *All Passion Spent*, 81.
93. *Ibid.* 66.
94. *Ibid.* 124.
95. *Ibid.* 181.
96. *Ibid.* 68.
97. *Ibid.* 65.
98. *Ibid.* 83–4.
99. *Ibid.* 79.

100. *Principia Ethica*, 238.
101. *Ibid.* 162.
102. *Ibid.* 48, 79.
103. *Mrs Dalloway*, 122.
104. *All Passion Spent*, 218, 57, 117, 149, 150.
105. *Ibid.* 136.
106. *Ibid.* 137.
107. *Ibid.* 150.
108. *Ibid.* 155.
109. *Mrs Dalloway*, 101–2.
110. *All Passion Spent*, 159.
111. *Ibid.* 169. Glendinning discusses Sackville-West's feelings of guilt toward her own wealth, during the Depression ("Introduction," 15–16).
112. *All Passion Spent*, 168.
113. *Mrs Dalloway*, 122.
114. *All Passion Spent*, 172.
115. Glendinning discusses Sackville-West's anger at the patriarchal family entail, and how she continued to walk the grounds of the property even after it passed to her cousin Eddy ("Introduction," 9). In her historical study *Knole and the Sackvilles* (1922), as in her novel *The Edwardians* (1930), Sackville-West memorializes the estate.
116. Sackville-West traveled with Woolf to Cambridge, to hear Woolf deliver the lectures on which *A Room of One's Own* is based (Glendinning's "Introduction," 11).
117. *All Passion Spent*, 136.
118. *Ibid.* 172.
119. *Ibid.* 173.
120. *Ibid.* 111.
121. Woolf's diaries (vol. 2) provide a wealth of detail on the composition history of *Mrs Dalloway*, from its early incarnation as the short story "Mrs Dalloway on Bond Street." Refer to the index entry for "*Mrs Dalloway*," (369).
122. *Mrs Dalloway*, 94.

CONCLUSION: THE PRESCIENCE OF THE TWO BLOOMSBURIES

1. *Mr Bennet and Mrs Brown*, 4–5.
2. Roberts, "51% of women."
3. On mixed-race couples, including their limited ranks and social impact, see Romano (*Race Mixing*, esp. 287–95); Kalmijn ("Intermarriage"). On dual-career couples, see Holmstrom (*Two-Career Family*, esp. 1–6).
4. *All Passion Spent*, 23.
5. See Lukács for a radical's indictment of modernist subjectivity ("Ideology").
6. Weiten, *Psychology*, 314; Chafetz, *Handbook*, 376.

7. Kinsey, *Human Male*, 639.
8. See Robinson's *Modernization of Sex.*
9. See Maier, "Can psychiatrists really 'cure' homosexuality?"
10. Walkowitz, *Cosmopolitan Style*, 90–1.
11. See *On Beauty* and "Forster, middle manager."

Bibliography

Abel, Elizabeth. "(E)merging identities: the dynamics of female friendship in contemporary fiction by women." *Signs* 6 (1981): 413–35.

Virginia Woolf and the Fictions of Psychoanalysis. University of Chicago Press, 1989.

Ackerman, Diane. *A Natural History of Love*. New York: Random House, 1994.

Adelman, Gary. *Snow of Fire: Symbolic Meaning in* The Rainbow *and* Women in Love. New York: Garland Publishers, 1991.

Allen, Peter. *The Cambridge Apostles: The Early Years*. Cambridge University Press, 1978.

Ardis, Ann. *New Women, New Novels: Feminism and Early Modernism.* New Brunswick: Rutgers University Press, 1990.

Armstrong, Paul. "E. M. Forster's *Howards End*: the existential crisis of the liberal imagination." *Mosaic* 8 (1974): 183–99.

"The narrator in the closet: the ambiguous narrative voice in *Howards End*." *Modern Fiction Studies* 47 (2001): 306–28.

Armstrong, Tim. *Modernism, Technology, and the Body: A Cultural Study.* Cambridge University Press, 1998.

Arnett, Jeffrey. "G. Stanley Hall's *Adolescence*: brilliance and nonsense." *History of Psychology* 9(3) (2006): 186–97.

Ascher, Carol, Louise DeSalvo, and Sara Ruddick, eds. *Between Women: Biographers, Novelists, Critics, Teachers, and Artists Write about Their Work on Women*. Boston: Beacon Press, 1984.

Atkinson, Charles. "Preface." *The Decline of the West*. By Oswald Spengler. Trans. Atkinson. New York: Knopf, 1926.

Austen, Jane. *Sense and Sensibility*. Oxford University Press, 1970.

Ayer, A. J. *Russell and Moore: The Analytic Heritage*. Cambridge, MA: Harvard University Press, 1971.

Bakshi, Parminder. *Distant Desire: Homoerotic Codes and the Subversion of the English Novel in E. M. Forster's Fiction*. New York: Peter Lang, 1996.

Ball, Stephen. "Linguistic intuitions and varieties of ethical naturalism." *Philosophy and Phenomenological Research* 51 (1991): 1–38.

Banfield, Ann. *The Phantom Table: Woolf, Fry, Russell and the Epistemology of Modernism*. Cambridge University Press, 2000.

Barthes, Roland. *The Pleasures of the Text*. Trans. Richard Miller. New York: Hill & Wang, 1975.

Bartley, Mel, David Blane and John Charlton. "Socio-economic and Demographic Trends, 1841–1991." *The Health of Adult Britain: 1841–1984*. John Charlton and Mike Murphy, eds., 2 vols., vol. 1. London: Stationery Office, 1997.

Beach, J. W. "Her characters' limitations." *Critics on Virginia Woolf: Readings in Literary Criticism*. Jacqueline E. M. Latham, ed. Coral Gables, Florida: University of Miami Press, 1970.

Beauman, Nicola. *Morgan: A Biography of E. M. Forster*. London: Hodder & Stoughton, 1993.

Beauvoir, Simone de. *The Second Sex*. Trans. H. M. Parshley. London: Jonathan Cape, 1953.

Bedell, Geraldine. "Coming out of the dark ages." *The Observer*. June 24, 2007. www.guardian.co.uk/society/2007/jun/24/communities.gayrights

Beer, J. B. *The Achievement of E. M. Forster*. London: Chatto & Windus, 1962.

Begam, Richard. "Making modernism matter." *CLIO: A Journal of Literature, History, and the Philosophy of History*. 30(1) (2000): 91–121.

Beja, Morris, ed. *Critical Essays on Virginia Woolf*. Boston: G. K. Hall, 1985.

Bell, Quentin. *Bloomsbury Recalled*. New York: Columbia University Press, 1995.

Bennet, Joan. "Characters and human beings." *Critical Essays on Virginia Woolf*. Morris Beja, ed. Boston: G. K. Hall, 1985, 37–52.

Bergmann, Gustav. "Logical positivism, language, and the reconstruction of metaphysics." *The Linguistic Turn*. Richard Rorty, ed. University of Chicago Press, 1992, 63–71.

Berlant, Lauren. *Intimacy*. University of Chicago Press, 2000.

Berman, Marshall. *All That Is Solid Melts into Air: The Experience of Modernity*. New York: Viking Penguin, 1988.

Bernheimer, Charles and Claire Kahane. "Biographical note: Dora's family." *In Dora's Case: Freud – Hysteria – Feminism*. Charles Bernheimer and Claire Kahane, eds. New York: Columbia University Press: 1985, 33–4.

Beynon, Richard, ed. *Icon Critical Guides: The Rainbow and Women in Love*. Cambridge: Icon Books, 1997.

Black, Max. "On speaking with the vulgar." *Studies in the Philosophy of G. E. Moore*. E. D. Klemke, ed. Chicago: Quadrangle, 1969, 220–6.

Bloch, Iwan. *The Sexual Life of Our Time in Its Relations to Modern Civilization*. New York: Falstaff Press, 1937.

Bloom, Harold. *The Anxiety of Influence: A Theory of Poetry*. New York: Oxford University Press, 1997.

The Western Canon. New York: Riverhead Books, 1994.

Bluemel, Kristin. "'Suburbs are not so bad I think': Stevie Smith's problem of place in 1930s and '40s London." *Iowa Journal of Cultural Studies* 3 (Fall 2003). www.uiowa.edu/~ijcs/suburbia/bluemel.htm

Booth, Alison. *Greatness Engendered: George Eliot and Virginia Woolf*. Ithaca: Cornell University Press, 1992.

Boucé, P. G., ed. *Sexuality in Eighteenth Century Britain*. Manchester University Press, 1983.
Bowdler, Roger. "Between the wars: 1914–1940." In *London Suburbs*. Introd. Andrew Saint. London: Merrell Holberton, 1999, 103–29.
Bradbury, Malcolm and James McFarlane, eds. *Modernism: A Guide to European Literature, 1890–1930*. London: Penguin Books, 1991.
"The name and nature of modernism." *Modernism*, 19–55.
Bradshaw, David. "*Howards End*." In *The Cambridge Companion to E. M. Forster*. David Bradshaw, ed. Cambridge University Press, 2007, 151–72.
Branca, Patricia. *Women in Europe Since 1750*. New York: St Martin's Press, 1978.
Bray, Alan. *Homosexuality in Renaissance England*. London: Gay Men's Press, 1982.
Brentano, Franz. *The Origin of the Knowledge of Right and Wrong*. Trans. Cecil Hague. Westminster: A. Constable, 1902.
Bristow, Joseph. "Fratrum societati: Forster's apostolic dedications." *Queer Forster*. Robert Martin and George Piggford, eds. University of Chicago Press, 1997, 113–36.
Sexuality. London: Routledge, 1997.
British Family Research Council. *Families in Britain*. London: Routledge & Kegan Paul, 1982.
Brown, Marilyn R., ed. *Picturing Children: Constructions of Childhood Between Rousseau and Freud*. Burlington: Ashgate, 2002.
Burke, Carolyn. "Gertrude Stein, the Cone sisters, and the puzzle of female friendship." *Writing and Sexual Difference*. Elizabeth Abel, ed. University of Chicago Press, 1982, 221–42.
Busfield, Joan and Michael Paddon. *Thinking about Children: Sociology and Fertility in Post-war England*. Cambridge University Press, 1977.
Caine, Barbara. *Victorian Feminists*. New York: Oxford University Press, 1992.
Cameron, Brooke: "Grant Allen's *The Woman Who Did*: Spenserian individualism and teaching new women to be mothers." *English Literature in Transition 1880–1920* 51(4) (2008): 421–38.
"Canada passes bill to legalize gay marriage." *New York Times* 29 June 2005. www.nytimes.com/2005/06/29/world/americas/29iht-web.0629canada.html
Canguilhem, Georges. *The Normal and the Pathological*. Trans. Carolyn R. Fawcett, and Robert S. Cohen. New York: Zone Books, 1989.
Carpenter, Edward. *Homogenic Love, and Its Place in a Free Society*. Manchester: Labour, 1894.
"The Intermediate Sex." Selected Writings. vol 1. London: Gay Men's Press, 1984.
Woman, and Her Place in a Free Society. Manchester: Labour, 1894.
Cavarnos, Constantine. *A Dialogue on G. E. Moore's Ethical Philosophy: Together with an Account of Three Talks with G. E. Moore on Diverse Philosophical Questions*. Belmont: Institute for Byzantine and Modern Greek Studies, 1979.
Chafetz, Janet Saltzman. *Handbook of the Sociology of Gender*. New York: Springer-Verlag, 1999.
Clarke, Colin. *River of Dissolution: D. H. Lawrence and English Romanticism*. London: Routledge & Kegan Paul, 1969.

George Ford, Frank Kermode, and Mark Spilka. "On 'Lawrence up-tight': four tail-pieces." *D. H. Lawrence: Critical Assessments*. 4 vols., vol. 2. David Ellis and Ornella De Zordo, eds. East Sussex: Helm Information, 1992, 297–316.

Coates, John. *The Claims of Common Sense: Moore, Wittgenstein, Keynes, and the Social Sciences*. Cambridge University Press, 1998.

Coleridge, Samuel Taylor. *Selected Poetry and Prose of Coleridge*. Donald Stauffer, ed. New York: Modern Library, 1951.

Comini, Alessandra. *Schiele in Prison*. Connecticut: New York Graphic Society Limited, 1973.

"Toys in Freud's attic: torment, and taboo in the child and adolescent themes of Vienna's image-makers." *Picturing Children: Constructions of Childhood Between Rousseau and Freud*. Marilyn R. Brown, ed. Burlington: Ashgate, 2002, 167–88.

Conrad, Joseph. *Heart of Darkness*. Robert Kimbrough, ed. New York: W. W. Norton, 1963.

Craft, Christopher. *Another Kind of Love: Male Homosocial Desire in English Discourse, 1850–1920*. Berkeley: University of California Press, 1994.

Cravens, Hamilton. "The historical context of G. Stanley Hall's *Adolescence* (1904)." *History of Psychology*. 9(3) (2006): 172–85.

Cruikshank, Margaret, ed. *Lesbian Studies: Present and Future*. New York: Feminist Press, 1982.

Cucullu, Lois. "Shepherds in the parlor: Forster's apostles, pagans, and native sons." *Novel: A Forum on Fiction* 32 (1998): 19–50.

Cunningham, Michael. *The Hours*. London: Picador, 1998.

Dangerfield, George. *The Strange Death of Liberal England*. New York: Capricorn Books, 1961.

Davidoff, Leonore and Catherine Hall. *Family Fortunes: Men and Women of the English Middle Class, 1780–1850*. University of Chicago Press, 1987.

Davies, Alistair. "Contexts of reading: the reception of D. H. Lawrence's *The Rainbow and Women in Love*." *The Theory of Reading*. Frank Gloversmith, ed. Brighton: Harvester, 1984, 199–221.

Dean, Jeffrey. "Clive Bell and G. E. Moore: the good of art." *British Journal of Aesthetics* 35 (1996): 135–45.

Decker, Hannah. *Freud, Dora, and Vienna 1900*. New York: Free Press, 1991.

DeSalvo, Louise. "Lighting the cave: the relationship between Vita Sackville-West and Virginia Woolf." *Signs* 8 (1982): 195–214.

Virginia Woolf: The Impact of Childhood Sexual Abuse on Her Life and Work. London: Women's Press, 1991.

Deutsch, Felix. "A footnote to Freud's 'Fragment of an Analysis of a Case of Hysteria.'" *In Dora's Case: Freud – Hysteria – Feminism*. Charles Bernheimer and Claire Kahane, eds. New York: Columbia University Press: 1985, 35–43.

DiBattista, Maria. *First Love: The Affections of Modern Fiction*. University of Chicago Press, 1991.

Dickinson, Goldsworthy Lowes. *A Modern Symposium*. London: George Allen & Unwin, 1962.

Dimrock, George. "Children's studies and the romantic child." *Picturing Children: Constructions of Childhood Between Rousseau and Freud*. Marilyn R. Brown, ed. Burlington: Ashgate, 2002, 189–99.

Dowling, David. *Bloomsbury Aesthetics and the Novels of Forster and Woolf*. New York: St Martin's Press, 1985.

Duckworth, Alastair. Howards End*: E. M. Forster's House of Fiction*. Twayne's Masterwork Studies 93. New York: Twayne, 1992.

Eagleton, Terry. "The ideology of the aesthetic." *Poetics Today* 9 (1988): 327–38.

Edel, Leon. *Bloomsbury: A House of Lions*. New York: Lippincott, 1979.

"Eight EU countries back same-sex marriage." *Angus Reid Global Monitor*. December 24, 2006. www.angus-reid.com/polls/view/eight_eu_countries_back_same_sex_marriage

Eliot, George. *Middlemarch*. Oxford University Press, 1986.

Eliot, T. S. *"Ulysses, order, and myth." Selected Prose*. Frank Kermode, ed. New York: Harcourt Brace Jovanovich, 1975.

Ellis, Havelock and John Symonds. *Sexual Inversion*. London: Wilson, 1897.

Ellis, Steve. *Virginia Woolf and the Victorians*. Cambridge University Press, 2007.

Ellman, Richard. *Oscar Wilde*. London: Hamilton, 1987.

Erikson, Erik. "Reality and actuality: an address." *In Dora's Case: Freud – Hysteria – Feminism*. Charles Bernheimer and Claire Kahane, eds., 44–55.

Eysenck, Hans. *Decline and Fall of the Freudian Empire*. New York: Viking, 1985.

Faderman, Lillian. *Surpassing the Love of Men: Romantic Friendships Between Women from the Renaissance to the Present*. New York: Morrow, 1981.

Feldman, Jessica. *Victorian Modernism: Pragmatism and the Varieties of Aesthetic Experience*. Cambridge University Press, 2002.

Finkelstein, Bonnie. *Forster's Women: Eternal Differences*. New York: Columbia University Press, 1975.

Ford, George. "An introductory note to D. H. Lawrence's prologue to *Women in Love*." *Texas Quarterly* 6 (1963): 92–7.

Forster, E. M. *A Passage to India*. London: Harcourt, 1924.

A Room with a View and Howards End. New York: Signet, 1986.

Aspects of the Novel. New York: Harcourt, 1927.

"The challenge of our time." *Two Cheers for Democracy*. Abinger Edition of E. M. Forster, vol. 11. London: Edward Arnold, 1972. 54–8.

Goldsworthy Lowes Dickinson and Related Writings. Oliver Stallybrass, ed. Abinger Edition of E. M. Forster, vol. 13. London: Edward Arnold, 1973.

Howards End. Oliver Stallybrass, ed. Abinger Edition of E. M. Forster, vol. 4. London: Edward Arnold, 1973.

The Longest Journey. Elizabeth Heine, ed. Abinger Edition of E. M. Forster, vol. 2. London: Edward Arnold, 1984.

Maurice. Toronto: Macmillan, 1971.

"Notes on the English character." *Abinger Harvest and England's Pleasant Land*. Abinger Edition of E. M. Forster, vol. 10. London: Andre Deutsch, 1996, 3–13.

"Virginia Woolf." *Two Cheers for Democracy*. Oliver Stallybrass, ed. Abinger Edition of E. M. Forster, vol. 11. London: Edward Arnold, 1972. 238–252.

"What I believe." *Two Cheers for Democracy*. Oliver Stallybrass, ed. Abinger Edition of E. M. Forster, vol. II. London: Edward Arnold, 1972, 65–73.

Where Angels Fear to Tread. Oliver Stallybrass, ed. Abinger Edition of E. M. Forster, vol. I. London: Edward Arnold, 1975.

Foucault, Michel. *The History of Sexuality*. 3 vols., vol. I. New York: Random, 1978.

Frankena, W. K. "The naturalistic fallacy." *Studies in the Philosophy of G. E. Moore*. E. D. Klemke, ed. Chicago: Quadrangle, 1969.

Franks, Gabriel. "Virginia Woolf and the philosophy of G. E. Moore." *The Personalist: An International Review of Philosophy* 50 (1969): 222–40.

Freud, Sigmund, James Strachey, Anna Freud, Carrie Lee Rothgeb, and Angela Richards. 1900. *The Standard Edition of the Complete Psychological Works of Sigmund Freud*. London: Hogarth Press.

Civilization and Its Discontents. Standard Edition, XXI, 59–145.

"'Civilized' sexual morality and modern nervous illness." Standard Edition, IX, 179–204.

"Femininity." Lecture XXIII. Standard Edition, XII, 112–35.

Fragment of an Analysis of a Case of Hysteria. Standard Edition, VII, 3–122.

The Interpretation of Dreams I and II. Standard Edition, 4 and Standard Edition, V, 339–625.

Jokes and Their Relation to the Unconscious. Standard Edition, VII.

"The paths to symptom formation." Standard Edition, XVI, 358–77.

"Postscript" to *Analysis of a Phobia in a Five Year Old Boy*. Standard Edition, X, 148–9.

"The psychogenesis of a case of homosexuality in a woman." Standard Edition, XVIII, 147–72.

"The psychotherapy of hysteria." Standard Edition, II, 255–305.

"The question of lay analysis." Standard Edition, XX, 183–250.

"Resistances to psychoanalysis." Standard Edition, XIX, 213–22.

"The sexual aetiology of the neuroses." Standard Edition, III, 263–85.

"The sexual enlightenment of children." Standard Edition, IX, 131–9.

"Some neurotic mechanisms in jealousy, paranoia, and homosexuality." Standard Edition, XVII, 223–32.

"Some psychical consequences of the anatomical distinction between the sexes." Standard Edition, XIX, 248–58.

"The taboo of virginity." Standard Edition, XI, 193–208.

Three Essays on the Theory of Sexuality. Standard Edition, VII, 125–243.

Froula, Christine. *Virginia Woolf and the Bloomsbury Avant-Garde*. New York: Columbia University Press, 2005.

Furbank, P. N. *E. M. Forster: A Life*. 2 vols. London: Secker & Warburg, 1978.

Garnett, Angelica. *Deceived with Kindness: A Bloomsbury Childhood*. London: Chatto & Windus, 1984.

Garnett, David. Introduction. "My early beliefs." *Two Memoirs*. By John Maynard Keynes. New York: Augustus M. Kelley, 1949, 75–7.

Garrett, Eilidh, Alice Reid, Kevin Schürer, and Simon Szreter. *Changing Family Size in England and Wales: Place, Class and Demography, 1891–1911.* Cambridge University Press, 2001.

Gay, Peter *The Bourgeois Experience: Victoria to Freud.* 5 vols., vols. 1 and 2. Oxford University Press, 1984 and 1986.

"Gays win marriage rights." *Radio Sweden.* January 4, 2009. www.sr.se/cgi-bin/International/nyhetssidor/artikel.asp?ProgramID=2054&Format=1&artikel=2739765

Gebhard, Paul and Alan B. Johnson. *The Kinsey Data: Marginal Tabulations of the 1938–1963 Interviews Conducted by the Institute for Sex Research.* Indiana University Press, 1998.

Giddens, Anthony. *The Transformation of Intimacy: Sexuality, Love, and Eroticism in Modern Societies.* Stanford University Press, 1992.

Gillis, John R. *For Better, for Worse: British Marriages: 1600 to the Present.* Oxford University Press, 1985.

Glendinning, Victoria. "Introduction." *All Passion Spent.* By Vita Sackville-West. London: Virago, 1983, 9–16

Leonard Woolf: A Biography. Free Press, 2006.

Vita: The Life of V. Sackville-West. New York: Knopf, 1983.

Gloversmith, Frank, ed. *The Theory of Reading.* Brighton: Harvester, 1984.

Goldman, Jane. "Forster and women." In *The Cambridge Companion to E. M. Forster.* David Bradshaw, ed. Cambridge University Press, 2007, 120–37.

Graff, E. J. *What Is Marriage for?* Boston: Beacon, 1999.

Gray, John. *Men Are from Mars, Women Are from Venus: A Practical Guide for Improving Communication and Getting What You Want in Your Relationships.* HarperCollins, 1992.

Grew, Tony. "Norway legalises gay marriage." *Pink News.* June 11, 2008. www.pinknews.co.uk/news/articles/2005–7926.html

Guiguet, Jean. "Characters and human relations." *Virginia Woolf: A Collection of Critical Essays.* Claire Sprague, ed. New Jersey: Prentice-Hall, 1971, 40–50.

"guy." second entry, third definition. *Oxford English Dictionary.* 1971, repr. 1975.

Haight, Gordon. *George Eliot: A Biography.* Oxford University Press, 1968.

Hall, G. Stanley. *Adolescence: Its Psychology and its Relations to Physiology, Anthropology, Sociology, Sex, Crime, and Education.* 2 vols. New York: D. Appleton and Company, 1904.

Haralson, Eric. *Henry James and Queer Modernity.* Cambridge University Press, 2003.

"'Thinking about homosex' in Forster and James." *Queer Forster.* Robert Martin and George Piggford, eds. University of Chicago Press, 1997, 59–74.

Hardy, John Edward. "*Howards End*: the sacred center." *Critical Essays on E. M. Forster.* Alan Wilde, ed. Boston: G. K. Hall, 1985, 113–20.

Hare, R. M. *The Language of Morals.* Oxford: Clarendon, 1952.

Harrison, Bernard. "Forster and Moore." *Philosophy and Literature* 12 (1988): 1–26.

Heilbrun, Carolyn. *Toward a Recognition of Androgyny.* New York: Knopf, 1973.

Heilmann, Ann. "(Un)masking desire: cross-dressing and the crisis of desire in new woman fiction." *Journal of Victorian Culture* 5(1) (2000): 83–111.

Heine, Elizabeth. "Introduction." *The Longest Journey*. By E. M. Forster. Heine, ed. Abinger Edition of E. M. Forster, vol. 2. London: Edward Arnold, 1984.

Helmstadter, Richard and Bernard Lightman, eds. *Victorian Faith in Crisis: Essays on Continuity and Change in Nineteenth-Century Religious Belief*. Stanford University Press, 1990.

Henke, Suzette. "*Mrs Dalloway:* the communion of saints." *New Feminist Essays on Virginia Woolf*. Jane Marcus, ed. Lincoln: University of Nebraska Press, 1981.

Herz, Judith Scherer. "The double nature of Forster's fiction: *A Room with a View* and *The Longest Journey*." In *Critical Essays on E. M. Forster*. Alan Wilde, ed. Boston: G. K. Hall, 1985, 84–94.

Himmelfarb, Gertrude. *The Demoralization of Society: From Victorian Virtues to Modern Values*. New York: Vintage, 1996.

Hobsbaum, Philip. *A Reader's Guide to D. H. Lawrence*. London: Thames & Hudson, 1981.

Hodges, Andrew and David Hutter. *With Downcast Gays: Aspects of Homosexual Self-Oppression*. London: Pink Triangle, 1979.

Holbrook, David. *Where D. H. Lawrence Was Wrong about Women*. London: Associated University Press, 1992.

Holmstrom, Lynda Lytle. *The Two-Career Family*. Cambridge, MA: Schenkman, 1973.

Holroyd, Michael. *Lytton Strachey: A Critical Biography*. 2 vols. New York: Holt, 1967.

Horn, Pamela. *Life Below Stairs in the 20th Century*. Stroud: Sutton, 2001.

The Rise and Fall of the Victorian Servant. Stroud: Sutton, 2004.

Horstman, Allen. *Victorian Divorce*. London: Croom Helm, 1985.

Hostettler, Maya. *D. H. Lawrence: Travel Books and Fiction*. New York: Lang, 1985.

Hundley, Tom. "Homosexual unions slowly gain momentum in Europe." *Chicago Tribune*. June 30, 2004. www.chicagotribune.com/news/nationworld/chi-0406300271jun30

Huxley, T. H. "Emancipation – black and white." In *The Essence of T. H. Huxley: Selections from His Writings*. Cyril Bibby, ed. London: St Martin's Press, 1967.

Hynes, Samuel. *The Edwardian Turn of Mind*. London: Pimlico, 1991.

Ingram, Penelope. "'One drifts apart': *To the Lighthouse* as art of response." *Philosophy and Literature* 23 (1999): 78–9.

Jackson, Holbrook. *The Eighteen Nineties*. London: Jonathan Cape, 1931.

James, Henry. *The Portrait of a Lady*. New York: Norton, 1975.

Joyce, James. *Ulysses*. New York: Vintage, 1986.

Joyce, Simon. *The Victorians in the Rearview Mirror*. Ohio University Press, 2007.

Kalmijn, Matthijs. "Intermarriage and homogamy: causes, patterns, trends." *Annual Review of Sociology* 24 (1998): 395–421.

Kennedy, Paul. *The Rise and Fall of the Great Powers*. New York: Vintage, 1987.

Kent, Susan. "Gender reconstruction after the First World War." *British Feminism in the Twentieth Century*. Harold L. Smith, ed. Amherst: University of Massachusetts Press, 1990, 66–83.

Kermode, Frank. *Lawrence*. Fontana: Richard Clay, 1973.
Keynes, J. M. "My early beliefs." *Two Memoirs*. New York: Augustus M. Kelley, 1949, 78–103.
King, Dixie. "The influences of Forster's *Maurice* on *Lady Chatterley's Lover*." *Contemporary Literature* 23(1) (1982): 65–82.
Kingsley, Charles. *Charles Kingsley: His Letters and Memories of His Life*. 2 vols. New York: AMS Press, 1973.
Kinsey, Alfred. *Sexual Behavior in the Human Female*. London: Saunders, 1953.
Sexual Behavior in the Human Male. London: Saunders, 1948.
Kipnis, Laura. *Against Love*. New York: Pantheon, 2003.
Klemke, E. D. "Introduction: did G. E. Moore refute idealism?" *Studies in the Philosophy of G. E. Moore*. E. D. Klemke, ed. Chicago: Quadrangle, 1969, 3–24.
ed. *Studies in the Philosophy of G. E. Moore*.
Lago, Mary. *E. M. Forster: A Literary Life*. New York: St Martin's Press, 1995.
Lambert, Tim. "A brief history of Tunbridge Wells." *A World History Encyclopedia: The History of England*. August 2, 2009. www.localhistories.org/tunbridge.html
"London in the 19th century." *A World History Encyclopedia: The History of England*. August 2, 2009. www.localhistories.org/london19th.html
Latham, Jacqueline E. M., ed. *Critics on Virginia Woolf*. Coral Gables: University of Miami Press, 1970.
Law, C. M. "The growth of urban population in England and Wales, 1801–1911." *Transactions of the Institute of British Geographers* 41 (1967).
Lawrence, D. H. Appendix III: The "Prologue" and "Wedding" chapters. *Women in Love*. Cambridge Edition of the Letters and Works of D. H. Lawrence. Cambridge University Press, 1987, 499–528.
The Collected Letters of D. H. Lawrence. Harry Moore, ed. 2 vols. London: Heinemann, 1962.
D. H. Lawrence: Selected Literary Criticism. Anthony Beal, ed. New York: Viking, 1966.
The First Women in Love. John Worthen, and Lindeth Vasey, eds. Cambridge Edition of the Letters and Works of D. H. Lawrence. Cambridge University Press, 1998.
"Foreword." *Women in Love*. By Lawrence. Cambridge Edition of the Letters and Works of D. H. Lawrence. Cambridge University Press, 1987, 485–6.
Kangaroo. Bruce Steele, ed. Cambridge Edition of the Letters and Works of D. H. Lawrence. Cambridge University Press, 1994.
Lawrence: Sex, Literature and Censorship. Harry Moore, ed. New York: Viking, 1959.
The Letters of D. H. Lawrence, Volume 2, June 1913–October 1916. Cambridge Edition of the Letters and Works of D. H. Lawrence. George J. Zytaruk and James T. Boulton, eds. Cambridge University Press, 1991.
The Plumed Serpent. L. D. Clark, ed. Cambridge Edition of the Letters, and Works of D. H. Lawrence. Cambridge University Press, 1987.

Psychoanalysis and the Unconscious and Fantasia of the Unconscious. New York: Viking, 1960.

The Rainbow. London: Penguin, 1989.

Reflections on the Death of a Porcupine and Other Essays. Michael Herbert, ed. Cambridge Edition of the Letters, and Works of D. H. Lawrence. Cambridge University Press, 1988.

Study of Thomas Hardy and Other Essays by D. H. Lawrence. Bruce Steele, ed. Cambridge Edition of the Letters, and Works of D. H. Lawrence. Cambridge University Press, 1985.

Twilight in Italy and Other Essays. Paul Eggert, ed. Cambridge Edition of the Letters and Works of D. H. Lawrence, vol. 10. Cambridge University Press, 1994.

Women in Love. David Farmer, Lindeth Vasey, and John Worthen, eds. Cambridge Edition of the Letters and Works of D. H. Lawrence. Cambridge University Press, 1987.

Lawton, Richard. "Census data for urban areas." In *The Census and Social Structure: An Interpretative Guide to Nineteenth Century Censuses for England and Wales.* Lawton, ed. London: F. Cass, 1978.

Leathard, Audrey. *Family Planning: The Development of Family Planning Services in Britain 1921–74.* London: Macmillan, 1980.

Leavis, F. R. *D. H. Lawrence: Novelist.* London: Chatto & Windus, 1955.

Lee, Hermione. *Virginia Woolf.* New York: Random, 1996.

"Legislation affecting official statistics on divorce in England and Wales," in "Publication details" for *Marriage, Divorce, and Adoption Statistics.*

Lerner, Lawrence. "Lawrence and the feminists." *D. H. Lawrence: Centenary Essays.* Mara Kalnins, ed. Bristol Classical Press, 1986, 69–87.

Levenback, Karen. "Virginia Woolf and returning soldiers: the Great War and the reality of survival in *Mrs Dalloway* and *The Waves.*" *Woolf Studies Annual* 2 (1996): 71–88.

Levenson, Michael. *Modernism and the Fate of Individuality: Character and Novelistic Form from Conrad to Woolf.* Cambridge University Press, 1991.

Levy, Paul. *Moore: G. E. Moore and the Cambridge Apostles.* New York: Holt, 1979.

Lewis, C. S. *"De Descriptione Temporum." They Asked for a Paper.* London: Geoffrey Bles, 1962, 9–25.

Lewis, Pericles. *Modernism, Nationalism, and the Novel.* Cambridge University Press, 2000.

Lindsey, Ben. *The Companionate Marriage.* New York: Boni and Liveright, 1927.

Locke, Nancy. "Beaudelaire's 'La Corde' as figuration of Manet's art." *Picturing Children: Constructions of Childhood Between Rousseau and Freud.* Marilyn R. Brown, ed. Burlington: Ashgate, 2002, 89–102.

Louÿs, Pierre. *Aphrodite: A Novel of Ancient Morals.* London: Fortune, 1928.

Lukács, György. "The ideology of modernism." *The Meaning of Contemporary Realism.* Trans. John and Necke Mander. London: Merlin Press, 1962, 17–46.

Macfarlane, Alan. *Marriage and Love in England 1300–1840: Modes of Reproduction.* New York: Basil Blackwell, 1986.

Magid, Barry, ed. *Freud's Case Studies: Self-Psychological Perspectives*. London: Analytic Press, 1993.

Maier, Thomas. "Can psychiatrists really 'cure' homosexuality?" www.scientificamerican.com/article.cfm?id=homosexuality-cure-masters-johnson August 4, 2009.

Masters of Sex. Basic Books, 2009.

Malcolm, Norman. "Defending common sense." *Studies in the Philosophy of G. E. Moore*. E. D. Klemke, ed. Chicago: Quadrangle, 1969, 200–19.

"Moore and ordinary language." *Linguistic Turn*. Richard Rorty, ed. University of Chicago Press, 1992, 111–24.

Malik, Charu. "To express the subject of friendship: masculine desire and colonialism in *A Passage to India*." *Queer Forster*. Robert Martin and George Piggford, eds. University of Chicago Press, 1997, 221–36.

Marcus, Stephen. "Freud and Dora: story, history, case history." *In Dora's Case: Freud – Hysteria – Feminism*. Charles Bernheimer and Claire Kahane, eds. New York: Columbia University Press, 1985, 56–91.

"Introduction." *Three Essays on the Theory of Sexuality*. By Sigmund Freud. Trans. James Strachey. New York: Basic Books, 1975, xix–xli.

Marriage, Divorce, and Adoption Statistics. Historical Series, 1837–1999. London: Stationery Office, 1999. July 18, 2009 www.statistics.gov.uk/statbase/explorer.asp?CTG= 3&SL=&E=4695#4695

Martin, Robert K. "Edward Carpenter and the double structure of Maurice." *E. M. Forster*. Jeremy Tambling, ed. New York: St Martin's Press, 1995.

and George Piggford. "Introduction: queer, Forster?" *Queer Forster*. Robert Martin and George Piggford, eds. University of Chicago Press, 1997, 1–28.

and George Piggford, eds. *Queer Forster*. University of Chicago Press, 1997.

Masters, William, Virginia Johnson, and Robert Kolodny. *Crisis: Heterosexual Behavior in the Age of AIDS*. New York: Grove Press, 1988.

Masters, William and Virginia Johnson. *Homosexuality in Perspective*. Boston: Little, Brown, and Company, 1979.

Human Sexual Inadequacy. Boston: Little, Brown, and Company, 1970.

Human Sexual Response. Boston: Little, Brown, and Company, 1966.

May, Brian. *The Modernist as Pragmatist: E. M. Forster and the Fate of Liberalism*. University of Missouri Press, 1997.

McBride, Theresa M. *The Domestic Revolution: The Modernisation of Household Service in England and France 1820–1920*. London: Croom Helm, 1976.

McClintock, Ann. *Imperial Leather: Race, Gender and Sexuality in the Colonial Context*. New York: Routledge, 1995.

McGregor, O. R. *Divorce in England: A Centenary Study*. London: Heinemann, 1957.

Meisel, Perry and Walter Kendrick, eds. *Bloomsbury/Freud: The Letters of James and Alix Strachey 1924–1925*. New York: Basic Books, 1985.

Meyers, Jeffrey, ed. *D. H. Lawrence and Tradition*. London: Athlone, 1985.

"'Vacant heart and hand and eye': the homosexual theme in *A Room with a View*." *English Literature in Transition* 13 (1970): 181–92.

Mill, J. S. *Enfranchisement of Women*. London: Virago, 1983.
"Utilitarianism." *Utilitarianism and Other Essays by John Stuart Mill and Jeremy Bentham*. Alan Ryan, ed. New York: Penguin, 1987.
Miller, Elizabeth Carolyn. *The New Woman Criminal in British Culture at the Fin de Siècle*. Ann Arbor: University of Michigan Press, 2008.
Miller, J. Hillis. "The critic as host." *Critical Inquiry* 3 (1977): 439–47.
"Virginia Woolf's All Soul's Day: the omniscient narrator in *Mrs Dalloway*." *The Shaken Realist*. Melvin J. Friedman and John B. Vickery, eds. Baton Rouge: Louisiana State University Press, 1970, 100–27.
Millett, Kate. *Sexual Politics*. New York: Simon & Schuster, 1990.
Minow-Pinkney, Makiko. *Virginia Woolf and the Problem of the Subject*. New Jersey: Rutgers University Press, 1987.
Moi, Toril. "Representation of patriarchy: sexuality and epistemology in Freud's Dora." In *Dora's Case: Freud – Hysteria – Feminism*. Charles Bernheimer and Claire Kahane, eds. New York: Columbia University Press: 1985, 181–99.
Moore, G. E. "An autobiography." *The Philosophy of G. E. Moore*. Paul Schlipp, ed. Library of Living Philosophers. La Salle: Open Court, 1992.
Commonplace Book 1919–1953. Casimir Lewy, ed. London: George Allen, 1962.
"A defense of common sense." *Philosophical Papers*. New York: Collier, 1962. 32–59.
The Elements of Ethics. Philadelphia: Temple University Press, 1991.
Ethics. Oxford University Press, 1971.
Principia Ethica. Cambridge University Press, 2000.
"Proof of an external world." *Philosophical Papers*. New York: Collier, 1962, 126–48.
"A refutation of idealism." *Philosophical Studies*. London: Routledge, 1960, 1–30.
Morris, R. J. and Richard Rodger. "An introduction to British urban history" 1820–1914." In *The Victorian City: A Reader in British Urban History, 1820–1914*. Morris and Rodger, eds. London: Longman, 1993, 1–39.
Murdoch, Iris. *The Fire and the Sun: Why Plato Banished the Artists*. Oxford: Clarendon, 1977.
"The idea of perfection." The Sovereignty of Good. New York: Schocken, 1970.
Murry, John Middleton. *Son of Woman*. London: Jonathan Cape, 1931.
Nakhnikian, George. "On the naturalistic fallacy." *Studies in the Philosophy of G. E. Moore*. E. D. Klemke, ed. Chicago: Quadrangle, 1969, 64–75.
Neuman, Shirley. "Heart of Darkness, Virginia Woolf, and the specter of domination." *Virginia Woolf: New Critical Essays*. Patricia Clements and Isobel Grundy, eds. New Jersey: Barnes & Noble, 1983, 57–76.
Nicolson, Harold. *Diplomacy*. London: T. Butterworth, 1939.
Peacemaking, 1919. New York, Harcourt, 1939.
Nicolson, Nigel. *Portrait of a Marriage*. London: Weidenfeld & Nicolson, 1973.
Nietzsche, Friedrich. *On the Genealogy of Morals* and *Ecce Homo*. Trans. Walter Kaufman. New York: Vintage, 1989.
Nixon, Cornelia. *Lawrence's Leadership Politics and the Turn Against Women*. University of California Press, 1986.

O'Carroll, Annette. "Tenements to bungalows: class and the growth of home ownership before the Second World War." *Urban History* 24(2) (1997): 221–41.

Office of Population Censuses and Surveys. *Census 1911: General Report, England and Wales*. London: HMSO, 1911.

Office of Population Censuses and Surveys. *Census 1931: General Report, England and Wales*. London: HMSO, 1931.

Page, Malcolm. *Howards End*. Critics Debate Series. London: Macmillan, 1993.

Panichas, George. "Introduction." *Thirtieth Anniversary Issue: Essays on the Crisis of Modernity. Modern Age: A Quarterly Review* 31(3–4) 1987.

Patmore, Coventry. *The Angel in the House; Together with the Victories of Love*. London: Routledge, 1905.

Phillips, Roderick. *Untying the Knot: A Short History of Divorce*. Cambridge University Press, 1991.

Pines, Davida. *The Marriage Paradox: Modernist Novels and the Cultural Imperative to Marry*. Gainesville: University Press of Florida, 2006.

Pinkney, Tony. *D. H. Lawrence and Modernism*. University of Iowa Press, 1990.

Plato. *Plato: Complete Works*. John M. Cooper, ed. Indianapolis: Hackett, 1997.

Pollock, Linda. "Foreword." *Picturing Children: Constructions of Childhood Between Rousseau and Freud*. Marilyn R. Brown, ed. Burlington: Ashgate, 2002, xv–xix.

Poovey, Mary. *Uneven Development: The Ideological Work of Gender in Mid-Victorian England*. University of Chicago Press, 1988.

Price-Williams, R. *Journal of the Royal Statistical Society* 43 (1880) 462–508.

Raitt, Suzanne. *Vita and Virginia: The Work and Friendship of Vita Sackville-West and Virginia Woolf*. Oxford University Press, 1993.

Regan, Tom. *Bloomsbury's Prophet*. Philadelphia: Temple University Press, 1986.

Regnery, Harry. "Foreword." *Thirtieth Anniversary Issue: Essays on the Crisis of Modernity. Modern Age: A Quarterly Review* 31(3–4) 1987.

Rieff, Philip. *Freud: The Mind of the Moralist*. 3rd edn. University of Chicago Press, 1979.

"Introduction." *Dora*. By Sigmund Freud. New York: Macmillan, 1963.

Roberts, Sam. "51% of women are now living without spouse." *New York Times*, January 16, 2007. www.nytimes.com/2007/01/16/us/16census.html?r=1

Robinson, Paul. *The Freudian Left: Wilhelm Reich, Geza Roheim, Herbert Marcuse*. New York: Harper & Row Press, 1969.

The Modernization of Sex: Havelock Ellis, Albert Kinsey, William Masters, and Virginia Johnson. Cornell University Press, 1988.

Roby, Kinley. "Irony and the narrative voice in *Howards End*." *Journal of Narrative Technique*. 2 (1972): 116–24.

Rogow, Arnold A. "Dora's brother." *International Journal of Psychoanalysis* 6 (1979).

Romano, Renee C. *Race Mixing: Black–White Marriage in Postwar America*. Harvard University Press, 2003.

Rorty, Richard. "Introduction." *The Linguistic Turn*. Rorty, ed. University of Chicago Press, 1992, 1–39.

ed. *The Linguistic Turn*.

Rose, Jacqueline. "Dora: fragment of an analysis." *In Dora's Case: Freud – Hysteria – Feminism*. Charles Bernheimer and Claire Kahane, eds. New York: Columbia University Press: 1985, 128–48.
Rosecrance, Barbara. *Forster's Narrative Vision*. Ithaca: Cornell University Press, 1982.
Rosenbaum, S. P. *Aspects of Bloomsbury: Studies in Modern English Literary, and Intellectual History*. New York: St Martin's Press, 1998.
ed. *The Bloomsbury Group: A Collection of Memoirs and Commentary*. University of Toronto Press, 1995.
Edwardian Bloomsbury. New York: St Martin's Press, 1994.
"Foreword." *The Bloomsbury Group: A Collection of Memoirs and Commentary*, ix–xiii.
Victorian Bloomsbury. New York: St Martin's Press, 1987.
Ross, Charles. *The Composition of The Rainbow and Women in Love: A History*. Charlottesville: University of Virginia Press, 1979.
Ross, Dorothy. *G. Stanley Hall: The Psychologist as Prophet*. University of Chicago Press, 1972.
Rothenbacher, Franz. *The European Population 1850–1945*. New York: Palgrave, 2002.
The European Population since 1945. New York: Palgrave, 2005.
Rougemont, Denis de. *Love in the Western World*. Trans. Montgomery Belgion. New York: Harcourt, 1940.
Rousseau, G. S., and Roy Porter, eds. *Sexual Underworlds of the Enlightenment*. Manchester University Press, 1987.
Ruderman, Judith. "An 'Englishman at heart'?: Lawrence and the national identity debates." *D. H. Lawrence: New Worlds*. Keith Cushman and Earl Ingersoll, eds. London: Associated University Press, 2003, 50–67.
Ruotolo, Lucio. "Mrs Dalloway: the unguarded moment." *Virginia Woolf: Revaluation and Continuity*. Ralph Freedman, ed. Berkeley: University of California Press, 1980.
Russell, Bertrand. *The Autobiography of Bertrand Russell*. 3 vols., vol. 1. London: Allen & Unwin, 1967–9.
"Introduction." *Tractatus Logico-Philosophicus*. By Ludwig Wittgenstein. Trans. D. F. Pears, and B. F. McGuinness. New York: Humanities Press, 1961.
Rylance, Rick. "Lawrence's politics." *Rethinking Lawrence*. Keith Brown, ed. Philadelphia: Open University Press, 1990, 164–80.
Sackville-West, Vita. *All Passion Spent*. London: Virago, 1983.
Aphra Behn: The Incomparable Astrea. New York: Russell, 1970.
Challenge. London: Collins, 1974.
The Edwardians. London: Virago, 1983.
Knole and the Sackvilles. London: E Benn, 1958.
The Letters of Vita Sackville-West to Virginia Woolf. Louise DeSalvo and Mitchell Leaska, eds. London: Virago Press, 1992.
Passenger to Teheran. New York: Moyer Bell, 1990.

Pepita. New York: Doubleday, 1937.
Saint Joan of Arc. New York: Doubleday, 1936.
Seducers in Ecuador. London: Hogarth, 1924.
and Harold Nicholson. *Vita and Harold: The Letters of Vita Sackville-West and Harold Nicolson*. Nigel Nicolson, ed. London: Weidenfeld & Nicolson, 1992.
"Same-sex marriage, civil unions, and domestic partnerships." *New York Times*, "Times Topics." Updated August 3, 2009. http://topics.nytimes.com/top/reference/timestopics/subjects/s/same_sex_marriage/index.html
"Same-sex marriage: re-defining marriage around the world." Pew Forum on Religion and Public Life. Updated January 22, 2009. http://pewforum.org/docs/?DocID=235
Sanger, Margaret *Motherhood in Bondage*. New York: Brentano's, 1928.
Saussure, Ferdinand de. *Course in General Linguistics*. Trans. Wade Baskin. New York: Philosophical Library, 1959.
Saville, John. *Rural Depopulation in England and Wales 1851–1951*. London: Routledge & Kegan Paul, 1957.
Schlack, Beverly Ann. "A Freudian look at *Mrs Dalloway*." *Literature and Psychology* 23 (1973): 49–58.
Schlipp, Paul Arthur, ed. *The Philosophy of G. E. Moore. Library of Living Philosophers*. La Salle: Open Court, 1992.
Seckel, Al, ed. *Bertrand Russell on Ethics, Sex, and Marriage*. Buffalo: Prometheus Books, 1987.
Sedgwick, Eve Kosofsky. *Between Men: English Literature and Male Homosocial Desire*. New York: Columbia University Press, 1985.
Seymour, Miranda. *Ottoline Morrell: Life on the Grand Scale*. Farrar, Strauss, and Giroux, 1993.
Shakespeare, William. *Cymbeline*. Oxford: Clarendon, 1998.
Sinfield, Alan. *The Wilde Century*. London: Cassell, 1994.
Smith, Anne, ed. *Lawrence and Women*. London: Vision Press, 1978.
Smith, Harold. "British feminism in the 1920s." *British Feminism in the Twentieth Century*. Smith, ed. Amherst: University of Massachusetts Press, 1990, 47–65.
ed. *British Feminism in the Twentieth Century*. Amherst: University of Massachusetts Press, 1990.
"Introduction." *British Feminism in the Twentieth Century*. Smith, ed. Amherst: University of Massachusetts Press, 1990, 1–3.
Smith-Rosenberg, Caroll. "The female world of love and ritual: relations between women in nineteenth century America." *Signs* 1 (1975): 1–29.
Smith, Zadie. "E. M. Forster, middle manager." *New York Review of Books*. 55(13) 2008.
On Beauty. London: Penguin, 2005.
Somerville, C. John. *The Rise and Fall of Childhood*. London: Sage Publications, 1982.
"South Africa passes same-sex marriage bill." Canadian Broadcasting Corporation. November 14, 2006. www.cbc.ca/world/story/2006/11/14/marriage-safrica.html

"Spain approves liberal gay marriage law." *St Petersburg Times.* By wire services. July 1, 2005. www.sptimes.com/2005/07/01/Worldandnation/Spain_approves_libera.shtml

Spengler, Oswald. *The Decline of the West.* 2 vols. Trans. Charles Atkinson. New York: Knopf, 1926.

Spilka, Mark. "Lawrence up-tight or the anal phase once over." *D. H. Lawrence: Critical Assessments.* 4 vols., vol 2. David Ellis and Ornella De Zordo, eds. East Sussex: Helm, 1992, 281–96.

The Love Ethic of D. H. Lawrence. Bloomington: Indiana University Press, 1955.

Sprague, Claire, ed. *Virginia Woolf: A Collection of Critical Essays.* New Jersey: Prentice-Hall, 1971.

Sprengnether, Madelon. "Enforcing Oedipus: Freud and Dora." In *Dora's Case: Freud – Hysteria – Feminism.* Charles Bernheimer and Claire Kahane, eds. New York: Columbia University Press: 1985, 254–75.

Sproles, Karyn. "Virginia Woolf writes to Vita Sackville-West (and receives a reply): *Aphra Behn, Orlando, Saint Joan of Arc* and revolutionary biography." *Virginia Woolf: Texts and Contexts, selected Papers from the Fifth Annual Conference on Virginia Woolf.* New York: Pace University Press, 1996.

Stansky, Peter. *On or about December 1910: Early Bloomsbury and Its Intimate World.* Cambridge, MA: Harvard University Press, 1996.

Stape, J. H. "Picturing the self as other: Howards End as psychobiography." *Howards End: Complete, Authoritative Text with Biographical and Historical Contexts. Alistair Duckworth*, ed. New York: Bedford, 1997.

Steinberg, Erwin. "G. E. Moore's table and chair in *To the Lighthouse.*" *Journal of Modern Literature* 15 (1988): 161–8.

"Stock of dwellings: by tenure: social trends 34." Dataset ST341005. *National Statistics Online.* February 13, 2004. www.statistics.gov.uk/StatBase/ssdataset.asp?vlnk=7320&More=Y

Stone, Lawrence. *The Family, Sex and Marriage in England, 1500–1800.* New York: Harper & Row, 1977.

Stone, Wilfred. *The Cave and the Mountain: A Study of E. M. Forster.* Stanford University Press, 1966.

"E. M. Forster's subversive individualism." *Critical Essays on E. M. Forster.* Alan Wilde, ed. Boston: G. K. Hall, 1985, 31–41.

Strachey, James. "Editor's note." *Three Essays on the Theory of Sexuality. Complete Psychological Works of Sigmund Freud*, Standard Edition, VII, 127–9.

Strachey, Lytton. "Does absence make the heart grow fonder?" *The Really Interesting Question and Other Papers.* Paul Levy, ed. New York: Coward, 1972.

Tatchell, Peter. *Europe in the Pink.* London: Gay Men's Press, 1992.

Taylor, Roger and Edward Wakeling. *Lewis Carroll: Photographer. The Princeton University Library Albums.* Princeton University Press, 2002.

Thompson, F. M. L. *The Rise of Respectable Society: A Social History of Victorian Britain, 1830–1900.* Cambridge, MA: Harvard University Press, 1988.

Timms, Edward, ed. *Freud and the Child Woman: The Memoirs of Fritz Wittels.* New Haven: Yale University Press, 1995.

Trautmann, Joanne. "The Jessamy brides: the friendship of Virginia Woolf and V. Sackville West." *Pennsylvania State University Studies* 36 (1973): 1–57.
Tredwell, R. F. "On Moore's analysis of goodness." *Studies in the Philosophy of G. E. Moore*. E. D. Klemke, ed. Chicago: Quadrangle, 1969, 53–63.
Trilling, Lionel. *Beyond Culture: Essays on Literature and Learning*. New York: Viking Press, 1965.
E. M. Forster. New York: New Directions, 1943.
Tsuzuki, Chushichi. *Edward Carpenter, 1844–1929, Prophet of Human Fellowship*. Cambridge University Press, 1980.
Ulrichs, Karl Heinrich. *The Riddle of "Man–Manly" Love*. 2 vols. Trans. Michael A. Lombardi-Nash. New York: Prometheus, 1994.
"unhinged." Definition 1. *Oxford English Dictionary*. 1971, repr. 1975.
University of Portsmouth. Department of Geography. *A Vision of Britain through Time: Including Maps, Statistical Trends and Historical Descriptions. c.2009* [began 2004]. August 9, 2009. www.visionofbritain.org.uk/
"Greenwich through time." *A Vision of Britain through Time*. August 9, 2009. www.visionofbritain.org.uk/unit_page.jsp?u_id=10171880&x=3336127.80402&y=2788087.23681
"Richmond upon Thames through time." *A Vision of Britain through Time*. August 9, 2009. www.visionofbritain.org.uk/unit_page.jsp?u_id=10084593&c_id=10001043
"Tunbridge Wells through time." *A Vision of Britain through Time*. August 9, 2009. www.visionofbritain.org.uk/unit_page.jsp?u_id=10099195&x=3344188.17835&y=2750201.33779
Vivas, Eliseo *D. H. Lawrence: The Failure and the Triumph of Art*. Evanston: Northwestern University Press, 1960.
von-Hallberg, Robert and Cassandra Laity, eds. "Men, women and World War I." *Modernism/Modernity* 9 (2002): 1–184.
von Krafft-Ebing, Richard. *Psychopathia Sexualis*. Trans. Charles Gilbert Chaddock. Philadelphia: F. A. Davis, 1894.
Vorachek, Laura. "Rebellion in the metropolis: George Gissing's new woman musician." In Spiers, John, ed. *Gissing and the City: Cultural Crisis and the Making of Books in Late-Victorian England*. Basingstoke: Palgrave, 2006, 118–28.
Walkowitz, Rebecca. *Cosmopolitan Style: Modernism Beyond the Nation*. Columbia University Press, 2006.
Waller, Philip. "Introduction: the English urban landscape: yesterday, today, and tomorrow." *The English Urban Landscape*. Waller, ed. Oxford University Press, 2000, 11–31.
Walvin, James. *A Child's World: A Social History of English Childhood: 1800–1914*. New York: Penguin, 1982.
Warner, Michael. "Introduction." *Fear of a Queer Planet: Queer Politics and Social Theory*. Warner, ed. Minneapolis: University of Minnesota Press, 1993.
Watt, Donald. "G. E. Moore and the Bloomsbury group." *English Literature in Transition (1880–1920)* 12 (1969): 119–34.

Watt, Ian. *The Rise of the Novel: Studies in Defoe, Richardson, and Fielding*. Berkeley: University of California Press, 1957.

Webb, Beatrice. *The Diary of Beatrice Webb*. 4 vols. Norman and Jeanne MacKenzie, eds. Cambridge, MA: Belknap Press, 1983.

Weeks, Jeffrey. *Coming Out: Homosexual Politics in Britain from the Nineteenth Century to the Present*. New York: Quartet, 1977.

Weininger, Otto. *Sex and Character*. New York: AMS, 1975.

Weintraub, Stanley, ed. *The Yellow Book: Quintessence of the Nineties*. New York: Anchor Books, 1964.

Weiten, Wayne. *Psychology: Themes and Variations*. Cengage Learning, 1997.

Welton, T. A. *Journal of the Royal Statistical Society* 73 (1913) 304–17.

Whelan, P. T. *D. H. Lawrence: Myth and Metaphysic in The Rainbow, and Women in Love*. London: UMI Research, 1988.

Widdowson, Peter. "*Howards End*: fiction as history." *Critical Essays on E. M. Forster*. Alan Wilde, ed. Boston: G. K. Hall, 1985, 121–31.

Wittgenstein, Ludwig. *On Certainty*. Trans. Denis Paul, and G. E. M. Anscombe. New York: Harper, 1972.

Philosophical Investigations: The English Text of the Third Edition. Trans. G. E. M. Anscombe. New York: Macmillan, 1968

Tractatus Logico-Philosophicus. Trans. D. F. Pears, and B. F. McGuinness. New York: Humanities Press, 1961.

Wollaeger, Mark. *Modernism, Media, and Propaganda: British Narrative from 1900–1945*. Princeton University Press, 2006.

Woolf, Leonard. *Economic Imperialism. New York*. Harcourt, 1920.

Empire and Commerce in Africa: A Study in Economic Imperialism. New York: Macmillan, 1919.

Imperialism and Civilization. London: Hogarth, 1928.

Woolf, Virginia. *The Common Reader*. New York: Harcourt, 1984.

The Death of the Moth and Other Essays. San Diego: Harcourt, 1970.

The Diary of Virginia Woolf. Anne Bell, ed. 4 vols. London: Hogarth, 1982.

Jacob's Room. London: Hogarth, 1990.

The Letters of Virginia Woolf. Nigel Nicolson, ed. New York: Harcourt, 1975.

"Modern Fiction." *The Common Reader*. New York: Harcourt, 1984.

Mr Bennet and Mrs Brown. London: Hogarth, 1924.

Mrs Dalloway. New York: Harcourt, 1981.

Night and Day. London: Hogarth, 1992.

Orlando. New York: Harcourt, 1956.

A Room of One's Own. New York: Harcourt, 1981.

To the Lighthouse. New York: Harcourt, 1955.

Index